BEFORE I HAD THE

ON BEING A
TRANSGENDER YOUNG ADULT

SKYLAR KERGIL

Skyhorse Publishing

Skyhorse Publishing books may be purchased in bulk at special discounts for sales promotion, corporate gifts, fund-raising, or educational purposes. Special editions can also be created to specifications. For details, contact the Special Sales Department, Skyhorse Publishing, 307 West 36th Street, 11th Floor, New York, NY 10018 or info@skyhorsepublishing.com.

Skyhorse® and Skyhorse Publishing® are registered trademarks of Skyhorse Publishing, Inc.®, a Delaware corporation.

Visit our website at www.skyhorsepublishing.com.

10 9 8 7 6 5 4 3 2 1

Library of Congress Cataloging-in-Publication Data is available on file.

Cover design by Jenny Zemanek
Cover art by Skylar Kergil and Levin Mayerhofer

Print ISBN: 978-1-5107-2306-1
Ebook ISBN: 978-1-5107-2308-5

Printed in the United States of America

Contents

Acknowledgments

To my grandfather, Spurgeon Struven, who taught me it's okay to have ice cream every night and who loved me even when he didn't understand.

To my mother, Stephanie Tyler, who protected me from a cruel world while also letting me create my own scars.

To my father, John Kergil, who gave me his X chromosome and, as I grew up, told me I was a good man.

To my brother, JT, who showed me that change can happen.

To Dr. Spack, my endocrinologist, who allowed me a chance at my true life.

To my best friends, Amy and Winnie, who were and are always there for the biggest moments I have gone through, delighting in the joys and facing the challenges as we navigate this complex world.

To Katie and Arin, whose honesty and stories help generations of LGBTQ youth.

To ABRHS, the high school that found space for me to evolve.

To Hank, Paul, Anna, Zane, and N—your love reached my bones.

To Barack and Michelle Obama, two compassionate leaders and personal role models, who served in office from when I began hormones until when I completed this work. Thank you for your endless hope.

To Janet Mock, Tiq Milan, and Chandler Wilson, for everything you have shared and continue to inspire others to share.

And to my community, my friends, family, followers, fans, and goofballs bopping their heads up and down at my shows: Thank you for encouraging me to write my truth and thank you for embracing me while I face my fears—you have held me together.

Disclaimer

WHEN I AM INVITED TO share my story, I spend about five minutes listing disclaimers. I wanted to write this memoir; no one forced me into it. No ghostwriters up in here. So let me list my usual disclaimers:

1. There is no one way to be transgender. There is not one path, one journey, set of guidelines or steps to get there. It is an individual path, full of choices based on feelings and experiences. There are options to physically transition, but not everyone has access to these options, even if they wanted them. Some people are transgender but don't ever "transition." It is pretty amazing how diverse the transgender community is. I can only offer one story, so I highly encourage you to explore the countless stories of transgender lives available online, in books, or other media. I've included links to resource and inspiration sections at the back of this book.

2. I am open about my experiences coming out, taking hormones, choosing surgeries, and much of what came along with my transition. However, had I been asked to write this book five or six years ago—a few years into my transition—there are a million things that would not be included that I feel comfortable enough to share now. Had someone inquired what my "birth name" was years ago, I would have been offended and given them an earful. These days, I explain why it is inappropriate to ask such a question and I caution them against asking it of anyone. However, I will also share my birth name, as it is something I am comfortable with after having been separated from it for so long.

When I answer a question or offer intimate information, it is not an invitation to expect answers from other transgender persons. I can stomach a blaring "So do you have a penis or vagina?" now because I have educated myself, learned along the way how to best answer these offensive inquiries, and gotten thicker skin. When I was coming out and beginning my transition, these questions made me feel awful, as they should. They made me feel depressed—even suicidal—to be reduced to my genitalia during a time when I was simply fighting to be seen as a sentient human being.

Hormones and surgery are personal discussions. They are not required for transitioning; they are options to help ease gender dysphoria,[1] but not every treatment is applicable to all cases. Even though I identify as transgender, I do not hold a free pass to ask any transgender person invasive questions. If there is something I want to know, I'll usually preface it with a "Is it okay for me to ask you about your transition?"

3. My experience transitioning lands me within the binary. Although I will always question what it means to be a man, I am comfortable being seen as a man and being referred to with he/him pronouns. When I see a form that just says "male" or "female," I can select "male" without feeling any sort of discomfort. It is important to appreciate and celebrate and remind others that many transgender people do not experience a binary transition that is female-to-male (FTM) or male-to-female (MTF). Gender exists on a spectrum and non-binary identities are valid. Gender also doesn't *really* exist, as it is a social construct. One of my most talented friends identifies as agender. They do not experience gender. They do not feel strongly as anything existing on, within, or around the binary genders "man" and "woman." They use they/them pronouns as that is what they are comfortable with. I love them.

4. My truth is solely mine. I write from memory and memory is not a perfect record, but I have tried my best to be as truthful as possible. I may forget some important moments, but they still existed. Furthermore, there are things I remember that I cannot disclose,

---

1 An overwhelming feeling that one's physical sex does not align with their psychological and emotional gender identity, often resulting in depression, anxiety, and discomfort.

mainly to keep friends, family, and others safe. Most names have been changed for this reason as well.

5. I started writing this book for my younger self. When I was fifteen, coming out as transgender felt like a death sentence. I had not met or seen a living, breathing transgender person that was over the age of eighteen. I doubted that I could graduate from high school, go to college, get a job, find love. I doubted that I could live a . . . not normal, because screw whatever "normal" is . . . I doubted that I could live a life. Any life, let alone my own transgender one.

This memoir is not meant to be a guide. It is a reflection of my experiences that I wish I could have shown my younger self back then. To inspire hope instead of fear. To expand rather than withdraw.

I finished writing this book for the transgender youth who have contacted me over the years. They inspired me to complete this project and send it out to the world. I have learned so much by listening to the youth of today and I cannot thank them enough.

Speaking

I believe that telling our stories, first to ourselves and then to one another and the world, is a revolutionary act. It is an act that can be met with hostility, exclusion, and violence. It can also lead to love, understanding, transcendence, and community. I hope that my being real with you will help empower you to step into who you are and encourage you to share yourself with those around you.

—Janet Mock, *Redefining Realness*

SHIFTING INTO PARK, I TOOK in a deep breath. Exhaling, I turned off the engine of my little yellow car. I named him Theodore (Theo for short) right after I bought him. The slow hum of the radiator faded away.

I flipped open my phone and called the number I had scrawled on a small piece of paper and stuffed in my left pocket.

"Hey! Are you here?" a man asked.

"Yeah, I think so." I noticed my palms were sweating.

"I'll be right out!" He sounded cheerful, but I wasn't sure.

I opened the door and buttoned up my flannel shirt; the temperature was both hot and cold on this breezy fall day. Slinging my backpack over my shoulder, I shuffled some notes around and grabbed my index cards.

You've got this, I thought, remembering the reassuring words of my best friends back at school.

Kaleb had these amazingly bright eyes. He greeted me with a handshake and then a hug.

"Not sure how to go about that," he said, laughing. "It's new to me."

"I got you." I smiled back. "The handshake part always feels forced even when I've known someone forever."

"We are so, so excited you are here! Can I show you around?" His energy calmed me.

As we toured a small part of the campus, he mentioned that it might be a small group, but that the work I was doing was still very necessary.

"It's a conversation we need to have—and let me tell ya, they are pretty tired of my voice. It's better for them to hear more stories and get a new perspective"—he looked up at me—"and anyway, I like your music and videos."

Knowing he had listened to my super low-fi, DIY college dorm recordings made me feel comforted. I knew he had liked my videos from his initial email—that was how I figured he had found out I was living nearby anyway. Albany, New York isn't too far from Saratoga Springs, where I was going to college.

We were heading down a hallway when someone ran up to greet me and told me how glad they were I had arrived. I blushed, feeling suddenly vulnerable but also flattered at the same time.

On a wall in the hallway, I saw a poster. It read:

IDENTITY PRESENTS: TRANS* WEEK GUEST SPEAKER SKYLAR KERGIL

A picture of my face was beside the lettering. The reality hadn't hit me yet. I had been invited here, warmly welcomed here, and expected to perform here. I tried to slow my beating heart, but time felt like it was racing past.

Entering the room, I met a few of the students who ran their LGBTQ club, Identity, and some other students who had heard about the event. Thankfully, everyone I chatted with seemed kind and conversation was easy—I mean, it made sense considering I was the same age as the seniors. We could all relate to that feeling of nearing the final semester of our college careers.

The clock kept ticking and it was time for Kaleb to introduce me. The room was a small classroom near the student center, but there were at least ten students there. Ten people. Twenty eyes.

I recalled the first time one of my YouTube videos ever got any random views. *Where are these people coming from?* I had thought at the time. *Twenty views—that's forty eyes. That's actually a lot of people.*

So whether it was ten or twenty or fifty million people, I was taken aback by the fact that, on this fall night, they were taking the time to listen to *me*.

"When I first saw Skylar's videos, I had no idea he was around the corner! He is twenty-one, a senior at Skidmore College, and identifies as a transgender man. He has been documenting his transition from female-to-male on YouTube since he was in high school in 2009. Here to share his story and college experience while transitioning, please welcome Skylar Kergil!" Kaleb announced, flawless in front of his friends and peers.

Beaming, Kaleb wished me luck. I walked toward the center of the room and looked out at the crowd of happy faces.

How did I get here? I thought.

Moments passed in a blink of an eye. After an hour, I heard clapping and had a line of students to chat with. Lots of folks I spoke to wanted to know if I had done this before.

"No, I haven't. I'm shy, honestly." I laughed it off.

"You should consider speaking more!" Kaleb was so encouraging. The student newspaper also wrote that students were honored theirs was the first school I had spoken at.

That night, for the first time in my life, I shared some of the story that comes after this. I mean, my story. It is . . . my story. Just one among infinite.

Every transition is unique. There are choices we all make every day that shape who we become. There is no right way or wrong way. There are no requirements for being transgender. Some people are transgender; until you hear their stories, you may not know what that means to them.

I am still learning.

"You Can
Call Me Mike!"

"AND WHAT'S YOUR NAME, LITTLE one?" a stranger asked, putting his hand down on my shoulder.

"You can call me Mike!" I exclaimed as I turned around to face the man.

"Well hello then, Mike." He had gray whiskers and a friendly smile. I smiled back up at him, my brown eyes barely showing underneath my new bowl cut hairstyle. Hey, it was the early nineties.

Wearing my bright yellow sundress, I followed my grandpa to the hardware store. It was April of 1996; I was almost four years old and up until that point, I had been called Katherine Elizabeth.

Never Mike.

Always Katherine.

When I came to this conclusion, announcing my identity in front of close family friends, my grandpa and parents were taken aback. But in a swift motion, all was laid to rest.

"Mike it is!" my grandpa chimed in. My parents didn't look worried; the moment passed in all of three seconds.

Except for the rest of the summer, I would only respond to the name Mike.

While I wish I could say I *knew* I was transgender at four years old, I didn't. I suppose I expressed myself however I saw fit at the time, and my parents let me. If I had not come out as transgender later in life, this early memory would likely be recounted as fun childhood exploration. A "silly couple of months" for me when I was younger. But, because that is not the case, I look back on it as my first coming out experience, one that would likely garner a different reaction from my parents in today's world.

Born on May 19, 1991, I am a Taurus. I am stubborn. I made sure every person called me Mike that entire summer. It ended when I went back to kindergarten and the teacher read my legal name off the roster. At recess, we lined up by two sandboxes—boys on one side, girls on the other. There was actually a sandbox in the middle, too, and, according to my mom, I often invited kids to that sandbox.

"The weirdos, the new kids, the oddballs, the lonely looking ones—you'd go right up to them and ask them to come play with you, to include them so they felt more involved, too," Mom told me recently. "It was pretty amazing. The other kids wouldn't even notice what was going on around them, but you cared so much for those outsiders."

While I could enjoy my weird friends in my weird sandbox, I couldn't quite demand the teachers call me Mike. I was too shy for that.

By default, I went back to being called my birth name. That's what the government documents said, and that's what I had been told many, many times: I was a girl. A girl named Katherine.

I was told I belonged in *that* sand box. The one for girls. I didn't know anything else.

Not Twins, but Close

OUTSIDE OF KINDERGARTEN, I TOOK up T-ball with my brother, JT. Dad would bring us to our sports practices behind the elementary school. It was a tiny field, the back of it pressed up against dark woods. I loved that I got to wear the same shirt as JT, black with white stripes. Even though my hair grew out from under the helmet, wavy blonde and reaching my shoulders, some people would still call me a boy.

Anyway, when it came to JT, I seemed to idolize him. He was my big brother and I liked following in his footsteps. JT is two years older than me and we look quite similar but his hair is darker and curlier than mine. One time, a lady swore we were twins. My mom had to argue with her, saying we weren't. The woman laughed and declared JT and I must absolutely be twins. My mom told her that she gave birth to us two years apart, so no, we were not twins.

Sometimes, I liked to think we were. Some top-secret government ploy to keep the truth from us or something. Back then, I imagined twins as being identical and that meant I'd get to be a boy, too.

One time, when I was about four, JT had run up a slide at the playground by the beach and I ran up right after him. Someone had gone down it in a wet bathing suit right after JT had climbed up, but I didn't pay attention. When I got to the top of the metal slide, I slipped. My mouth crashed down on the top corner and, essentially, I bit my teeth down into steel.

JT ran down the beach to get Mom and Dad, leaving me at the top with a mouth full of blood. A stranger saw me and came up.

"Are you okay, little girl? Come here." She reached out her hands to lift me off the top of the structure.

Once I saw my parents, I opened my mouth to start crying and blood dribbled out all over my swimsuit. It probably looked awful. My mom laid me down in the station wagon (that car always smelled like rotten banana milk) and tried to keep me calm as we drove to the emergency room. My teeth were practically swimming around in my mouth; for whatever reason, my mom instinctively tried to push them back into place.

At the hospital, the doctor marveled that she had done the right thing. My gums turned black for months, yet my teeth stayed in for years. It took four years for my last baby tooth to finally come out in a bowl of Fruit Loops I ate at our dining room table, across the country, in San Ramon, California.

Even after the slide incident, I kept following JT around, annoying the heck out of him as we got older. He'd make fun of me, punch me sometimes. My parents insisted it was just brotherly/sisterly fighting. I didn't know any other "sisters" who got punched as often (or at all), though. Lots of "brothers" got punched by their older brothers, it seemed. Regardless, it was more the yelling and name calling that bothered me, but I don't remember why we snapped at one another. Sometimes, we'd be having fun playing video games and then he'd be pissed at me. It was what it was.

I figured it must be because I was secretly a boy and everyone knew it that my parents would let him hit me, like the other brothers I'd seen on TV and whatnot. And, I figured, once I grew up a little bit and was bigger, the punching would stop.

I was wrong. Writing about the impact that my brother's issues have had on me is difficult. It spans twenty-three years of my life: uncertainty, violence, pain, heartache, concern. But those were also his years, his life, his choices, his reasons. I was not an entirely angelic little sibling, and I'll be writing about some of the hardest moments he and I had together.

In the end, it was my brother who came the furthest to show me he respected and loved me. One night, after so many years of turbulence, he was sober and he came to me with open arms. I was already a year on testosterone.

"I always wanted a little brother," he said, looking down at me from underneath his curly hair, "and out of all the transgender little brothers in the world, I'm glad I have you."

I hugged him, as closely as I had when visiting him while he was in rehab.

"I love you, Sky," he whispered.

Until that moment, he had never called me Sky.

"I love you, too." I did and do.

Cross Country
Doesn't Feel Super Far
(When You're Six)

It is not the strongest of the species that survives, but rather, that which is most adaptable to change.

—Leon Megginson

RIGHT BEFORE I ENTERED FIRST grade, my parents moved us from New York to California. It was for my mom's job, but I didn't understand it at the time. I was going to miss eating butter and salt sandwiches with my close kindergarten friend, Cam. I was going to miss playing Frisbee with Kara. Begrudgingly, we left our little forest off the highway and settled into a new home in a giant cul-de-sac in the suburbs of San Francisco. I adjusted. I made new friends. I got my knee stuck in a fence at day care. I avoided the lice plague at that same day care. I found a solid small group, a handful of girls I met when we were all signed up for softball. I joined the Girl Scouts, got my Brownie brown sash, while I followed JT along to the Boy Scouts events, wishing I could race in the Pinewood Derby.

My grandparents lived an hour away from our new home. I'd go up to their house and be amazed by the giant tree in their living room. They named him Raphael and had to trim him when he started taking over the ceiling. JT and I would make boats out of driftwood and pull them along the street when it rained.

One afternoon, out doing some errands with my grandparents, I heard a stranger say something behind me.

I turned around. "What?"

"Sorry, thought you were my son. He has long blond hair, too!" The stranger was an older man with a mustache, awkward but non-threatening.

His son ran up right behind him. He was about the same height as me but maybe was a year or two younger. Tucked behind his father's leg, he peeked out and looked at me with the same wide eyes I had been looking at his dad with.

"Dad, he has my hair, too!" Sam chimed to his father.

I froze, not knowing what to say. *Do I correct them?*

I didn't have to say anything.

I smiled and walked back to my family.

Cool Bike, Yo

ORTY FEET IN THE AIR, gravel and tiny bushes disappearing underneath my wheels, had I ever felt more alive? Thankfully, I wasn't quite forty feet in the air, more like three or four, tops, but that's how I *felt*—alive and forty feet in the air. As the rush of freedom surrounded me, my bike turned sideways, my eight-year-old body also turned sideways, and I began a vertical drop perpendicular to the gravel underneath me. My left knee sank into the ground as my handlebars forged their own scar into the earth. My arm ripped open to share what I kept inside, outside.

When I was a kid, pain felt different. It felt like picking scabs and bragging at recess about how we got them. Catching a baseball with a shoulder was painting a green, purple, charcoal landscape that I could show off the next day. Falling on my face during a game of hide-and-seek after school in the first grade left me with a pretty amazing mustache-shaped scab on my upper lip and, the next day, a concerned teacher who gasped and took me to the counselor's office. I never perceived how much my parents had to explain my injuries to teachers. I was fortunate enough to have a home safe enough that I knew my scars, scabs, and bruises were okay to share. I knew where they came from and, luckily, they came from the benign part of growing up that many kids experience—learning how fast I could go on rollerblades, learning not to blindly chase a butterfly through poison ivy, learning how quickly blood can rush to the surface of a scraped elbow, learning not to build a half-pipe out of plywood propped up on air conditioning units.

Most of my time spent in California involved motion. We lived very close to the elementary school I attended. Montevideo was a fun place, where the classrooms had outdoor walkways to connect them and a huge playground with many foursquare spots, concrete, wood chips, ropes, splinters—the whole nine yards of nineties playground construction that had many risks alongside many gains. Even when I was in the first grade, my parents sometimes let me walk to and from school with my brother or friends. A lot has changed in our world since then; parents with a similar loose approach to their children may face criticism in allowing the same freedoms I was given. It's sometimes hard to remember that the world has not become a scarier place, but our ability to absorb it instantaneously, to access news all day long—that has made it a scarier *seeming* place.

For example: on midnight of New Year's Eve, 1999, we held our breath thinking the world might end. A lot of theories in the news had forecast an apocalypse. There were tons of predictions about what would happen when the clock struck midnight. Excited, we all waited up until the countdown. As the year turned to 2000 . . . nothing changed. We pulled strings on a few small confetti toys. The next day, everything was how it had been before, although it took a while to get used to writing 2-0-0-0 rather than 1-9-9-9.

I was glad life continued on, because that year, my parents got us new bicycles. A couple of months before Christmas, they took JT and me to a bike shop nearby. There were bikes everywhere of every shape and size—it was better than a toy store. I was overwhelmed with options, but immediately gravitated toward the shiny silver trick bike in the middle. It felt heavier than my own body, big for me, and had these blue and silver striped pegs on the front and back wheels that were huge. In my mind at the time, it was the most badass bike I had ever seen. JT pulled up a red bike with pegs that he was fascinated with.

My dad appeared and looked at my current obsession.

"Well, what about these bikes over here?" He gestured toward a wall of bikes that I had not even seen.

"Ummmmm . . ." I followed him in that direction.

The wall was full of girl bikes. It hadn't even crossed my mind that this bike shop had sides which now, looking back, were entirely gendered. I knew a little bit about gendered stores, especially clothing ones—but my mom often let me go wherever JT went and so I rarely entered the girls' side unless there was an item deemed necessary (a bathing suit, for example.)

The girl bikes didn't intrigue me at all. Pink camouflage paint, blue and pink sparkle paint, purple striped paint, all with bright white seats and big baskets on the front to carry flowers home. I kept thinking about the silver and blue trick bike. At the end, I explained that was the one I wanted. We left the store empty-handed, but I had a feeling that that those blue and black wheels would be under my feet someday.

A few months later, I couldn't sleep. It was Christmas morning and I could tell by the little bit of bright gray sunlight outside that JT would be rushing downstairs soon. He was usually the first one up on Christmas, unlike every other day of the year. We both emerged from our rooms at the exact same time and started running across the expanse of white carpet that cascaded down our stairway right onto the living room landing. Many mornings were spent slipping down the stairs in oversized socks—I used to ride my giant stuffed lion down those stairs.

As we bounded from point A to point B, we saw two extra-large wrapped things in the living room.

"YESSSSSSSSS!!!!" JT yelled out, knowing without even opening them.

I uncovered my bike—it was the shiny silver blue and black one with all four pegs (two on the front wheel and two on the rear). I had gotten the boy bike of my dreams, even as a little girl! I felt so special and so rad and so chill and so kewl and so awesome. I felt on par with JT because in front of us were two bikes meant for boys to ride around the neighborhood, doing tricks, causing ruckus. And those boys were going to be us!

Upon careful examination, I realized the bike had been modified. Turns out, since it was made for boys my age and I was a little bit smaller than the guys around me, my dad had had a friend help him bend the seat so that it sat forward rather than further back. He smiled as he let me know that he did this so that I could actually reach the handlebars comfortably. I grumbled, likely because I was sad I wasn't big enough yet to ride without it being modified, but got over myself quickly. The most important thing was that I was able to ride it and *it was mine*.

A fantastic part about California winters was that it was still warm enough out during the day that we could venture outside. After opening the rest of our presents and enjoying family time, we rushed out toward the driveway, circling around on our new bikes. My mom and dad both had bikes too; sometimes we would bike to the pool together in the summer.

The novelty of this bike didn't wear off for years; the many scars it gave me from trying new things, the scabs all over my shins because I kept hitting them into the pegs as I got used to them, then standing on the back pegs going downhill as if I weren't even biking, just soaring . . . much of my childhood centered around this bike. I learned new things, but in some ways, this bike taught me a bunch too.

One weekend in February, I was heading toward my elementary school down the neighborhood paths. The jumps (those ones that I often skinned my knees on) were beyond the expanse of concrete that surrounded the playground. That playground was huge—felt like five football fields to me. As I was biking through the middle of it, there was an older kid dressed in all black hanging out in the center. He had a bike, too, and was doing a couple of tricks up on some of the ledges.

Alone, I didn't want to approach him. Although my tomboy appearance gave me some confidence—my shoulder-length hair tucked under my helmet, my cool cutoff pants that could easily zipper into shorts, and my black and yellow fuzzy hooded sweatshirt—I knew better than to interact with strangers alone. But he shouted hi to me I biked past.

"Hey, that's a sweet bike!" he boomed with a thick accent that I couldn't place.

"Oh, haha thanks, I got it a few months ago," I replied as I came to a stop nearby him.

"It looks pretty sick actually, can I try it for a second?" he said, gazing at the wheels.

I looked around. It was a gray, cold morning. Not many people were around, at least nobody nearby. I felt this moment of hesitation—he was a stranger after all; yet being young and naïve, I quickly hopped off my bike.

"Sure! It's hella neat. Check out these pedals too." I rolled it over his way. The pedals had spikes on them to give a better foot grip when doing tricks.

"Hmmm. Okay boy, here, hold this." He handed me his pager as I handed him my bike.

He was probably sixteen or seventeen; I was half his age. I had no idea what this pager thingy was. It was the size of an egg, black, not very shiny, had a green screen that would show like ten characters of text; it was meaningless to me. I had no idea why he handed it to me, why I was holding it. As he got on my bike, all I could think about was that he had called me boy.

After a couple of circles around, he did a few wheelies and tricks on it that I definitely wasn't able to do, he came back up to me and hopped off. I handed him his pager back while he told me about how the bike was much more legitimate than he thought from a distance.

"Honestly I was thinkin' this was going to just be some kid's bike painted fancy to look tricked out. It's heavy but it's actually solid—that's a cool bike, yo," he said.

"Thanks!" I probably sounded overjoyed at the compliment.

I continued on my way, beaming—I felt proud and thrilled to have this bike that even the older kids thought was worthy. The whole experience left me daydreaming, free and blissful, like when I hit the jumps to soar into the sky.

When I got home an hour later, I wanted to tell my dad all about the interaction I had had because it confirmed that the bike was awesome, and I figured my parents would want to know that *everybody in the world* thought the bike was awesome too!

"Umm. You shouldn't have done that, Katherine," he said. "That's your new bike, and he could've taken it. That's why he handed you his pager, and you're lucky he did, because you wouldn't have asked for that, and had he not, he would be riding your new bike down Contra Costa Avenue right now!"

He pointed at his pager that he wore clipped to his belt.

"Ooooooooooh." I now understood that the guy had handed me it as collateral to reassure me he wouldn't take off with my bike.

"So don't do that again, but I'm glad you had fun and yes, it's a good bike."

Although I went from feeling wicked cool to immensely stupid in one moment, I had learned, I had lucked out, and I had been affirmed all in that morning. Not a bad Saturday.

Talent Shows in 1999

I DIDN'T NEED TO DO IT.

I wasn't forced to.

It wasn't a requirement of entering third grade to perform in it, but here I was.

Fall of 1999, I ended up in a talent show. Any elementary schoolers could try out and most got accepted. Somehow, I got swept into being in two acts.

The first was with a random girl in one of my classes who always wore pigtails. I think we were friends, or maybe friendly, because she was the younger sister of one of JT's friends. Anyway, her name was Cathy and she wanted to do a dance to ABBA's "Dancing Queen." Yeah.

In my baggy shorts and T-shirt, I groaned, giving in. She and her mom came up with a dance routine and I went over to her house after school one day. I tried my best to learn it. I did. But the day before the show was when things got confusing.

"So we're going to wear these tight white sparkly shirts and pants, okay?" She paraded around her bedroom.

"What?" I hadn't heard about this until now.

"Yeah! Mom says we should match. We'll look better!" I could tell I was going to lose this battle.

"Okay, I guess I'll change clothes in the middle then," I thought out loud, remembering the second act I was in.

I was also going to sing karaoke to "All Star" by Smash Mouth, my favorite band at the time. It had been released in May of that year. When I had gone to tryouts, I had sung along to a recording. Standing there, uncomfortably still, I tried my best to loosen up but felt intimidated by this other act. A trio of guys were also trying out, playing Blink-182 covers. I loved Blink-182. This cover band sounded godly to me. I felt envious and starstruck. Wow. When the supervisors heard my performance, they asked if the boys would play the song and then I could sing with a band and loosen up.

Sure. I'll totally loosen up with some strange boys surrounding me. No big deal.

But I was in my sweatpants, baggy shirt on, and I don't think they gendered me as something other than them. Voices were all on a similar plane and mine seemed neutral to me and likely others. I tried, while singing, to sound like I had a deeper voice anyway. It was sung by a dude, so.

The night of the talent show, I could tell my mom and dad were proud of me; Dad was recording me on his video camera and Mom was beaming from the audience. I attempted to "fake it 'til I made it" when it came to our "Dancing Queen" routine. Cathy was happy I had squeezed into this shirt with sleeves that felt waaaaaay too short, just for her, and I was glad it was over.

A few acts after, I was with the boys, in my comfortably androgynous clothes—singing my heart out to "All Star."

And all that glitters is gold, only shooting stars break the mold . . .

Tomboy

IN 2001, I TURNED TEN years old. Mom flew us out to Massachusetts to take a look at houses. We stayed in a hotel in Waltham for a few days as we were driving around in a rental car to visit properties with the realtor. Mom's job was going to transfer her to somewhere in Boston, but the reality hadn't hit me until that moment. *We were moving, again.*

On our first day there, I read a sign on the highway that stated MIDDLESEX COUNTY. Sitting in the backseat, I had no words to describe it and while I was reading every name off the signs, I skipped that one so I didn't have to read it out loud. It made me feel uncomfortable to see that on the signs, the word "sex."

Instead, I distracted myself with the fact that Worcester was pronounced "Wooster" and that Leominster was "lemon-stir" rather than "Leo-Mine-Stir" as I would have assumed. The towns all had weird names and it especially confused me that they had to indicate Concord, Massachusetts from Concord, New Hampshire because they weren't creative enough to come up with different names for different towns in different states.

"California is unique, these Massachusetts people are boring with their names," I thought.

Heading into the suburbs on one of the outings we took to peruse houses, we went down a street in Acton that ended with this barn-like house. It had a large backyard with a pond and hills. I liked that it looked campy, like something out of a movie; it was starkly different from any house I had seen in California.

JT and I followed along with Mom and the realtor, noting the things that ten- and twelve-year-olds look for—enough kitchen counter space wasn't as important as imagining where our N64 and our beanbags would get to live, for example. The issue was that it was a two-bedroom house. The master bedroom was clearly set up for the adults, and the second bedroom had peaked ceilings with exposed beams. Coming from stucco and white walls and ceilings, I thought this bedroom was the coolest in the world. Plus, they had two or three kids, so there was a bunk bed in there.

"Mom! Mom! I love this one!" I gushed.

"Well, there are only two bedrooms . . ."

"It's okay! I'll share with JT! I don't care! It'll be fun!" I was optimistic.

In the end, Mom didn't like the house that much. I tried to fight for it because I liked the rustic nature and I *really* liked the idea of sharing a bedroom with JT so we could be bros. In retrospect, I don't think JT would have been down with that, but it was Mom who made the call—my dream of two brothers sharing a bedroom wasn't going to come true.

Turns out, JT started puberty the following year, and I was heading straight that way, too. I didn't realize it would be weird for JT and me to share a room because I didn't realize what puberty was about to do to us both.

JT was about to become a "man." And within a few years, I was expected to become a "woman." A brother and sister sharing a bedroom wouldn't make sense; my reality, the one I didn't speak about, had been that we were brother and brother. And maybe, had I articulated that to my mom, she would have heard me before puberty.

I just didn't have the words.

When all was said and done, we settled on a four-bedroom house that was one street over from the barn-like house I had adored. Then, we headed back to California for the final few months of school before packing everything up.

My friend Maria and I took a trip to our local skate park one last time.

"We will be even better next time you're here," she said.

"Heck yeah. We'll be doing backflips!" I tried to stay optimistic.

While I was lacing up my skates, she took off down a smaller ramp and went up on the island. I was always nervous going down any ramps, much preferring to enter the park on level ground rather than jump right in. But it was our last time. As soon as I hopped over the edge, I knew I was about to get the wind knocked out of me. I had leaned backwards while going down, thus tilting entirely backwards and landing flat on my ribs. There were tons of other kids around, too; I looked at some of the guys over in the bowl doing tricks and wished I could do that but instead I was lying, splattered on white concrete. With no breath in my lungs, I felt like I was dying. Thankfully, I knew from previous experiences that I wasn't.

"Dude! You okay? What happened?" Maria rushed over to my side. Gasping, I gestured with my hands.

"Oh, I thought you learned not to do that last time, jeez," she said, laughing as she reached down her hand to help me up. She reminded me of the time I had knocked the wind out of myself in her back yard and been super freaked out while her dogs licked my face.

"I still want to skate," I announced, giggling once I had gotten my breath back.

"You sure?" she asked, concerned.

"Yeah . . . I don't know when else I'll get to be back at a park like this with a friend as good as you." I slid down into the bottom of the bowl and did my usual routine of trying to get up on some of the edges but not doing anything spectacular. I never went to the skate park with my board, just with my skates, because I knew I couldn't do anything on a board except get major speed, fall off, or get from my house to a friend's house around the block. I didn't even have enough skills to get out of the bowl without using my elbows to prop me up. And yep, I wore wrist guards, knee pads, and elbow pads. My parents required it.

"Dude, I wish I could get some Roces," Maria said.

They were these sick skates she loved. They had been the latest fad in the roller-skating community. I made a mental note that I wanted them too; if not for myself to get better at skating then to remind me of her when I felt lonely in Mass.

When we finally had our actual goodbye, just the two of us, I felt I was losing my best friend forever. The distance was going to be too far; we still had so much time left ahead of us in school to make new friends and form new bonds. I hoped I could meet people like her in Massachusetts; I wrote in my diary that I was worried I wouldn't. We had had everything in common, from Girl Scouts to being on the All-Star team in softball, and although I felt like nothing would change that, I began to feel defeated and alone.

One night in the hotel, days before we got to Massachusetts, Mom sat JT and me down.

"Your dad isn't going to be with us anymore," she said, as if she were telling us a secret.

Assuming something awful had happened, like Dad had died, we started crying and getting confused and angry. Mom clarified that she and Dad would be getting a divorce once we arrived in Massachusetts, but we were convinced he must be dead. We were in hysterics.

Dad actually turned his van around to come back to us and prove he was alive. He was there the next day. With both of them, we went over what would happen on the East Coast. Dad was looking for a job and a place to live, potentially hoping to own a motel. Part of the reason he drove cross country was so he could stop and look at different opportunities.

JT and I understood this, but perhaps JT understood better what it meant. In my mind, not much was going to change, but I was so very, very wrong.

I called Maria super quick and let her know what was happening.

"I'm so sorry," she said. She still sounded so close by. I wished we hadn't said goodbye as early as we had, but she and her family were going on a trip the next morning. As we hung up the phone, I began to cry. I opened up my journal, picked up a blue sparkly pen, and wrote:

Sometimes life doesn't seem so fair and I'm not happy about it. I can't breathe, like when I fell skating the other day with Maria and I don't want to keep moving this fast. Will I ever even come back to San Ramon? What if I don't? Will Maria forget me?

We arrived in Massachusetts in August of 2001. I had been afraid to leave, but in reality, moving into the new house was exciting, especially since it was the summertime. One of the first things I remember is that we had to figure out what to fill the base of the basketball hoop with. In Cali, it had been weighed down with water, but here we were deciding if we should put water or sand in it. JT and I wanted it on the street but Mom insisted it had to be in the driveway until we were older or we knew how busy the street was. Something like that.

I settled into the smallest bedroom, right at the top of the stairs. Even though our guest bedroom was bigger, I liked this one because it had huge built-in bookshelves along the wall. Plus, the window in the corner overlooked our garage roof, something I knew I'd want to climb out on someday. Mom had let me get new bedroom furniture that I was so excited about. The brass bed set I had had before was not going to do.

I chose a lofted bed from a local furniture store, so it was like a merge between the bunk bed I actually wanted and something that would fit in my small room. The bed was about four feet up and so I would be sleeping right in the middle of my window, able to look out through it to the backyard. Underneath it, I had a small dresser, a sliding-door chest that was perfect to store all my mini skateboards and Legos, and a desk table that could roll out. There was space for my giant stuffed lion that I used to ride down the stairs in Cali. I kept him under there to keep me safe; he fit perfectly. I also used pipe cleaners twisted together to tie a small baseball bat to the railings by where I slept, just in case. In some way, because my dad wasn't around anymore and because I was right at the top of the stairs, I wanted to be sure I could protect the family.

The cats we had adopted when I was a baby, Thelma and Louise, liked to sleep on my bed lots. But right when we moved in, we couldn't find Thelma. Dad happened to stop by around that time and he helped us to look for her. She legitimately wasn't anywhere to be found; JT and I began thinking we would have to post MISSING CAT posters already and we had just moved there! It was so scary and it was hard to remain calm.

The basement creeped me out, but of course we had to look there too, as it had the most nooks and crannies. The gross faded brown carpet matched the dark wooden paneling that ran halfway up the walls. The rest was painted off-white, and the ceiling had those dropped tiles combined with fluorescent lights that I originally thought were reserved for schools.

We heard something in the wall and looked into one of the electrical outlets in the corner that we could pop open for some reason. Thelma had squeezed herself in between all the wood paneling and the structure of the house, with all the wires and pipes running through it too. Seeing the bare bones of the house was confusing to me, since Cali had felt like it ended with the white stucco walls. Way creepier, for sure. Thelma looked spooked in between all this dust and rubble with the flashlight in her eyes, and JT and I called for help. Being a cat, she was stubborn, and unlike a dog, wouldn't come when we called her name. Dad had a pretty great idea of spraying her with one of our water squirt guns to scare her and get her to run out the other side where we'd opened a small door. Dad would talk about that genius idea for years because it was quite smart.

She ended up bolting right on out of there and we sealed up the way to get into the wall space. Soon after, we also had to seal up the workshop-type room that had this awesome graffiti: a giant smiley face that simply read "SMILE AND THE WHOLE WORLD WILL SMILE BACK!" However, that room didn't have a finished ceiling so my other younger kitty, Tiger, had managed to get himself up in it and walk around in between the floorboards and the basement ceiling, causing little white bits of it to break off and fall, until he got his butt stuck under a support beam right above the washer and dryer. That time, it was alarming but also pretty hilarious to have to pull the rascal out by removing the ceiling tile under him.

Dad wasn't around much after that. That's the thing about divorce; everyone seems to go about it differently. My parents had never had any huge fights around us before we moved, but after getting to our new home in Massachusetts, it was clear that this was my mom's space and that Dad wasn't supposed to be in it.

One of the last times I remember Dad being at our house was when he had dropped off a box on our front porch at the end of August. The cats had been staring at it through the window when I came home. I opened the box. Inside was a tiny turtle. It had a spiky tail, its shell no bigger than the palm of my hand. I knew it must have been Dad who had dropped it off because in the box there was one piece of green vegetation and a bright orange cap to a milk carton filled with a little bit of water.

When Mom got home, she was pissed about it. She didn't want a turtle and she wasn't thrilled that Dad was still coming by and adding to our house when it was clear he was supposed to be off finding his own. I called Dad and told him we had to bring the turtle back to wherever it came from. Oh, also, it was a baby snapping turtle.

Dad came back in his van and picked me and the turtle up. I sat down in the big gray passenger seat. I loved that it had arm rests; they were huge and could go up or down. It was a super cushiony vehicle overall and anytime I rode in it, I felt like we must be on some type of space adventure.

We drove back to the Walmart where Dad had found the turtle. He had been sleeping in the parking lot one night near this fenced-in area when he had found the baby snapper. As we approached that same area, I could tell right away it was infested with giant snapping turtles. I laughed, knowing my dad would have totally ignored the potential danger in search for a critter.

"Everything isn't changing, right?" I wondered aloud to Dad.

"Some things are changing, Katherine. That's the way life works. Things are constantly changing. But I'm going to be your dad forever, no matter what. This is what is best for you and JT."

"What do you mean, what's best?"

"For you to be with Mom. I want you with me always, of course, but I always knew. It makes sense for the children to be with the mom when a divorce happens. Mom is amazing, I'll always love Mom, and it makes the best sense for you guys to be with her," he explained.

When he dropped me back off at home, that was the last of him coming around to the house. Soon after, he found a motel in New Hampshire, about an hour and a half away, that he was going to own and operate. Mom dropped us off there every other weekend, but once school got busy, visits to Dad's were limited to holidays or other long weekend trips.

While Dad had mentioned some things would change, it felt like everything had. Holding the landline phone to my ear every other night, I'd call Dad to see what was up with his days. Once I hung up, I missed him immediately. But even though I seemed to favor my dad, I wasn't mad at Mom. Somehow, even though none of my friends' parents were divorced, and it was still pretty taboo, I knew that this made sense. I didn't expect to have a "normal" life and this seemed to reinforce that. The pieces, although jumbled several times, still fit together. I was working with what I'd been given. I opened up my journal for the first time in this new state.

December 2, 2001—MASS :,(

Dear Journal,

Sorry I haven't written for so long! I moved from San Ramon Calif to Acton, MA! I left all my best friends back there! Douglas is a cool school, but my teacher, Ms. Francine keeps staring at me as if I have 2,000 heads! Yesterday, Maria called! Cool! Today I hope I can call Betsy!

I have a good friend here in Mass, her name is Amy. Even though my parents got a divorce, I'm still stuck living here! Because if I moved back to CA, my dad would still be in New Hampshire. I wish they'd go back together! Hopefully, they won't get married to other people!

California is my most favorite place in the world. I'm glad I can visit there in the summer.

Midway through the fifth grade, we were told that were about to begin a series of videos and talks about puberty in the coming weeks and that we needed our parents to sign off on a permission slip. Or something like that. I was not paying attention.

I was too busy kicking some serious butt in kickball. Amy and I were often the best girl players on the kickball field and we got close because of that competition against the boys in many ways. We also got involved in baseball during recess and were pretty good at that, too.

At some point, my uncle gave me a shirt he had gotten from a Cheerios box. It was a bright yellow shirt (my favorite color) and had the logo across it. People began calling me "Cheerio Girl" instead of Katherine. I didn't mind it because I didn't like the name Katherine. Plus, people hadn't been making fun of me or anything, but they jabbed a bit at my outfits from California. First, I wore those pants that could be zippered off into shorts; to my own detriment, yes, I liked to wear them like every single day. I also had a bunch of skateboard shirts with ELEMENT across the front. I had a few California-specific skate shop shirts that I loved to wear. I wore a lot of JT's hand-me-downs. Although I had fit in a little bit more with the folks in Cali, it was clear that here in Massachusetts, I was a tomboy.

The word "tomboy" back then meant simply a girl who likes to do what boys do. There was no word like "tomgirl," though there ought to have been. But maybe because in many ways, American society favors men, they could understand why a girl would act like a boy. The idea of the opposite, however, likely seemed preposterous.

I loved being called a tomboy because it had the word "boy" in it. Before I had the words, I knew I loved being called a boy. It was a feeling, deep down inside of me, that smiled, and felt awakened, when people called me a boy. Even if it was in the context of a girl who liked to do boy things. It meant so much to me, but at the time, I had no idea why.

Mom had hung a calendar whiteboard up in our kitchen pantry. She used JT's initials for his events and she would use KE for mine. I didn't like the look of KE. Listening to NSYNC, I heard the name KC. I asked Mom if she could write KC instead of KE. She was fine with it and that was the last we saw of KE on the board. KC felt more androgynous to me.

So basically, when the puberty class was about to happen, I felt grossly uncomfortable. First, they had to divide us up into boys and girls and separate us. Sitting with a room full of all the fifth-grade girls in a classroom had me nervous. I made some jokes to try to be more comfortable. Joking around always helped me lighten up situations and I had long used laughter as a way to get me out of a nervous funk. Part of me wanted to be the class clown too, but I was definitely too shy for that.

The female teachers were all with us. They started playing a film, something with a name like "Just Around the Corner." It was about puberty for girls. It talked about what girls' bodies were about to go through; what *our* bodies were supposedly about to go through. There were some cartoons. The intro cartoon showed a black girl, a white girl, an Asian girl, a girl with blonde pigtails, a girl with long black hair, a chubbier girl, a very short girl . . . all holding hands dancing in the street as they rounded a corner to a big exclamation point.

They basically looked at it like "WHAT IS THAT?!" with their hands over their mouths, giggling or gasping.

The little dot on the exclamation point introduced itself as a period. Then, the narrator began to talk about what to expect every month. What a period is. What it does to the body. How getting your period is a "huge step to womanhood." These were all the feelings I was left with, at least, whether or not they were entirely truly the message of the video.

There was a 3D model in that class, or maybe later on at the nurse's office, that showed the vagina and how everything is inside and outside of there and how it all works and how to put a tampon in that to stop the bleeding or how to use pads. It looked graphic, and I felt horrified. I felt embarrassed. I felt like I was a creepy boy sitting in this classroom full of girls learning about their bodies. I felt like I was learning something I wasn't *supposed* to know. I was accidentally admitted into the secret "Girls to Women Club" and it wasn't cool.

After I managed to get past the initial shock of blood and period talk, the movie also talked about other factors of puberty. Breasts growing, for example. What a bra is/how to handle that. How hair may grow places. Where, when, why, and how this would all come together. I covered my eyes for some parts.

After the female movie was over, we were told to switch class-rooms with the boys, but they did it in such a way that we couldn't interact with the boys very much. They must have expected some awkwardness between the two genders mixing in the midst of this very educational day. Turned out, we had to learn about what would happen to boys' bodies next. Sitting in the room with all the girls, though, it was more of a snickering, laughing moment than in the previous room. While learning about female puberty was informative to this group, the male puberty was something to laugh at or poke fun at.

A cartoon showed a boy skyrocketing in height. His voice cracking and then finally dropping. Skin getting oily, pimples popping up. Feet needing larger shoes. I could see that JT was probably starting puberty. The videos clarified that female puberty came before male puberty in a lot of cases.

Seeing what the boys could expect, I realized I had expected that for myself too. I had seen JT growing taller. His voice cracking and how funny that was. How he had been growing out of a lot of his clothes, which worked out well for me because I got to pick through bags of hand-me-down shirts and shorts before they went off to Goodwill. I'd even started seeing some of his Lakers basketball jerseys in there; not that I knew anything about the Lakers, but I liked the purple and yellow mesh tank tops and figured he would have never gone to donate one. Since he had been growing out of them, though, more had trickled down into my happy wardrobe.

At the end of the videos, we were allowed to ask questions.

All I wanted to ask was, "So . . . how can I go through *that* puberty instead of *this* one?"

That day was a wake-up call for me. The future I had imagined, where my androgynous body would go through the male puberty, had been proven to be a misunderstanding. And while I could see right in front of me what was to come for my body, I had this gut feeling that *nah, they just put me in the wrong group and they'll see they were wrong to think I was going through that one, hahaha.* At least I knew what *could* happen. I had a strong feeling that it *wouldn't* happen to me.

I felt this pit in my stomach, and it wasn't about upcoming puberty. It wasn't about the ways my body was going to change. It's just . . . I had been having such a great time playing kickball and baseball with the boys at recess. Amy and I had been doing so well, fitting in as tomboys. As I climbed on the bus home, even though people weren't talking seriously about the films, I felt like everything had changed. I worried that, the following day at recess, kickball wouldn't be the same. That I would be looked at as this body about to go through this, that, and the other thing. And with all of those changes, that the boys would no longer see me as one of them.

November 15, 2002

Now I'm in the 6th grade. Ugh. My teachers Miss H and Mr. C are soooo nice. Same with Miss B and Mrs. D, the assistants. Mrs. O is EVIL! I dread writing except that it is right before recess. I love recess. I play baseball with the boys and 3 other girls. A person named Hunter said I had hit the longest home run, except for Enrique because he's a year older than everyone else. Also, Hunter and Jeremy said I made the best play, in which I ran and dove for a ball in right field because no one was there, and I caught it. I've caught most of the fly balls in my area. They even say I'm better than most of the guys. They even let me bat because every time I hit it, I at least get a double. I'll keep you informed on baseball for a while.

Oh yeah and I got a 5 month old Bernese Mountain puppy named Toby. He's cool, too.

I didn't write too much in my journal during fifth grade, but with this update in sixth, I knew things had continued on as normal. Amy and I kept at it; recess was our savior. I had joined the soccer team too, often wearing my Cheerio shirt to practices. Because I was bright yellow, I'd sometimes be put as goalie. Having played defense before, it seemed okay to switch off since no one liked being goalie on my team. I started to like being goalie and Mom allowed me to get this young boy's goalie shirt for my new role. It had little elbow pads for when I would dive after the ball. I loved pulling it on before a cold, frosty morning practice. It gave me an extra layer of protection; I could live inside my fantasy of being on the Olympic men's team someday by hiding my body that way.

Massachusetts and I had a rough start. First, I couldn't spell "Massachusetts" during the spelling bee. Second, I had no idea what the state capital was. These were things others had learned from the get-go, and when I couldn't catch up quickly, I realized I was on the outside and missed California.

It turns out that not many people say "hella" on this coast. In California, everything was hella cool! Or hella rad! Or hella nice! But here, that wasn't a phrase. "Wicked" was the word. Wicked, like the winters.

Being a sunshine kid, I wanted nothing to do with the ice and snow that poured down during this season. However, it did present me with an opportunity I had not expected: snowboarding.

Snowboarding looked similar enough to skateboarding that I figured I should try it out. Plus, back in Cali, I had always wanted to learn to surf. Never having the access or guts (sharks? No thanks!) to take on that idea, snowboarding seemed great.

There was a little mountain—well, more like a hill—nearby our town that people could ski or snowboard on. They also had lessons there and as part of our Christmas that year, we received lessons to snowboard, which was very exciting!

Dressed in snow pants, a snow jacket, helmet, and goggles, I knew one thing was for sure; once I was bundled up and ready to board, no one had any idea of my gender. My hair barely stuck out the back of my helmet. I got a black and blue winter coat—the blue was an instant symbol of "boy" to me.

Bundled and on the mountain, falling on my butt every five minutes, I felt free and unrestricted. Like putting on an outfit for a job. Or putting on a costume for a show. I could get into all my gear and I'd become something else, like a transformer. Often, people would yell, "Little dude, get out the way!" at me because I looked like a boy on the slopes, and I loved it.

At the time, I didn't know anyone else who skied or snowboarded. I'd find friends later on, in high school, but prior to that—snowboarding was a fairly solitary activity for me, unlike all the sports I played. It became something I looked forward to, even at night in December after Christmas when it was icy and cold. Even through March, stretching out the last bit of snow dirt (snirt).

For a long time, I repeated "I'm a boy" in my head or wrote it in my journals. I never spoke it out loud, because looking at my body and everything, it seemed unrealistic. It seemed impossible. While I knew it to be true, I didn't think anyone else would believe me or know what I meant. It felt impossible to describe—even "I'm a boy" didn't seem to sum it up. And without the words, I continued on, full swing into puberty.

I entered the seventh grade, middle school, and people around me began getting their periods. It was partially hush-hush, especially for the first girls to get theirs. Something about it being shocking for the early ones. But no one wanted to be "too late" either—something might be wrong. Some people talked openly about it, others were tight-lipped. It was awkward.

Months before puberty reared its angry head at me, I recall being at my dad's motel and playing my favorite game alone in the woods, which was "Boyfriend/Girlfriend." I'd pretend to be the boyfriend of my imaginary girlfriend.

Walking through the trees and boulders, I'd pretend to hold her hand and guide her around rocks, saying things out loud like, "Make sure you don't trip! I'd pick you up if you did though, don't worry!"

I wasn't hallucinating; it was a full-on roleplay fantasy out in my dad's many acres. I'd flop down on the hill and imagine having a girlfriend curl up under my arm, like in the movies. I felt like a country boy up in the middle of nowhere New Hampshire and wanted to be a true gentleman, living up to the books I'd read.

My dad always had a bunch of guitars around, too. I had learned four basic chords and Dad encouraged me to learn more. I wanted to write love songs someday, I had decided. I took one of Dad's guitars home with me from that school break and began playing it almost every day. Just in time to cope with the impact of a pubescent body.

I got my period sometime during the seventh grade and my body began changing, like the movie had said it would. When I saw the blood in my underwear, I wanted to cry. It felt like a huge inconvenience and the beginning of an irreversible time of life.

I told Mom about getting my period and that I needed some supplies for it. She asked if I had any questions. I muttered a no. And then sometime later on, my mom told me she would buy me a razor at the pharmacy.

"Why? For what?"

"You know, girls your age will begin to shave their legs."

My face blushed with embarrassment. Girls shaving their legs? What's wrong with leg hair? I had little knowledge about these expected standards and no desire to learn.

"No thanks, I'm all good."

She shrugged and moved along. I always appreciated that about Mom. If she suggested something and we didn't roll with it, she wouldn't harp on it or try to convince us. Sometimes, maybe, she would rephrase it later for us to think about differently. I appreciated that a simple decline of a razor did not cause a preteen girl versus her mom screaming match.

Mom did give me one razor, in case I wanted to use it. Instead of shaving my legs with it, though, I was curious about my face. Girls around me had begun trimming their eyebrows. Not knowing about tweezers, I assumed they used the razors they shaved their legs with too. One day, in the shower, I decided I'd do the same. I presumed that I could shave in the direction of the hair and it would leave behind a nice thin line of an eyebrow left. Seemed easy. I didn't look any info up beforehand, but to me, it seemed likely that would be the way it was done.

I immediately felt like something was wrong after I shaved my right eyebrow. There was no mirror in the shower; I reached up to feel my face. There wasn't much hair there, just little stubbles. I ran out of the shower and wiped the steam off the mirror.

I had shaved off my entire right eyebrow.

My jaw dropped. I looked up closer. It looked weird, of course. And my eyebrows hadn't been that bushy before. Why did I have to ruin a great thing?!

I took a deep breath, knowing I'd have to own this. And that I'd likely have to explain this. I didn't shave the other eyebrow to make it even. I came up with an excuse.

The following day, my neighbor on the bus pointed at me. "What happened to your face?"

"Oh, I ran into a tree branch when I was running outside and it took out my eyebrow hairs!" It seemed like a totally legitimate excuse. Regardless, I had one eyebrow for a week or two and it was definitely embarrassing when I thought too much about it.

Personal grooming came at the onset of puberty for a lot of the people around me. If I had been privy to some female knowledge, I might have had makeup that I could've used to fill in my missing eyebrow; but alas, I was not knowledgeable. Deodorant became a regular daily chore. I went from the women's section to the Old Spice section midway through high school. But before that autonomy, I was at the mercy of Mom's bulk Secret deodorant hauls from Costco.

With the onset of puberty came a change in my wardrobe. JT's old clothes weren't going to fit my body as it changed. On trips to the mall with Mom, we ended up in the girls section most of the time. I didn't like looking at bras; my chest was barely growing. Sports bras seemed to be the best bet; I also dug a few of these tank tops that were undeniably feminine, but less feminine than a straight-up bra.

I got some tight jeans as well, a couple of pairs. A few shirts that were cut for women—shorter sleeves, tighter fitting. As my body began to change, I tried my best to accommodate it. I didn't feel I had any other choice.

I also began dating boys. Just a few parent-approved dates and an "i luv u _____" in my AIM profile. I kissed like four different boys, dating them for a couple of weeks to a few months. Relationships didn't last very long in middle school. A lot of my guy friends stuck to dating the girls in our friend group, and then as we expanded, it wasn't too uncommon to expect them to try to date the newcomers.

Simultaneously, some of my friends began questioning if they were bisexual. At sleepovers, we would talk endlessly about what that meant. Girls kissing girls and boys kissing boys became a sort of trend for teens at the time, at least on MySpace, where posts and videos and pictures ran rampant. We also began to lean more toward emo music. The likes of Hawthorne Heights, Brand New, My Chemical Romance, Avenged Sevenfold.

While my friends were experimenting with kissing one another, I claimed I was 100 percent straight. Not a doubt in my mind. I didn't experiment with friends (besides a kissing video you'll read about in the next chapter).

But I did love the new gothic clothes some of my friends were trying out. We went to Hot Topic in the mall together. I got these big baggy black jeans; they were pretty androgynous overall, but they had holes and chains and metal studs decorating them. They even had suspenders that I never wore as actual suspenders, leaving them to dangle behind my butt and restrict my walking. It was awesome and I wanted to wear them every single day.

The nice thing about the aesthetic that my friends and I were getting into was that it was primarily dark colors. Black shirts, black jeans, black shoes. Black is a slimming color in a lot of ways and it also didn't carry any big gender weight to it, like blue or pink seemed to. Other people in the emo and goth scene embraced androgyny. It was perfect timing, as my chest had decided to become full grown and I wanted to run away from dealing with it. Baggy black clothes did the trick.

In the eighth grade, Amy and I practically lived for Friday afternoons, when we could go down to the Bowladrome, a run-down bowling alley/arcade nearby. They had the giant Dance Dance Revolution machines that, being sporty but also musical, Amy and I loved. Amy was a beast at DDR and could beat most of the boys. I loved it too—hopping around and stomping on tiles to a song repeating "la diddy daaai my little butterflyyyyy" made me feel better.

The Bowladrome was also a popular spot for going on dates. There was a dark corner that was carpeted even on the walls, with this black speckled galaxy theme that glowed in black light. Friends that were seeing each other could often be caught making out in one of the dark corners. It was grimy, it was gross, but it was our little group's safe space.

With two years as tumultuous as middle school and puberty could possibly be, hiding out with my friends on the outskirts of society felt right. It was like a little home. A little dysfunctional, but wonderful. As we moved into high school, we still visited our space for a few months. Then, a spot called Danny's Place opened up at the school. It had video games, a stage for concerts, and musical instruments. Danny's Place was a less sketchy version of the Bowladrome, and it had been set up to help provide entertainment and a safe space after school for students.

The goth phase fizzled out as we entered high school. With 2,000 students, it was a behemoth of a building. I didn't want to attract unnecessary attention.

A/S/L?

B ACK IN THE THIRD GRADE, when I wasn't sneaking around or riding my bike, my parents would let me use the Internet for a half hour in the evenings. It was a treat to get to climb onto the big wooden chair on the big wooden desk that my dad often sat at. The Internet was a small thing—computers still loaded with blue screens, took ten minutes to boot up (if not longer), and the Internet was dial-up. Dial-up meant that it used the phone line in order to connect to it. I had no understanding of what it was or how it worked or why it affected the phone. But it made sense, because at least it was attached to a cord, like the phones. In my mind, all this information was traveling through a cord connecting right to the other person. Magic. Now, wireless Internet blows my mind.

When I started using Neopets, a site where you can play games and earn coins and have a shop, I found out people there also used AOL Instant Messenger (AIM). It was my first gateway to the Internet. Neopets also began to teach me HTML—they had these spaces called "guilds" which was like a personal page or website that one could code and manage. I wanted a sparkly font in mine and so I had to learn how to code images in and put them on the left, center, or right—I could talk about this for ages. It was fascinating.

"A/S/L?" was used to ask someone their age/sex/location. At first, mine would read 8/f/CA if I was being honest. I often bumped myself up to 10 or 12 and changed my location to Florida because I knew my parents would be so mad if I gave out any personal information on the computer. So as I began to use AIM, I was 10/f/FL. Sometimes 12/f/TX. Depended on my mood, I suppose.

All my chats were quite innocent. Nothing scandalous. This was before smartphones and easy picture taking—there was no selfie so there was no one asking to see one. That type of anonymity intrigued me. One day, when I created a new AIM screen name (you could have an infinite number), I became 12/m/CA. At some point, I began telling people I was 14/m/CA. Guys would talk to me about guy stuff, although the guy stuff was really the same stuff I'd talk about to any of my friends, such as Pokémon and sports. It felt awesome. One day, in a random chat room with the topic of Nintendo, this 16/f/MA girl messaged me. We began chatting back and forth and I was like *holy shit I'm talking to a girl omg she thinks I'm a boy omg this is so cool.*

It was my first time ever "being" a boy. I was a real boy to someone else. I didn't have any words in my head—gender? That wasn't a word I knew. I was being . . . a different version of myself online. A truer version. I was exploring my identity. But I didn't have those words.

It was so impactful to me, I can remember exactly what we talked about over AIM that first time. She was asking me what I like to do in California since she had never been there. I told her I was basically your typical skater boy kid. That I could do ollies and kick flips (I couldn't and I can't). That I was a legend around the local skate park. That I played guitar (I do now, but I didn't then), and sang songs to my girlfriend often. Then she told me about how her boyfriend had stayed over that last Friday night, and I was all concerned as to why her parents would allow that and she mentioned it wasn't like they actually "did" anything, they just slept, and her parents trusted her and him.

I felt what was, I guess, a pang of jealousy about her having a boyfriend. Did I think that some sixteen-year-old girl across the country was going to long distance have a crush on a "fourteen-year-old boy" in California? (Never mind the fact that I was a nine-year-old girl at that point.) We talked lots over the course of a year. Things ended abruptly when my parents told my brother and I that we would be moving to the East Coast—specifically, to Massachusetts. I remember complaining about this to my online friend, but she got super excited thinking our paths would cross and we could be real life friends. She told me she lived in Wakefield—we were moving to somewhere near Waltham, not far from her. Then, I totally stopped talking to her. I didn't want her to want to actually meet me and then be disappointed to find out I wasn't who I said I was. I didn't want her to meet me and see that I was a girl in real life.

A few years later, living in Massachusetts, I found myself creating a MySpace page under the fake name Brandon. The issue was that I had been IMing a few people saying I was 14/m/MA (when in actuality, I was 11/f/MA) and now technology had caught up to me. People had begun having "profiles" on websites like MySpace, and a picture was pretty much required. As I created Brandon's profile, I kept most of the details true about me aside from my gender. To solidify that I was a guy, I wrote that I had done Boy Scouts. Truthfully, I had watched my brother race in Pinewood Derby and thought it was the coolest thing ever, so it wouldn't be a stretch for me to talk about it if questioned.

But then it came time for the picture and I had no idea what to do.

Rummaging about on the Internet, I pulled up a band I had been hearing lately, the surf rocky poppy McFly group from over in the UK. They had come together that past year, and in early 2004 they had their first hit single. At this time, I gathered not many people in the US knew about them or who they were. I thought Danny looked like what I'd look like if I swapped one of my Xs for a Y chromosome. He had ear-length straight brown hair and an oval face and brown eyes.

I picked a photograph I found of him in a yellow shirt. I stored a couple of lesser known pictures of him—one of him playing his acoustic guitar, one of him with shorter hair—in a folder on my computer so I had some I could show to people if they didn't believe my pictures were actually me. It was a super complicated time for me. Living each day in the real world as a seemingly happy, hyper girl. At night, I was down in my basement on my computer, pretending to be a boy.

I kept all of these things top secret. I made sure JT couldn't see my computer screen at any time. I wiped my browser history daily. I deleted stored AIM conversations. I would have felt humiliated if anyone had seen them, if anyone had made me feel uncomfortable about it. I knew it was not necessarily *right*. But I knew that this part of my life was super important to me. I looked forward to logging on at the end of a day. I looked forward to reading the messages I would get from folks. I posted a shirtless picture of Danny at one point. I remember thinking I would never be able to post a shirtless picture of myself, ever. But that somehow felt okay, because I was living vicariously through a person who was born male and didn't have to worry about many of the things I would have to worry about later on.

Everything was kept so secret that I can't even log back into my accounts now to check them out, and many of my profiles were private out of fear that the actual Danny would see I was stealing his stuff. One evening, I saw a comment saying I looked exactly like Danny Jones from McFly. Before they could get further, I blocked them.

Whew, I thought, *That was a close call!*

Just like how I could hide behind my computer screen, I could also hide those who were trying to expose my world. I had a heightened sense of fear of being discovered—even if it was by my parents seeing my MySpace left up or a stranger on the Internet calling out my appropriation of images. I would have been mortified, as I assumed others would make me feel bad about something that was making me feel so good.

Brandon, in many ways, existed from when I was in elementary school to when I came out as Skye in high school. He lived in California and in Massachusetts with me. Although I didn't know it at the time, I had actually found a fantastic source of relief for my gender dysphoria. While I moved through my day-to-day interactions as Katherine, whom I still felt I *was*, my evening interactions reinforced my idea of Brandon, who I felt I was becoming. And when I, as Brandon, interacted with folks online, through messaging and MySpace and even Neopets, I felt incredible. It was an alternate reality to escape into, but it was also my reality. I was living dual lives—one that went to school with her friends and one that existed online with his acquaintances.

When I was in middle school, my fake online boy life and my real life intertwined in such a strange way, I almost didn't want to write about this. Gender exploration happens in a lot of ways, some of which are unusual and uncomfortable. For me, this is one of them.

My friends and I were bored in my basement after school. We had the lower half of my brother's bunk bed down there and on Fridays we often went to my house. My mom got home later than other parents, and the huge downstairs space was a good spot to hang out away from adults and people's siblings.

We all had recently joined this online community called Bat Caves. Very similar to MySpace but more gothic and definitely more diverse in that sense. They also had this "Top Rated" guys and girls feature. It was a weird combination of online networking, dating, and having your own website. You could have friends and followers. And everyone got a small page they could post pictures, likes, dislikes, personality quiz results . . . the usual for that simple old format of a social network site.

Someone, or somehow a few of us, came up with the idea that my friend Cassandra and I should pretend to be emo boys kissing for a video. I got excited about the idea and she did too. It seemed like an artistic social experimentation project—we would film the video and put it up on the accounts that we would create for our new identities as emo boys.

So here I was, with three of my closest friends in my basement, right near the computer that I pretended to be Brandon on, merging my real life with my fake life in front of others. It was both exhilarating and terrifying. Now, it was out of my control. My secret life? They would be a part of it and we would talk about it in the cafeteria and it would become a reality in a way . . . I was nervous but way too thrilled not to forge ahead.

I don't remember what name Cassandra picked for her emo boy alias, but I simply chose Brandon out of familiarity. We also had to take a couple of pictures in order to fully fill out our profiles. Even with straightened long-ish hair and a bunch of eye makeup, we were able to pull off an effeminate boy look and passed as such by taking drastically angled pictures that hid any feminine features . . . like our breasts. Mine had started growing that year and though I didn't have the word dysphoria to describe my intense discomfort, I already wanted them to disappear.

With our most masculine clothes on, chests hidden, hair styled perfectly —we pressed our hands in front of our mouths to fake the kiss. It did look pretty real on film. It was a short video of the kiss, but we were all quite pleased with the content we had created. We put it up online and sat back to see the results. And people were wild about the video, as we had hoped.

But like, really, *really* wild. My Brandon page started to get lots of friend requests and comments. Many private messages gushing over how cute my friend and I were. It was awesome. And the best part? My friends and I could all talk about it together.

"Oh my god, look at what this person wrote!"

"Katherine they think you're SOOOOO hot omg!"

"Should we make another video?!"

"How's it feel to be a famous emo boy?!"

After we had our fun, we took the video down, deciding it wasn't worth the risk of our parents finding it. I kept some of the pictures I had taken for the profile and stored them in a hidden folder on my computer. Eventually, I went back to being Brandon on a new social media page where I used the new images.

Immediately, I felt more authentic. At least no one would be able to pull up my page and call me out for being Danny from McFly. Katherine, dressed up as a boy and pictured at drastic angles—even with long hair—had become Brandon in these photos. I had created a version of myself.

And a year or two later, after I cut my hair off, it became even easier to take these types of photos. I specifically remember making a paper clip chain necklace, duct taping my breasts to my chest, and sneaking into my brother's room to steal a thick white T-shirt. At fifteen, I looked like an eleven-year-old boy. But it was something.

I'd get compliments on MySpace about how cute I was as a boy. I had conversations that lasted weeks, months. I had friends, folks with crushes on me, folks wanting to hang out in person—Brandon had all this. It was like he was as real as I was. But what he did not have is what I had to juggle—school, sports, real life friendships, being a daughter, being a sister, being a cat parent. I had so much going on all at once— when I think about it these days, I wonder where I found the time.

Later, when I cut my hair short, I joined an online community called "birls" on LiveJournal. It was meant to be for girls who looked like boys (a.k.a. "birls") to share pictures and stories. I began posting on there under my normal, real account and became connected with others who were androgynous like myself. For a year, I went on the page almost daily.

Slowly, over time, I let that community drift into the back of my mind as I figured out I was simply a boy who looked like a boy. Not a girl who looked like a boy. Not a girl pretending to be a boy online. Just . . . a boy.

Holding fake identities online helped me to explore my gender. It gave me a release from the boxes I tried to squeeze myself into during the day. At night, I could be myself. And while I didn't realize it at the time, having that outlet likely saved my life. The acceptance I felt from strangers helped convince me that transitioning wouldn't be as scary as I thought it might be. I had been accepted as a boy, even if by folks who weren't looking right at my face. The confidence I gained helped shape the person, the transgender man, I am today.

Cancer

FEBRUARY IS COLD. IT'S A cold month—the coldest month of the year some years.

Mom usually left the house at five in the morning. Now, it was seven and I was packing my school bag in the dining room.

"I'm going to the doctor today," she explained when I looked at her curiously in the kitchen.

"Okay, cool," I said, kissed her on the cheek, and went off to catch the bus.

Weird, I thought, *but it's probably just a usual checkup.*

Mom didn't mention anything about her appointment, but a few days later, she got a phone call. I heard her answer it from her desk and I wasn't trying to eavesdrop, but I happened to be nearby.

"Oh." She sounded sad. "Well, what's next?"

I couldn't hear whatever the doctor was saying.

"Okay, I'll schedule that ASAP."

At dinner, nothing was mentioned. I dipped chips into our favorite succotash. The challenge was to eat the whole dinner with just the chips and not use the spoon. Challenge: completed.

A few more phone calls came to the house over the next few days. Mom also found out she needed to leave the start-up that she had recently been a part of. She began looking for jobs and seemed hopeful.

One day, a few weeks into February, Mom sat us down.

"The doctors have explained that I have something called multiple myeloma. It's quite rare, and unusual in someone so young as me, so we're figuring out what to do about it now. But there's nothing to worry about." She had a tear in her eye, though. How could I trust there was nothing to worry about?

I didn't look it up online. I didn't want to read about it or hear stories Mom had made it clear—MM was an incurable form of blood cancer. Cancer with a big C.

Her doctors initially gave her three to four years. A lifespan defined. A lifespan set to end right before I graduated from high school. A life nothing could be done to save.

There were chemo options, however. Some people went into remission for several months or even years after chemo. The side effects were awful, but at least it was something she could try.

I went out on my roof a lot that spring. I thought about what it would be like to not have my mom around. I built a wall up in my heart that told me I could be independent and survive and be a part of this world, but I knew that I would fall apart without my mom. She was so strong. She didn't look sick.

Amy and I had a sleepover soon after I heard the news. I remember trying to explain it to her, and neither she nor I knew how to react. There wasn't much we could do, you know? No one in our friend group had experience with cancer, either, so we didn't know much of what to say.

"Maybe they'll find a cure for it?" Amy suggested.

"I hope so," I replied.

"What does MM do?" she asked.

"It's a cancer of the blood cells, like these evil blood cells attack the healthy ones. And then it creates holes in the bones, like Swiss cheese. And eventually, it attacks the organs so they can't function. It's so messed up." I felt like *I* was dying.

In stark contrast, Mom was optimistic and believed she had many years ahead. I saw that in her. She talked about adopting another Bernese Mountain Dog down the line. She talked about me and JT— attending our college graduations, our future marriages, the births of our children. She reminded me that this wasn't a death sentence.

Because of what she was going through, I wanted to do my best to not cause any problems. I wanted to support my mom and make things easier.

I wanted things to be easier.

Like they had been when I was younger.

Blending In

I WANTED TO BLEND IN AT high school, yeah. But I had a funny idea about blending in at high school. Blending in meant straightening my hair, putting it into a half ponytail, ditching my goth pants, and wearing handmade, marker-colored shirts. One, I had drawn a rainbow llama and labeled it "HYPER LLAMA" on the front.

Needless to say, I didn't blend in.

However, I did find the right people. While I was still friends with my main crew, I was also branching out into other groups of people. High school felt so much bigger. Also, JT was a junior while I was a freshman; this would be the first time we would be in school together.

Two weeks into the school year, someone caught my eye as I made my way through the quarter mile–long hallway that connected the whole building. Among the sea of faces, many of which I had never seen before, I spotted this jubilant, curly-haired person in a blue jean jacket decorated with pins and patches. She was wearing what looked like a navy blue–striped train engineer's hat, as she was leaning up against a locker, surprisingly quiet considering how loudly her outfit screamed, *Notice me or be reckoned with.*

She had this sticker on her notebook, a picture of Woody Guthrie smoking a cigarette and holding his guitar, on which he had painted THIS MACHINE KILLS FASCISTS. She wore baggy clothes, was taller and older-seeming than most of the other freshman, and I couldn't figure out where she had come from. She had an energy about her that I was immediately drawn to. Luckily enough, she started going to the high school's Gay-Straight Alliance right away. My best friends and I had already decided we were *definitely* going to attend.

The first few GSA meetings were mainly ice breakers. Girl with the hat and the sticker turned out to be Ashley. Ashley had an aversion to authority that I didn't see in many others until college. It was as if she had already learned she could trust only herself, that even teachers didn't have her best interests in mind, and that sometimes, the right option is to fight alone for what is right. It made sense—in one of our first conversations, she told me that she had transferred from a town almost an hour away. The reason being that she was gay, and the teachers at her old school did nothing to prevent the harassment she faced from her peers.

I pegged her in my mind as a queer hero. She had gone through a lot more than any of us were going to understand as fourteen-year-olds. She was almost sixteen and seemed more mature than the rest of my peers. I was always drawn to folks older than I was. I felt, I guess . . . special, when she said she wanted to hang out with me more.

One day after school, Ashley was waiting for her mom to pick her up. She asked me to wait with her.

"I can't wait until I get my license," she said. "I'm going to be so much more free, gah. Won't need anybody. Maybe I'll drive off somewhere and never even drive back."

She pulled out a black cigarette looking thing from her backpack (a clove cigarette, I later figured out).

"They're better for you," she gestured. "Not as bad as real cigs, though those are great too."

"Smells pretty good, honestly," I said. She offered me a puff but I declined. She smoked it down to the filter, smiling, as we continued waiting. Once her mom got there, we hugged and she left for the day. I felt butterflies in my stomach, having spent the short, cherished after-school freedom with a girl I found super intriguing. She had stories. She seemed . . . cool.

At this time, I was dating a boy I'd met in middle school. I technically had dated another boy for several months, but we only saw one another outside of school once and during school, he pretended like I didn't exist. Very serious stuff. One time I asked another guy to go snowboarding with me. He was way shyer than me so I decided to make the first move. Everyone assured me I was "out of his league" so I expected a yes. He said no. It was awkward.

So when my good friend, Tyler, who I played some guitar with, asked me out? I was thrilled. I got a cell phone during my freshman year, but I was limited to one hundred text messages a month. I spent them all on Tyler in the first week, of course. We'd been dating for a month when, at a party, he fell for this girl I knew. I was upset for a week or two before I collected my thoughts—he was my friend, first and foremost—and if supporting his new relationship meant he and I could still be buds, I was down.

Then Tyler left that girl and began dating a boy. When he told me about it, he was super nervous and felt pretty alone. Funny enough, at the same time he was coming to terms with his sexual orientation, I was also discovering mine.

As fall rolled into winter of freshman year, I followed Ashley around more closely, much to the detriment of my other friendships. I began only seeing my friends during the periods before school where we would arrive early and chat before class started at 7:27 a.m.

In January, Ashley asked me to be her girlfriend. I gleefully said yes. I was fourteen and felt like she was becoming my whole world—I *wanted* her to be my whole world. I *wanted* someone to work hard for, to impress, to woo. She acted like she desired the same for me.

As we began to hold hands in school, people began calling us lesbians, lesbos, freaks, faggots. While it was hard, I faced worse name-calling at home from my brother. Having been called "stupid" my whole life, I clung to the saying "I'm rubber, you're glue, anything you say bounces off of me and sticks to you." Yet much of this hatred got internalized, and it began turning school—a place where I had always felt safe—into a place where I felt judged, humiliated, and unwelcome.

Strangely, no one asked me about my sexual orientation. I had gone from dating boys off and on throughout middle school to now dating a woman who very much identified as a woman. She dressed androgynously, but she was visibly a woman. Me with my half ponytail and tight jeans? Yep. I certainly looked like a woman as well. Two women dating/holding hands? Default interpretation: lesbians.

We kept our relationship hidden from our parents for over eight months. I've got to give my mom some credit; she knew, but never brought it up. I'm thankful that she didn't, because I felt embarrassed to a certain degree. I wasn't embarrassed that I was in a seemingly gay relationship, but I was ashamed of how others were treating me and how I wasn't sticking up for myself. I didn't know how yet.

And at the same time, I was intrigued by this new world unfolding around me. Queer club meetings. Queer dances. LGBQ youth and activism began to surround me; I began to be a part of this new world. And after some time, I began to realize the differences between gender identity and sexual orientation. Within the year, I would finally meet the "T" in LGBTQ.

JT

O N MY SECOND DAY OF high school, I bumped into my brother in the halls. He barely acknowledged me. On the third day, he sneered when I walked by instead of saying hi. It wasn't how I expected our school experience would be.

At home, he was barely present. Some nights, he would come home after Mom and I had gone to bed. Sometimes, we didn't know where he had been. Some mornings, Mom would ask me to make sure JT got to school with me on the bus because she left around five in the morning to beat rush hour traffic into Boston. Most mornings, JT would either yell at me and threaten me or not say anything to me at all as he just barely made it to the bus stop.

In October, JT became more physically violent to me than he had been in the past. Previously, punching would happen occasionally, but would be one punch. Now, one small issue and I would be pushed up against a wall and strangled, not understanding what I had done to be there, gasping for breath and hoping he would let go. He always let go, but things began to escalate to threats of killing me, as well. JT wasn't acting like himself. He got suspended for bringing a milk jug with vodka in it to school. We didn't even have any alcohol in the house.

Toward the end of October, JT hadn't woken up pretty late on a weekend morning and we had plans so I went to go get him. I found him passed out in his bunk bed with an empty paper bag pressed into his face, presumably in case he puked. He looked dead.

Mom called an ambulance and JT woke up during that time not feeling well, but arguing he was fine. When the paramedics got there, Mom made them take him away, while he tried to fight them. We never used our front door in our house, always the side door by the garage. I'll never forget them bringing him out through there, restrained on a stretcher. I held Toby back while we locked the cats in the basement and tried to stay away from the situation.

On November 1, I woke up for school to find that Mom was still home.

"Should I go get JT up?" I had finished pouring a cup of coffee to take with me. I started drinking coffee younger than I would have liked, but it was needed after many nights of not sleeping for various reasons, both unknown (insomnia) and known (like JT coming home late.)

"No, it's okay, Katherine. Just go to school," Mom replied, sounding completely fine. It seemed like any other day.

Except JT wasn't in school that day. Maybe he had had an appointment? When I came home, Mom was still there. She hadn't gone to work. I was confused.

"Honey, JT won't be living with us for a while," she said, her tone firm.

"Is he okay?" Even though he scared me, he was my brother and I needed him.

Mom explained that he had been taken to a rehabilitation program, against his will, so that he could get healthy again. That he would be fine. That he would be back to the JT we had always known him to be, the kind, smart, funny, non-addicted brother whom I could love easier knowing he was healthy.

"Taken?!" I sobbed uncontrollably, not knowing what was going on.

"It's part of the program, sweetie. Two very kind, buff men came this morning and yanked JT out of bed and off to the wilderness in New York. Of course, he didn't take it lightly and was yelling and screaming the whole way out. However, the two guys called to let me know that he was very amicable for the ride and seemed to cheer right up. They did get him McDonald's, though, so you never truly know . . ."

"When will I see him again?"

"We'll get to visit him in a month and a half at the program, around Christmas. For now, you can write letters."

The first letter I got from JT was an apology letter. He scrawled, "I'm sorry for the pain I have caused," but then moved on to telling me about how he had learned to build a fire or something. He sounded different in the letter. I don't know that I'd ever read his writing before

47

then, but I liked it. A lot of my initial pain and suffering began to go away.

We visited during a blizzard. Mom and I drove during the night to get to this sketchy, small, haunted-looking hotel in the middle of nowhere in New York State.

JT looked better. He was sober, of course. He showed us how he learned to pick chamomile and make tea. He barely complained, not even about the ladybug infestation in his sleeping bag. He seemed calm, but of course, he was itching to leave.

When he graduated from that program, he went to a therapeutic boarding school for over a year. We, along with my dad, were able to visit him several times there. On some of those visits, I finally felt like we were becoming a "normal" family. We all attended his graduation from high school there, too. I'd never seen him look so proud. He had helped other kids to get to graduation, too.

He looked healthy and I can't wait for him to come home, I wrote in my journal the night he graduated.

Peter Pan

"**G**IRLS CAN HAVE SHORT HAIR, too, you know," a classmate mentioned casually.

I was in art class during the winter of freshman year when I saw a picture of Audrey Hepburn someone was drawing for their portrait project. A friend sitting nearby mentioned I looked like her, at which point, another person argued I definitely looked more like Peter Pan, especially in the classic film starring Mary Martin. I laughed it off, saying it was probably because of my pointy nose.

Secretly, I had been brewing up an idea of a haircut and these comments rained down on my ears like encouragement. After I had seen a lesbian-identified gal with super short hair at a Pride meetup shindig, I realized it was a possibility. I hadn't seen a real live girl with short hair before. My long hair that I was holding up in a half ponytail was frustrating—I straightened it every day because otherwise it got more curly and wavy than I could handle.

When I had begun straightening it, I'd get comments from family and older family friends like "Why are you straightening your beautiful waves?!"

So I'll look straight . . . I jokingly thought.

But in reality, it wasn't something I wanted to discuss. My "beauty" routine was nothing—just straightening and tying back half my hair. I hated shaving my legs and stopped after a dozen attempts. Occasionally, I retrieved my tweezers from behind a box in the bathroom cabinet to get those stray eyebrow hairs. Some days, hoping I looked okay in one of my three tight T-shirts—I would wear baggier ones on off days, but primarily circulated three tight ones. Other nights, praying that you couldn't see the lines of my bra underneath my clothing. My beauty routine was a silent wish at night that my chest would *stop* growing. I had a small figure. I did not need some big heavy things making me all unbalanced. My "beauty" routine was a nightmare.

As fall progressed into cooler weather, I recall Mom taking me to the mall. I'd pretty much graduated from buying all of my clothes at Hot Topic, figuring that high school meant "maturity" meant "adult," which somehow meant Hollister. The perfume radiating out drew me in. It was dark. I could slink from the women's section to the men's without anyone noticing me.

I found a men's hooded sweatshirt I liked. It was forty-two dollars, which, to me, was a million dollars. I knew I couldn't ask Mom to get me that. I wandered over to the women's area and saw this dark green skirt that seemed . . . okay. The fabric was soft. It was earthy. It was something that I could maybe see myself wearing. A semiformal dance was also coming up. I figured I should prepare myself for the potential of actually going and wearing something that classified as semiformal. The green skirt looked all right. There was also a girls' version of the hoodie I liked, except with much less fabric. I picked it out in brown, knowing full well I'd be an upside-down tree in the outfit.

Surely enough, a month or so later, that outfit was exactly what I wore to the dance with Ashley. That dance was one of the last times I can recall wearing super feminine clothing with long hair. I remember being the only visibly queer couple at the dance. I wore my skirt, Ashley wore huge tuxedo pants that were too big on her. She had gotten them from the Salvation Army years back.

A few weeks after the dance, I pleaded for Mom to take me to SuperCuts. I had printed out a picture of a girl with short hair and shown it to my mom, telling her I wanted that haircut. She said she didn't care about how I cut my hair; I was ecstatic.

I had straightened my hair that day as I always had. Once the hairdresser started spritzing the water on my hair to cut it, it began to get wavy, curly, and looked like an overall mess in the mirror. That was the last time I saw my face with hair that fell past my chin. As she began to chop away bits and pieces, I felt a quite literal weight being lifted. Within a half hour, I felt transformed in a way that I can't articulate. The way that hair alludes to gender, the way that hair frames and changes a face, the way that others would comment on my hair—all of these things changed in an instant.

I looked different and I felt different. I felt more confident. There were no other girls in my school that had super short hair, so I knew this would seem irregular around my town. But that was fine. I got used to being irregular back in the goth phase anyway.

Later that day, while picking up some things at the pharmacy, someone behind me said, "Excuse me, young man."

When I turned around, she quickly apologized about the "mistake."

That would be the first of many misgenderings that began to help me define what was going on inside of me.

Sneaking to Youth Pride in Boston

I**T WAS POURING RAIN, BUT WE** were committed to our plan. There was no way we were going to miss Youth Pride. Ashley's mom had been resistant to the idea, and although unsure of her final decision on the matter, my mom had given a definitive no.

"Mom, can I go to Youth Pride in Boston?"

"Are you going on a school trip?" she replied.

". . . No."

"Will there be any parents or guardians there?"

"Probably. I mean, it's for people twenty-four and under, but I'm sure other people's parents will be there . . ." I began to realize where this was heading.

"No, you can't go," was the final answer.

But—young, queer, and in love—we needed to get our rainbow on. I needed it, for sure. My queer circle was the suburbs of Boston. I needed the nitty, gritty, dirty, sparkly, glittery mess that happens when a bunch of young LGBTQ+ [2] folks get together. I needed that beauty to encompass me and swallow me whole.

---

2 Lesbian, gay, bisexual, transgender, queer or questioning, intersex, asexual, pansexual; often abbreviated to LGBTQ+ or LGBT, standing for a wide variety of gender and sexual minority identities. Similar to how "transgender" is an umbrella term for many identities, LGBTQ+ aims to encompass them as well.

I also really needed to see other queer relationships blossoming in public so that I could feel more secure about Ashley and me. Being stared at or talked about was exhausting. Every time someone called us lesbians or made a comment about us, I felt so off. Like *why are they staring at us? We're a young couple in love!* I still didn't quite have the words for it, but I saw us as a straight relationship—me being the boy and she being the girl. I had no idea what that meant, but I had begun to put my finger on the fact that I definitely identified as straight and needed to figure out what that meant. *A lesbian likes women and is a woman, but a straight woman would like men. And a straight man would like women . . . so am I a straight man?*

The thought kept clouding my mind. It felt too complex and impossible. I wanted distraction. I needed normalcy in the form of a spectacular array of colors and identities and chaos. I wanted to see some of the friends I had met at the local queer dance. I wanted, needed to go.

Ashley slept over the night before Youth Pride. In the morning, we lied about our plans for the day. Instead of doing whatever we had made up, we snuck out of my house and walked down High Street toward the train tracks. Climbing on board the big purple commuter rail, I felt a sense of purpose. I fumbled in my jeans pocket for enough change for the ticket.

Ashley was wearing flannel and jeans; we almost matched. I had a brick of a cell phone stuffed into my back pocket and that was about it. Otherwise, a paisley bandana and I was ready to roll.

It started pouring rain before the marching even began. And then it did not stop raining. It rained, rained, rained. It seemed to fuel the fire and the community though—everyone seemed to go pretty wild. I don't quite know what I was expecting, but it was more chaotic than even I had wanted. A kid walking behind me was clutching this empty water bottle, his eyes looking everywhere as he muttered. His friend or maybe his boyfriend, probably about fourteen or fifteen years old too, was giving him hickeys on his neck and talking about whatever drug they had taken. I managed to ignore all that noise as we sloshed through the puddles chanting "1, 2, 3, 4—OPEN UP THE CLOSET DOOR!"

Some schools had bused in full Pride Alliances and there were a fair number of parents and guardians nearby. I could imagine why my mom did not want us there without any parents around. It would have been easy to get involved in underage drinking or sexual activities or anything our minds imagined—but that wasn't so much a product of Youth Pride itself as it was a general truth that a bunch of youth, unsupervised or loosely supervised, wishing to be adults, may stray toward those vices.

While breaking rules and laws definitely gave me a sense of excitement—the "rush" of getting away with something—I knew how much it could destroy people and families. I had seen my brother make a bunch of the mistakes that others, wanting to rebel, might have idolized him for. My focus of the day wasn't to be a delinquent; it was to be surrounded by young queers, and I definitely got what I wanted.

Although we didn't talk to too many people, we definitely bumped into a lot of outgoing folks alongside lots of drag queens hugging us and leaving sparkly body prints left behind. Inside the church where there was half a dance party and half a soaked queer refugee situation, there were many organizations with tables and goodies. Rainbow stickers, ally pins, beads, patches, you name it.

We were still completely soaked to our bones and it had started to get colder out. It was definitely time to head home. Splashing in puddles on the way to the train felt so freeing, even though my toes had been pruney and cold all day. Giggling, joyous, empowered, we got on the commuter rail with barely enough change to get back home.

In our own world, completely immersed in the day's events, walking into my house didn't raise any red flags for me. But my mom knew right away. I had violated her trust, gone against her wishes. I was grounded. And by the end of the night, Ashley was grounded by her mom, too.

We snuck onto the phone that night, still giggling from the day's events. I had learned so much. No regrets.

You Can't Always Get What You Want

O N DECEMBER 14, 2006, I was walking home from school along a main route through our town. I had stayed after for a club meeting with friends and meandered about until it was getting close to four, chatting and talking about the weekend. I had a bunch of homework stuffed into my backpack, dreading the long night ahead, but looking forward to taking our big Berner pup, Toby, out when I got home.

Everything was as it always was. Rush hour traffic, but my sidewalk lane was quite empty. Winter hadn't quite reared its head yet—and I was thrilled. I was plenty warm in my usual black zip-up hoodie with patches and baggy jeans with patches. It felt more like September than December. This was the first year that my hair was short, although it had grown out a few months, making me look a little less like Peter Pan and a little more like early Bieber.

I could fit a decent chunk of songs on my green iPod mini, and since a few friends had recently made me some mix CDs that I'd uploaded onto it, I had it on shuffle so that I could get a taste of everything. As I was walking past the abandoned church I used to take guitar lessons in, the Rolling Stones' "You Can't Always Get What You Want" came on.

I was walking against traffic, but still on the sidewalk, up over the bridge as the sun was heading toward the golden hour of light. The intersection's light had turned and cars had started accelerating up the bridge, passing me, on their way to wherever. I dragged my left hand along the black fence that separated the bridge from the train tracks below. Mick Jagger was singing into my ear, "you can't always get what you want, but if you try sometimes, you just might find . . ." when I heard something loud, then felt an intense pain on the right side of my face. I withdrew my hand from the fence next to me, raised it up to my eye, and touched something way before I should've touched my face. A softball sized egg had formed on my eyebrow within milliseconds. Everything fell silent for a moment.

Not knowing what the hell happened—these things happen so fast—I hear Jagger in my earbud finishing his line, ". . . you get what you need."

Before I had a chance to look up from my hand cradling my eyes, my head sinking down low in pain, chin against my chest, I heard a car stopping next to me. A station wagon appeared in my vision, as I stood there, still very confused.

The driver quickly popped open the passenger door from inside and said, "We saw what happened. Get in so you're safe."

I'm not one to get into strangers' cars, but considering I had just been physically assaulted somehow, some way, I took my bag off my shoulder and slunk down into the passenger seat of a strange man's car.

"Are you okay? We're calling 911. My daughter's on the phone now. We can sit here until they get here." I took a look at him. He was in his forties with dark hair and a beard.

I turned around to see a young girl, hair pulled back in a ponytail, probably about eight or nine years old, holding her dad's phone to her face and yelling into it, "A BOY'S BEEN HIT! A BOY HAS BEEN HIT IN THE FACE ON ROUTE 27. A CAR THREW SOMETHING AT HIS FACE, A BOY'S BEEN HIT!"

He grabbed the phone back from her, now that he was safely pulled over, and sputtered, "A teenager has been assaulted on this road, we have her in our car now please send the police and an ambulance . . ." followed by details about his car.

While he was on the phone, the daughter tapped me on the shoulder. "Would you like a cookie?"

I looked down to see that she had a plate full homemade iced cookies on her lap and responded with a "No, thanks, though."

My head still swirling, I smiled at the awkwardness of this man's daughter calling me a boy to the emergency responder and then the man clarifying that he could tell, once up close, that I was a girl. My short hair, baggy clothes, and accessories had clearly read "boy" to his young daughter. But because my backpack was a single shoulder bag, sometimes the strap fell right between the two mountains on my chest, highlighting them even underneath dark layers. Upon hearing my voice and seeing me up close, the father had quickly registered that I was female and, possibly thinking that I was offended at his daughter's misgendering, had tried to remedy the pronoun situation.

Sitting in that front seat for all of five minutes, I became fixated on having been called a boy. Not even thinking about what had happened. I still hadn't arranged any thoughts, my head was pounding. But that young girl yelling "BOY" into the phone brightened the whole situation. I didn't know why at the time, but I knew something felt right amid all this chaos.

A few moments later, the police and an ambulance appeared, sirens wailing. My head hurt. We had been clogging up traffic, since it was a two-lane bridge with no shoulder. The father had told me he had seen the license plate number of the offending truck. He mentioned they were a few cars behind him on the bridge when he started accelerating and they saw a man in the passenger seat yell something and throw a metal object out the window at my face.

I got up out of the car while he conveyed the information to the police officers. I thanked the man and his daughter for their kindness as the paramedics gestured me toward the ambulance.

"No, no, I'm fine, I'm fine." I insisted, turning away.

"That bruising looks bad. We can't know unless we take you in," one of the paramedics responded.

"I really, really don't want to go to the hospital. I have a lot of homework—my mom is going to be home in an hour. Can I go home?"

"How old are you?"

"Fifteen."

"Because you're a minor, we have to take you to the hospital unless we can get a hold of a parent or guardian."

I pulled my phone out of my pocket and called Mom. She didn't answer, so I left her a voicemail letting her know I'd been hit in the head on the bridge and they wanted me to go to Emerson Hospital via the ambulance and how much I really did *not* want to do that.

"She's probably already on the subway heading home now. My house is four hundred yards that way, can't I just go home?"

"You understand you have been assaulted, correct? We will need to evaluate you for your own safety and in case this goes to court, especially since we already caught the guy."

"What? You did? How?"

"You got people looking out for you, it seems—many cars called in to 911 about an object hitting you on this bridge and several cars reported the truck's license number. It wasn't hard to find him in a matter of minutes. Route 27 is pretty backed up this time of night."

I stepped up into the ambulance, knowing full well that it costs $500 per emergency ride. It didn't occur to me that I could charge that copay to the assailant. I had no idea how these things worked.

As I sat there, the paramedic handed me ice for my face. I was feeling calm—happy in some way—and we had a friendly chat. I told him I'd stayed after school for the GSA meeting. I pulled out my phone and texted Ashley what had happened, figuring she was already on her way home from school with her mom. She responded with concern and how she could help; I wanted a normal day and for this hassle to be over with. I texted Mom real quick to let her know I was en route to Emerson's ER and to meet me there.

It was strange to get to the hospital, jump out of the ambulance, and be able to walk into the emergency room. It made me feel like it wasn't really an emergency. The paramedic had already screened me for potential concussion, so I didn't know what the doctors were going to recommend. Mom called and let me know she was on the way and would be there as soon as possible.

They signed me in, and I sat on a chair in the waiting area. Looking around, it seemed the ER had fewer crises than I expected (my imagination fueled by the medical/doctor/law TV shows I love). A few people getting checked in seemed to be going through some mental health issues. I didn't see any ghastly wounds or traumatic injuries, but people definitely noticed my eyebrow, which had stopped swelling and settled at the size of an egg.

"Whatcha got on your face there, son?" a chipper, bearded hospital employee inquired.

Instead of speaking, I smiled and demonstrated with my hand an object hitting my face.

"Ah, you're young, buddy, you'll be fine," he said and walked on.

Thanks, doc.

A nurse led me to an exam room and left me there with no word of when they would be coming back. It felt like hours, and I pulled out some of my homework to start working on it, right as a police officer entered the room with the doctor.

"It's time to take a statement," the doctor said as the police officer pulled out a notebook.

The doctor took a look at my eye, noting that, had the object hit me half a centimeter lower, I would likely be blind or in emergency surgery at the moment. Lucky duck, I was!

"We believe the object was an Altoids tin," the police officer chimed in.

"Someone threw an Altoids tin at my face? Why?" I began to feel the pain of a migraine slowly seeping up my neck.

Shrugs all around. "He may have been trying to scare you," the officer said, "but frankly, I think it was very stupid as it is considered assault with a dangerous weapon."

I gave a statement to police that detailed how I was walking home from school, where I was walking, what time it was, why I was walking, what side I was walking on, exactly where I was when I remember feeling something hit my face, if I remember the driver yelling anything, if I remember the vehicle. All I could recall was exactly where I was and at what time, that I thought it was a tallish truck-type vehicle, and that I did remember someone yelling something.

"Did they yell a slur, potentially?"

I didn't know. I had been too busy listening to the Rolling Stones.

By the time I went through that, my mom had arrived. I was ready to get the heck out of there. The doctor told me to ice the eye to keep swelling down and, if any new symptoms appeared, to check in with my primary care doc.

I got home and got straight to my homework. Ashley called to catch up but sounded less concerned so I played the whole ordeal lightly. I told her about the girl in the car yelling that I was a boy. Ashley didn't seem too amused by this, thinking it was disrespectful, so I didn't let her know that that was the highlight of the whole experience. That's the main thing that I remember. How those words made me feel awkward because they made me question myself, but overall, made me feel more free than mistaken.

A few months later, I was summoned to court about the incident. Truly, I had forgotten that I'd have to go to court. Once the swelling had gone down and I'd told the story to all my friends, it pretty much left my mind. I had to take a couple hours out of school to go to court, and Mom took the day off to drive me. Unfortunately, the defendant did not show that day so we the trial was rescheduled. Shortly after my sixteenth birthday, he showed up to court.

Wearing my best jeans (the ones without any holes), I sat in the pews next to Mom. We had to listen to a few other cases before mine—I honestly found it fascinating. When my assailant came out, I was surprised at how normal and young he looked. I had tried to google him beforehand but nothing had come up online. He didn't look over eighteen, though it turned out he was.

After the judge and the public defender questioned him, they needed me to come to the stand. A police officer had already detailed where I was walking, at what time, the information people had called in about the assault, what I was wearing, what the injuries were—it was a lot of information. The judge wanted to ask me some questions about myself and my reactions post-incident.

"Do you feel that the defendant may have targeted you based on you wearing the hooded sweatshirt and the baggy jeans?" he asked.

"No, I don't think so," I said, trembling.

"Do you feel that the defendant may have targeted you based on your short haircut?"

"No, I doubt he could have even seen it." I was feeling more confident.

"Do you feel that the defendant may have targeted you because of your sexual orientation or gender expression?" The bombshell.

"No, I don't think so."

"You chose to make a Victim Impact Statement and also came to court this second time to speak. Is there anything else you may want to say?"

"I don't believe the defendant should go to jail for his actions. I wanted to come here today to show him I am a human being and that his actions have consequences, in the hopes that he will never do something like this again."

The rest of the conversation went by without issue. At some point before the actual court date, I'd received a letter from the defense attorney. I wasn't pressing any charges, so long as the hospital bill was covered. The attorney informed me that I could write a letter to dismiss the more severe charges against him so that he wouldn't have to serve jail time. Basically, the town of Acton wanted to prosecute him to the fullest extent of the law for assaulting me on that bridge. I was young, and somewhat naive, but Mom and I had agreed that I'd write that letter because I didn't feel right about someone going to jail for "assaulting" me when it hadn't really affected that much of my life.

From everything I gathered at the courthouse, he may or may not have thought I was a gay male teenager walking by and targeted me as a hate crime. The thought of that sickened me but at the same time, if I passed as a gay male, the word male was in there, and I was beginning to question how I felt about that word being associated with me. The other theory was he was throwing the can out the window to hit the big metal street sign that was behind me—like throwing a basketball into a hoop, it was some game. I figured, he's some eighteen-year-old kid. Why wreck his life? He was lucky my eye didn't get injured and I had no lasting repercussions. In a sense, we both lucked out.

The whole event faded away until late one night in the summer between high school and college, when I woke up to a phone call at 1:30 a.m. JT had been living at home, up to his usual shenanigans but calmer, sometimes respecting my chosen name of Sky and honoring my pronouns after I came out as a transgender man. When I saw it was JT calling, though, my heart sank into a deep dark pit of doom. Any time he called me, he was in trouble. And in trouble meant *serious trouble*. His voice was slurred and I braced myself for the rest.

"Skyyyyyyy! Yo you wouldn't BELIEVE what just happened!" he yelled into the phone.

"Oh? What?" I was still groggy even though my alarms were heightened.

"Yo so I'm at this party and I'm waiting in line for the keg and this guy in front of me and I, we got to talkin' about if we'd ever been to jail or we'd ever been arrested and he mentioned that one time he threw an Altoids tin at some girl in south Acton out of his truck when he was a teenager and when he said that—I turned to him and yelled 'HEY THAT'S MY BROTHER THAT YOU ASSAULTED ACTUALLY' and I got so mad, I was about to beat this kid up because no one assaults my family okay, but then he started crying, no joke he's still crying, cause I guess you saved his fuckin' life by writing some letter, and he wants to talk to you okay? Can I put him on the phone?"

"What the hell? Small world, haha, why not." I celebrated the simple fact that JT was okay and this phone call was turning out to be a positive one.

The guy who assaulted me, Samuel, got on the phone, drunk and blubbering, "Dude, oh my god, thank you so much you don't even know how thankful I am that you wrote that letter and I am so so so so so sorry I never meant to hit you in the face—it was a total stupid accident—but you had the power to completely ruin and wreck my life, and you didn't, and I am so so so sorry and so thankful—so fucking thankful, thank you so much."

Small world. I felt taken aback that he remembered this; that he remembered and truly regretted the incident. It was a moment of clarity for me and for him—we had made amends.

But most important, that was one of the first times in two years that I'd heard JT call me his brother to someone else. Two drunk guys on the phone had never been so lovely in my life. Sure, you can't always get what you want—but if you try sometimes, you just might find . . . you get an Altoids tin to the face and years later your brother defends you for the first time because of it. ;)

Ice Cracks,
Hearts Break

O NE MORNING, WINTER BREAK OF my sophomore year of high school, my dad and I took off to Bradford Junction, the best diner around. Wearing a hoodie with black jeans and a beanie, I climbed into my dad's Jeep as he turned on oldies CDs he had burned for himself. Years later, when I finally got a car of my own, he gave me some of his mix CDs because I had a bunch of punk/metal/rap he couldn't tolerate.

"I think JT will be able to work it all out after he graduates," Dad thought aloud was we drove down the snowy highway. Not many cars were around.

"I hope so . . ." I never knew how to talk to my parents about the situation. Being parents and all, I figure they have their minds set and know what's best.

As we pulled into the junction restaurant, we noticed it wasn't super crowded.

"Must be because of the snow—people probably think it's closed!" Dad said.

We sank into a booth by the window. This diner felt like Christmas, always. It was a couple days after Christmas, but the essence remained in the smell of wood fire. The frosty windows contrasted with the warm sounds of a model train running on a track up high along the walls.

The waitress came over, greeting us with a cheery, "Hey gentlemen! What can I get ya today?"

My eyes grew wide. I looked across at my dad, who had a delayed reaction of confusion, then requested coffee. It was in this subtle interaction that I knew my androgyny still made him uncomfortable. He shuffled in his seat a little bit. I tried desperately not to talk—my feminine voice was my biggest source of insecurity, and I wanted to savor this moment of passing for a young boy out with his father.

Dad didn't say anything. Should I have pretended to be offended that the waitress had thought I was a guy? Would that have been the most reassuring reaction for my dad, saying don't worry, I'm still your daughter? Should I have told him that it's cool, no big deal? Most likely the latter, but regardless, the interaction both thrilled me and terrified me with the implication that I could have been a boy. Dad wasn't ready to know.

That afternoon, Ashley called.

"I need to talk to you about something when you get back," she said, her tone distant.

"What? Are you okay?" I felt my heart rate increase. I began to panic, to be honest.

"Nicole slept over last night because of the storm. I need to talk to you before she does."

Nicole was a mutual friend of ours.

This sounds . . . bad, I thought.

"Why can't you tell me now?"

"Trust me, Katherine, let's talk in person tomorrow." She hung up.

Confounded, I ran into my dad's office and said I was going to walk up to the dam.

"Be careful," he said. "The ice may not be safe."

I pulled on my snow jacket and headed out into the drifts. It was a fifteen-minute walk through the woods; I had done it a million times. In elementary and middle school, I had played my "Boyfriend/Girlfriend" game in those woods. The memory filled my mind as tears began to fall down my face.

Ashley probably just cheated on me, I thought. It's what the phone call sounded like. I had never been cheated on, but I'd had friends who had been. I walked out onto the ice, wishing I knew the answers at that very moment.

I heard the ice crack. My heart sank in my chest as I looked around for someone nearby. Nobody. I got down on all fours and started crawling toward the shore. The big chunks of ice that had broken off and refrozen in these stormy, sculpture like figures were making deep groaning noises. For a moment, I stayed still and held my breath.

Why did I even walk out here? I began to breathe again.

Slowly, I made it back to shore.

Calm, quiet, and peaceful again, I wandered through the forest and didn't tell my dad about the ice cracking on the lake. I didn't tell him about the rush of excitement, followed quickly by horror and fear. I didn't tell him that I was afraid my girlfriend had potentially cheated on me while I was away. I didn't tell him that I was beginning to realize I might be a boy. I didn't tell him much at all, except that the nachos were delicious as usual.

Mom picked me up the next afternoon to take me back home. I turned on my cell phone in the car, eagerly awaiting any news. I knew it would be about twenty or thirty minutes before I got cell reception. We chatted in the car but once I felt my phone buzz twice, I quickly entered my own world.

Bombarded with notifications, I started flipping through the texts I had gotten that week. A bunch from my friends, mainly asking to hang out or organize plans. Ashley knew I was up in New Hampshire so she hadn't texted me. I was, however, surprised to see one from Nicole.

Hey umm we need to talk when you get a chance. It's important.

For the rest of the car ride, my head imagined all sorts of stories, benign to grotesque. I braced myself to be let down.

I got home and it was dark outside. I petted Tiger, picked him up, and snuggled him close like I always did when I got back from New Hampshire. I especially loved floofing his stomach (blowing air into his fur and flab so that it jiggled). I don't think he liked that as much.

I took the living room phone up to my room and called Ashley as I started unpacking my duffel.

"Hey, Katherine," she mumbled.

I asked her to cut to the chase.

"So when I invited Nicole over, she ended up sleeping over. When we were going to bed, she out of nowhere pounced on me and kissed me and I couldn't stop it from happening." She dropped it so casually.

I took a moment to process in silence. My head felt stuffy. A kiss is a betrayal, obviously. A betrayal is a betrayal. Violence is violence.

These things exist on spectrums and scales, and though I trusted it had stopped at that, I felt violated. I let her know I needed some time to process, that I was pissed at Nicole, and I was, I guess, still excited to see her tomorrow. Maybe talking in person could clarify this nonsense.

I got into bed. And I didn't tell anyone.

When we talked in person the following day, she dissuaded me from asking Nicole about the facts.

"Why?" I asked.

"She will lie," she replied, sternly.

Nicole ended up texting me to talk. She told me an entirely different version of events. Spinning around in circles, I didn't know where to look or go. But since I didn't know what the truth was, I didn't make any decisions to end my relationship. My friends cautioned me to stay away from both of these people, but I still chose to try again.

Ashley and I went to an Ani DiFranco concert that winter. She has this song, "Hour Follows Hour," which Ashley had put on a mix tape for me.

One of the lyrics: "Nobody's lying, still the stories don't line up."

That practically summed up a whole year for me.

Unitarian Universalism

IN A JOURNAL ENTRY I wrote a few weeks after returning from New Hampshire, titled "cloudy or not, I'm just glad to know there is a sun," I wrote:

and as i stand naked, about ready to hop into the shower
i hear the phone ring, and press my ear against the door
as mum says softly "hello doctor"
and the seconds are a hundred for every real one
until she laughs "i'm so relieved"
and i smile as i climb into the water
sure that she'll call the rest of the family
and we'll all smile
this time
it's like we all escaped it.

this weekend will be good.
little kids are insane, but music is worth it
and basketball holds so many smiles and hands and handshakes
    and hugs
and some people just deserve second chances

One of the things that is so difficult for me to remember is that I always had so much going on. With my mom, with schoolwork, with sports, with babysitting in exchange for drum lessons. With my brother, with my friends, with my relationship, and all that comes with being a teenager in those years. Through everything, I was so very thankful to have the queer community. Meeting other LGBQ+ folks helped me immensely with grounding myself, finding a sense of stability, and another type of family.

Before Ashley had been unfaithful, we had begun looking at local churches to be a part of and hopefully get involved with the youth group. While the GSA was a safe space, we both wanted more of a challenge. Or more of an adventure. I'm thankful I stuck it through with her for a few more months, because after looking around a few different towns, we finally found one in nearby Littleton that seemed to fit.

And that's when I was introduced to Unitarian Universalism.

Like a light at the end of my intro-to-being-queer tunnel, a world unfolded full of beautiful, vibrant LGBTQ+ youth and adults. Ashley had been part of a UU church when she was younger. She had gone to youth conferences and she told me stories of how queer they could be. She spoke of drag balls, dances, crafts, community building, farming—all activities I was drawn to at the time.

Although it may have seemed strange to have fifteen-year-olds exploring their faith without any parental involvement, there is something about the queer community that makes a chosen family important. That something is the high amount of rejection that LGBTQ+ youth face from families. Research has shown that family acceptance is one of the most influential factors in a child's well-being. When a family rejects, disowns, or kicks out their LGBTQ+ child, that child's rate of dropping out of school, depression, suicide, drug abuse, alcohol abuse, being a victim of violent crime, and homelessness skyrocket. Queer culture has long fashioned families of choice together in order to create the space that a family should provide. A space where you can be yourself. A place where people love you unconditionally. It is of utmost importance for members of the community to stick together, provide for one another, and help out when we can—these risks are too serious for us not to.

Aside from the GSA and the handful of other pride events I had participated in with Ashley, this was my first community outside of school that I had chosen to belong to. I had been to church before; in California, Dad had taken JT and me to Sunday services and Sunday school. Mom would often cook dinner while Dad took us out to church. I went through Communion wearing a poofy white lace dress and pearls, walking down the aisle with a boy named Jacob (whom I thought I had a crush on but actually wanted to *be*).

At First Parish in Littleton, the music was alive, relevant, and performed by the minister himself. His name was Fred, and he had written acoustic albums of story-like songs. He performed several songs during the first service Ashley and I attended and I felt awestruck. There was a point when Fred was talking about recent bills to advance gay rights in the state. He mentioned how he was thankful to the community for supporting his choice to not perform any marriages until it was legal for same-sex couples to get married in all states. Massachusetts had legalized same-sex marriage in 2004, but because hardly any other states recognized it, Fred had chosen to stand in solidarity with all couples in the US.

I was amazed—this church was as accepting of queer people as Ashley had promised it would be.

The youth group at the church was energetic. It turns out, we had missed the past year which had a program called OWL (Our Whole Lives) to educate on relationships, safe sex, and gender and sexual orientations. What I would have given to have been there for that! With my recent realizations, I'd been struggling with the thought, *what took me so long to figure this out?* Maybe some open and honest discussion about bodies and lives and gender and sex would have helped. Darn.

Squeezed into a small room, there were many teenagers of all walks of life. Some boisterous, some visibly queer, some there because their parents encouraged them to be. There were many friendly faces in the crowd, but I stood nervously next to Ashley, who was more comfortable than I was because she was more familiar with UUism. Yet I didn't need to lean too far onto her as the other youth reached out right to us to help us feel included. I received more introductions and hugs in five minutes than I had in months. It was heartwarming. I had unconsciously started keeping my arms closer to my sides—the result of growing dysphoria about my chest—but found myself reaching out again and being reached out to.

That afternoon, a boy named Hank approached me. He was short, had long black hair, and truthfully—he had come off as a wise person. I don't know why, but he had this look to him.

"Hey, do you live in Acton?" He had many questions—a very outgoing guy.

"Yeah! Do you?" I smiled.

"Yep! Right in south Acton, by the old church."

"Dude! That's right near me!"

I gave him my phone number. He texted me later that night.

hey, it's hank. Want 2 meet @ the playground?

It was two in the morning on a Monday, but school had been cancelled due to snow. My insomnia had been bad that night and I just so happened to hear my phone buzz.

I snuck out of my house pretty easily; Mom slept with earplugs in and Toby was a heavy sleeper for a dog. As I approached the playground, the streetlights scared me. The scene looked haunting, snow coming down in an apocalyptic way. My shoes were filling up with snow and water. I wished I had worn my boots.

"Hey!" Hank called as I got closer to him. I hadn't seen him in the shadows, but he was on one of the swings.

"So tell me more about you." He lit a cigarette in the snow storm, but it kept getting extinguished by the big wet flakes. "Want one?"

"Sure." I didn't like the taste, but the act made me feel warmer.

"Where'd you meet Ashley?"

"She transferred into our high school, so I met her freshman year, last year. Wow, time flies." It felt like it had been forever.

"Do you guys say I love you and all that?"

"Yeah, but I don't know that I love her. Sometimes, I don't know that I feel much for her, and it sucks. We probably won't be together for long." Something about Hank made it okay to say that out loud.

"The opposite of love isn't hate, it's apathy. Not feeling strongly about something versus feeling very strongly about it," he mused.

"What keeps you up at night?" I asked. I wanted to figure out my own demons.

"Hating this world. It's all messed up, isn't it? What's the point of the future? What should I even do? Why do people all suck?" He giggled, but he was being honest.

"Sometimes I hate this world too, but I feel it can change. Or maybe I can make a difference or you can or someone can."

"You're too optimistic for me, dude," he said, looking right at me, "but I think I like that."

We left that night after pledging to meet up again next time one of us couldn't sleep. It ended up happening almost weekly.

Even though going to UU church had been so wonderful, Ashley and I hadn't been doing so well. We were regularly getting into little arguments. She had gotten her license and had been able to drive around more; there were times in the car that were so tense I wanted to get out and walk home. I had a hard time trusting her after what happened with Nicole. No matter how badly I wanted to believe her intentions when she promised she would be kinder, better, nicer, I couldn't shake the previous incidents from my shoulders and that influenced my reactions to many of her behaviors. I wasn't quite innocent either; although I wasn't cheating on her, I wasn't honest with her about who I was hanging out with or what we were doing.

For example, a friend of mine and I had recently gotten high with her brother out on a golf course behind their house—he had offered to smoke us up for our first time. I am so very thankful he did; I felt safe with their family. Part of me had wanted to try out weed and to get high because it was something Ashley had done a bunch and something I had felt excluded from when folks at church would talk about having done it. I wanted to have an experience, and overall, I enjoyed it.

I was also hanging out with Nicole after school sometimes. She would be in between drumming and meeting up with someone to go home, and we would plan to chat in the hallway. I showed her my art a few times and it felt oddly intimate. She opened up to me about her boyfriend problems and I felt weirdly protective of her. Her past with Ashley aside, she was a great person. And since I'd decided I couldn't definitively tell the truth of either party, there wasn't much point in judging her. Plus, she was really, really nice to me.

"Nicole mentioned you guys hung out?" Ashley said one day. "Not cool, Katherine."

"Oh, well, didn't you two hang out over last winter break? And if I remember correctly—didn't you two hook up? So what—I can't even talk to Nicole in chorus class?" I snapped back at her.

Things with Ashley were fizzling out. I didn't trust her and was tired of being put down or made to feel like no one else would ever love me. Plus, I was simply overwhelmed at the time and wasn't devoting much attention to the relationship. Other things had come up.

During that time, I was also playing in a punk band.

And I had begun thinking about my gender identity.

And I had recently met a transgender person for the first time.

So . . . yeah.

I had a lot going on.

The Word: Transgender

"I'm not giving up the claim that I can save the world and all I need is my friends"
                    —Against Me!, "All or Nothing"

S OPHOMORE YEAR OF HIGH SCHOOL was a time of musical exploration. Music had long been a way of expressing myself; I made
mix CDs for Ashley and other friends all the time. Ashley often
shared her taste in ska music with me, whereas I would typically go
for more lyric-focused, subliminal message stuff like Bright Eyes and
Johnny Cash.

Having only played acoustic guitar, I began playing keyboard again.
I wanted a better electric guitar than the starter one I had had forever
and my dad offered to look at some options with me when I was up
visiting. We went to a nearby town and visited this cute, hippie-type
shop. It had incense (so it smelled like a comfortable basement), clothing, records, amps, instruments, you name it. One area was designated
"18+ ONLY!!" and I could see an array of glass pipes for smoking
"tobacco." It was a funny little place.

I ended up with an awesome sunburst guitar. My new friend, Sam,
had been learning the drums and would often play along while I played
my new guitar and wrote some rough drafts of songs. As he got more
into punk type stuff, he met Marshall (Marsh for short). We all started
hanging out after school most Fridays. Mainly, we would lurk around
and either get slushies from 7-Eleven or go on long walks while drinking Arizona Iced Tea.

One day, feeling inspired while listening to Against Me! and Black
Flag, we decided to try to write music together. Our first session was

after school in Sam's house with me on guitar, Marsh trying bass, and Sam on drums. Marsh and I often sang, but I let him take the lead since I wasn't particularly fond of my voice at the time. We tried our best to create what we thought was punk music.

One of our songs was called "Punky Punk Punk, Hey Hey Hey." I'd yell out the "hey hey hey!" and sometimes "gay gay gay!" to make it queer friendly. And that was about it for lyrics.

One night, after band practice, I posted a picture of myself Marsh had taken. I chose the online community, Birls, as I felt safe there. People liked my picture and commented on it, more than my other posts. I felt a rush of confidence in "looking like a boy" and wanted to respond to everyone. As I did, some conversations continued and some ended. I saw someone's icon that captivated me. He looked intriguing, and I wanted to learn more about him.

When I clicked on him, it was super clear he identified as male from his profile and his posts. Actually, he seemed to be like any other guy. I felt silly for ending up there, but also drawn toward this dude.

Finding his MySpace wasn't hard. When I was looking through what I could see without adding him as a friend, I saw some groups he belonged to. One of them had "LGBTQ" in it. Another appeared pride related. Another was something about being "transgender."

Sitting on my chair in the basement, hands resting on my desktop while my cat purred in my lap, my jaw pretty much dropped. I went back to his journal and reread one of the only entries I could see. There, he had stated he was transgender, but that he was "just a regular guy." He mentioned being born female and the pain he had been through.

Though I still did not quite understand what it meant, my mind was spinning with the realization that this guy had been born a girl. It felt so wild and crazy and impossible to me that he looked so much like any other guy but had been born female. Something new to me. Something exciting. Something clicked in my head—I related to this so much.

I went up to my bedroom and listened to some of our band's music before writing in my journal. I wanted to write down the information I had seen online when I briefly googled "transgender" moments before.

It was February 25, 2007 at 9:59 p.m. when I wrote:

Transgender is still classified as a mental disorder.

No surgeon will operate on transgenders[3] until they have 2 notes from 2 different therapists that have treated them for at least a year.

No surgeon will operate on transgenders until they have lived as the stereotype of their true sex for at least a year.

No surgeon will operate on transgenders until they are 18.

Roughly 50% of transgender teens live to see 18.

I closed my journal and went to bed, wondering how I felt. Wondering what this all meant. The word felt medical. Technical. I didn't even know how the word would sound out loud.

In a few weeks, we were set to play a small punk show. Practicing lots, we had even gotten a friend to play bass and started trying to take ourselves a little bit more seriously, even though we weren't very serious at all. At one meetup, I briefly mentioned something to Marsh about this guy I had found online.

"Oh! Kayden? I know him!" he interrupted, practically yelling.

My heart started pounding. Marsh knew I was pretty androgynous. He was supportive of my masculinity, I figured, or at least he treated me way differently than he treated girls. He would never casually invite a girl to hang out late at night, wandering the streets and the train tracks. He didn't respect most girls (I think because they weren't that into him, but he claimed it was because they were dumb). A few months prior, in the fall, he and I had started sneaking out at night and going for late-night walks around south Acton. He once picked up a half-smoked cigarette off the sidewalk, put it to his lips, and lit it.

"Seriously? Is that a thing?"

"Yeah dude! Why let it go to waste?" he replied, casually.

I tried it out. Forget how disgusting it is to pick up something off the ground and put it to my mouth—smoking cigarettes at fifteen is

---

3 "Transgenders" is incorrect. I didn't have the appropriate language at the time and want to be honest that I have not always known the correct terminology. "Transgender people" would be correct, as transgender is an adjective, not a noun.

definitely not something I'm proud of. I don't have any excuses for it except that I thought it would lower my voice. Any time I smoked in the future, I was motivated by that thought.

He offered to introduce me sometime after going on about how cool Kayden was and about knowing Kayden had once been a girl. He said it so casually.

"You kinda remind me of him, you know," Marsh said as he played around on my guitar, attempting a new riff. "Kayden was born a chick, isn't that messed up? No one would ever see him that way now," He said.

"Woah, yeah, that's so weird man. Is it like a medical condition?" I had no clue what to say, not wanting to reveal my new knowledge.

"Changing your gender? Yeah, I think it is, but it's fixable somehow. Hormones I think? As for your Mohawk, that is not a medical condition." He cracked himself up some more.

Sam had been buzzing my hair lately and he liked the look of a Mohawk. I'd bleached it and dyed it hundreds of times, once as a rainbow, but my favorite was a teal/green/purple combo.

The night of our show, I spotted Kayden standing in the corner of a room, arms crossed. He wore a ragged flannel shirt and black pants with patches. I was way too nervous to say anything to him. I hadn't let myself look at his stuff online after that first night because I was worried I'd have too many questions or feel sad that I wasn't him.

Marsh came up, me over and introduced me to Kayden.

"Cool name, dude, where does it come from?" I attempted to be casual. I was probably trembling.

"I picked it. I'm transgender, a transgender guy, and the name I was born with sucked. My mom doesn't like this one either, but whatever," he said, half smirking.

It was the first time I had heard it out loud. I was probably standing there awkwardly laughing, let's be honest, but I can remember the impact. He went on to talk about how he had been on hormones for several months and was planning to get a surgery that would take away his breasts. He had acne and his voice cracked when he spoke. There were a couple of hairs sprouting on his chin.

This world unfolded in front of me when he said the word "transgender" out loud and explained his identity. I felt I was no longer alone, that someone else felt like I did. I couldn't believe it was physically possible to transition genders. And I felt amazed that it was socially possible, too. That there existed a community I could belong to.

I instantly knew the word described how I had felt for my entire conscious life. I felt connected, present, and certain in that moment.

I wasn't trapped inside a girl's body. I had a choice. I could be free.

It became possible that I could be myself in this life.

I wasn't alone in this. I was a transgender person.

Thinking, Thinking, Crying, Thinking, Hoping

D AYS AFTER THE PUNK SHOW, with Kayden on my mind and new galaxies forming in my heart, I had almost entirely forgotten about an important event that the GSA had planned to be a part of. The faculty of the high school had asked if any students would speak at the faculty meeting about the impact of words like "gay" and "fag" in school and the effects of bullying on the gay community. At GSA, we had gone around to see who wanted to speak and I volunteered to say something.

Speaking to the teachers rather than the other way around for one of the first times in my life, my voice shook. I was articulating an important topic to me. Ending bullying and harassment was crucial to our community. Understanding helps humanize the cause and the teachers wanted to learn; sharing some of my thoughts and story felt very personal but also critical to creating a safer high school space. I wouldn't want any other kids to feel as alienated as I had at times because of my relationship with a girl.

I stayed up all night writing my speech.

After sharing my story, I concluded by saying, "I ask that you open your ears, your hearts, and your minds to help us. If you hear harassment or bullying or these words, speak up. We need your help to set the example that intolerance is not welcome here."

Afterward, a few of my teachers hugged me and thanked me, leaving me trying to hold back tears. I didn't want to cry in public. I felt strong and vulnerable in the same moment. I felt exhausted but empowered.

Being able to confidently stand in front of them helped me take ownership of many of the experiences Ashley and I had when we had been one of the few visible "gay" couples in the school. This, while also realizing my gender, made me the happiest and most confused human bean in the world.

After school that day, Ashley and I held hands and hung out, chatting with others that were leaving. Someone in theatre mentioned how they were trying to get *The Laramie Project* to be performed at school the next year. Ashley seemed stoked about the news. The theater kid described the play, which told the saddest story about a gay teen being beat to death in Wyoming.

My grandfather had recently passed away, and I'd been thinking about life and death. I was happy at school, sure, but what about my future? Mom's cancer, sorting through words to tell others about my recent gender discoveries, and general life anxiety. The weight on my shoulders felt unbearable.

Later that night, I sat down and wrote in my journal:

> *because the music plays louder and louder*
> *caved in caves dancing mindlessly in the middle of nowhere*
> *salt under the skin of an ocean*
> *you haven't seen yet*
> *sneakers and pavement sitting*
> *together in love*
> *tap as the music gets softer and softer*
> *tap as the veins sink in*
> *tap as you're ready to wade in.*

I was thinking about life or death because I knew now what I was and it was scary. There wasn't much information about being transgender online. I looked through other people's journals again and found a couple folks who seemed to tread the line of possibly being trans guys. Most seemed angry, depressed, or had bleak outlooks.

Being transgender did, in some ways, feel like a lifelong sentence. Of what? I didn't know. I felt I'd have to take a huge risk by telling my parents or friends. I'd then have to take a huge risk with my body and safety in order to transition. And honestly, it might be super expensive and maybe I wouldn't pass whatever "tests" they had and then maybe I wouldn't be able to transition at all and then maybe it would have been better to go back to feeling like there were other girls who felt like how I did—felt like boys—but stuck it out and dealt with it. That there was nothing I could do about it. Before, when there was nothing to do about it, I couldn't beat myself up over the possibilities and choices.

Now, I was beating myself up over the possibilities and choices.

In stark contrast to the experience of meeting a trans person in real life, the online world was clinical and unapproachable, full of heavily worded medical or anthropological studies. The information I found about being transgender wasn't about identity. It wasn't about community. It was about medical procedures and mental health diagnoses.

My own selfish worries bubbled up again. Who would love me? Would I ever love myself? How could I do this to my mom and dad?

They wanted a son and a daughter, I thought, *and plus, the doctors say Mom may not make it that long. Shouldn't I keep being her daughter until then to make her happy? I don't want to break her heart and make life any more difficult. Plus, what if they disown me?! Where would I even go?*

Dissection and the Constructs of Gender

WHEN I WAS FIFTEEN, I had been vegetarian for a year. I had become quite fluent at explaining it— I had realized I wanted to be veg after seeing the conditions that chicken, cows, pigs, and other animals were in before slaughter. And how slaughter worked. Once I knew what happened, I knew I didn't want to support that in any way.

Even though it had been talked about at the beginning of the year, the biology class frog dissection snuck up on me. Thankfully we were able to elect to not participate in it. Instead, we were told to sit in the classroom doing a simulated dissection that was kind of like a mini computer game.

I sat in a small circle of desks with a few other students while the rest went to the lab tables. Our teacher pulled the frogs out of formaldehyde and the smell overwhelmed me. It was rancid; I almost felt like puking right then and there, but besides crying in public, vomiting in public was one of my biggest fears.

Wanting to get it all over with without making a big stink, I kept plugging away at the video game dissection. It was quite cartoony and fine. Behind me, the students weren't being very mature about taking apart a previously living animal and my blood felt like it was about to boil.

"This one is pregnant!" one girl screamed out.

"Look at all the eggs, ew!" a guy squealed back.

I turned my head to see some kid with a scalpel digging into his group's frog. People were laughing, maybe because it was awful and awkward, but also because it seemed like they didn't care at all.

Feeling sick, angry, and profoundly sad at the whole situation, I felt tears welling up in my eyes. I wasn't doing well. I left to go to the bathroom without getting permission.

Once I was out in the hallway, tears kept pouring down my face. I felt grossed out by the frogs. I felt grossed out by my own identity. I felt grossed out by my relationship with my body. I felt grossed out by cancer, by my classmates' drama, by the world I was learning I'd have to be living in forever. I felt awful.

I went into the girls' bathroom real quick and got stared at by a freshman who was in there, as if I didn't belong. I wiped my eyes in the stall and decided I'd head over to my drawing teacher Mrs. McDonough's room. The art hallway was around the corner from the biology wing. It was a place I felt safe. I had taken all the art classes I could every year so far, including drawing, painting, and sculpture.

When I saw her through the small window in the door, she seemed to be alone. I slowly walked in and she stood up from her desk.

"Is everything okay? What can I do to help?" She hugged me.

I fell apart. I don't think I actually did, but I certainly felt like I fell to the ground in a puddle of mush and wallowed in that. I started crying the nasty, hiccup tears that made it feel like I couldn't breathe.

"It's okay, Katherine, take a deep breath. It's okay. What happened?" Mrs. McDonough had the kindest voice.

"They made us dissect frogs in biology—I'm still in biology actually, I probably have to go back—oh no—and everyone's laughing at it, and it was disgusting, and it was mean, and it wasn't kind, and they forced me to still be in there with it all happening." I went on as she listened attentively.

"And then I also don't know how to deal with my mom having cancer, and my brother is supposedly doing better, but I don't know, and next year is time to start planning for college, and I don't even know who I am let alone anything about the future, and it all feels impossible. It all seems so impossible." I burst out crying even more.

Mrs. McDonough did the right thing in that moment. She helped lift me up and offered to take a walk together to the counseling center. She gave me reassuring words and promised they would be able to help ease some of the burden I had been carrying.

I got to schedule an appointment with the school counselor for the following day. Mrs. McDonough walked me back to biology class, where we informed my teacher that I would be missing the rest of class and I'd make up the dissection segment another time, in study hall or after school. Then, I got to spend the rest of the period, which wasn't very long, in the art room talking to Mrs. McDonough about current events and my own life. I brought up some of the things I'd learned in church as well as online.

"Gender is a social construct," I stated, using my newfound language.

"Hmmm, tell me more about that," she said, entertaining my ramblings.

"Well, when we are born, they designate our sex on our birth certificates. Like, mine says F. My mom's says F. And my dad's says M. But that's just biology. When people showed up at the hospital with all this pink stuff, pink blanket, pink hat to wrap around my head—that was gender. That was when they gendered me: *Because this child has XX chromosomes and we marked it as an F, we will call it she and her and she will be a beautiful baby princess girl!*"

"Fascinating." Mrs. McDonough seemed genuinely interested, maybe partially taken aback by my mentioning this out of the blue.

"It's something I've been thinking about. I met a boy who was born female and . . . I realized something, I guess." I paused.

"What is it, Katherine? You realized something?"

"I think that's like me. You know, I hear my own voice in my head, it seems like a lot of people do, but my voice is a man's voice. It's deep. It's not the one that comes out of my mouth right now. And when I look at myself, when I look at boys, I'm comparing myself to them. I thought I liked boys for a while because of that . . . but I wanted to *be* them. Does that make sense? I probably sound crazy, but I swear, others feel this way. Gender is a construct and I feel like I haven't had a chance to construct my own," I truly paused now, wanting to gauge her response.

"Makes sense," she said. "Gender starts when we are all very young. I believe it means different things to everyone, but also, that the majority of people feel comfortable with their gender and with the way society has been. The gender roles are made for physical and societal reasons—like the Bible—to guide our ways. You've never been one to fit into the box, this one or that one or any one, and I'm not surprised you're thinking about this stuff. But take it slow. You don't need to answer anything right now."

"I think I know my answers, Mrs. McDonough. I think I do." I wanted her to believe me.

"I trust that you do." She smiled.

That day, she truly saved my heart from thinking that no one would listen or understand me. That I'd be in all of this alone. I saw then what I needed to do.

Questioning
While Certain

ICAME OUT TO MYSELF WHEN I was a few weeks shy of turning six-teen. I accepted it fully, even with all the questions I still had left. I knew how I felt, and I now knew there was a word for it. After many years of having the release of "pretending" to be a boy online, I now knew I simply *was* a boy. A transgender boy, in fact. And if I wanted my life to align with the stars the way it was supposed to, I needed to start making moves in the right direction.

Since only a few months had passed since I had found the word, I knew others might be shocked if I bluntly announced it, this word: transgender. They might have the same reaction I did—fear, worry, and despair. Plus, no one knew too much about how much I had explored my gender identity in the past and how long this had been brewing. Well, Grandpa definitely knew about the Mike phase and continually brought it up, but you know.

Because of this, I decided I would come out as "questioning" first to my family and some friends to test out the waters. I mean, I *was* tech-nically still questioning. What if I asked to be called by male pronouns (he/him) and found they didn't actually fit? A lot of trial and error was about to begin, and I wanted to leave a little leg room for growth.

First, I figured I should tell my girlfriend. It seemed like informa-tion she should know. I told her when we were on the phone one night after school. I was standing in my bedroom by my fish tank. I had a couple of panda catfish that ate all the gunk at the bottom and sides of the tank—watching them go around cleaning it up always calmed me down. Looking at the fish, happy and content in their little fake ocean world, I gathered up the courage to turn my "fake" world into a real one.

"Hey Ashley, there's something I've been thinking about for a while that I wanted to tell you."

"What? Are you breaking up with me or something? You sound so serious." She was on the defense, as usual.

"No no no. I haven't been able to form the words for this in the longest time and I'm nervous these words won't come out right too, but I think I'm a boy. I've been questioning my gender pretty seriously these past few years, and when I was younger, and I think this makes sense. I didn't know it was possible until I met someone who seems like me and he's transgender . . . " I started to get excited, but tried to keep myself calmer since this could be a shock to Ashley.

"Ohhhh, huh? What?"

"I think I want to go to therapy," I said. "Remember that lady Ursula in church, how she told me she was a gender therapist or at least she had worked with cross-dressers? I'm going to ask her for a recommendation for one and ask them questions about my gender and explore it further, especially options for maybe transitioning . . ."

"Seriously? Where did this come from?" Ashley seemed apprehensive. Even though she knew about gender through her experiences with folks she knew from her old church, it was still over her head.

"It's been on my mind for a long time . . ." I trailed off.

After what felt like forever, Ashley said, "Well, I guess this is the end for us then, yeah?"

I was baffled.

"Well . . . since I'm a lesbian and that means I'm attracted to women, you know?" She was blunt.

It made sense.

So yeah, that was the first time I'd told anyone.

And that was also the end of my first relationship.

I felt like I was going to crawl out of my skin: so miserable, so unhappy, and so full of anger, that I had to move. I hopped out onto my rooftop.

You're unlovable. That was what I had taken away from it all.

Stars began to appear in the sky. More popped out the longer I gazed into the infinite abyss.

I love the sky, I thought. *Sky could be a cool name, actually.*

I typed "sky as a name" into my computer. "Skye" seemed to be a more common spelling, like the island over in Scotland. It was also androgynous; about seventy percent of folks with the name were girls and thirty percent were boys. *Sort of like me, right now.* I laughed thinking about it, before quickly remembering the conversation with Ashley.

I may not find love, but maybe, just maybe, I will find love for myself.

What Is a Name?

AFTER EXPLORING OTHER NAMES, LIKE Brandon and Mike, I had a realization.

It was time to start anew.

Tucker was a name I had long liked, but there was a guy named Tucker in my grade at school. And even though it's so small and petty now, I didn't want anyone to think I was a poser or copying him or anything like that. You know, teenage drama.

I also wanted something more neutral; something that didn't hold a lot of gendered weight. I tossed around ideas relating to my family but nothing fit. One afternoon the summer after sophomore year, when I was walking outside with Toby, I looked up at the sky.

Skye seemed nice. Androgynous and could be lengthened to Skylar or Schuyler down the line, perhaps.

I asked my closest friends to call me Skye. Amy and Eli were on it fast, which was incredible. Hearing it, plus male pronouns I had asked them to try out, immediately affirmed my feelings of being a man. I felt recognized.

There was one another step I needed to take to help me feel more complete while I was questioning. I wanted to bind my chest to make it look flatter. One of the tips I had read online was to get spandex undershirts a size or two too small so they would tightly bind across the chest area. I was already pretty narrow in my frame so I got an XS tight undershirt that I cut to fit like a tank top. It helped hide my chest a little, but I found combining it with a tight sports bra also helped keep everything down.

I began to layer my shirts to hide my chest even more. I felt more confident when facing myself in the mirror. One afternoon in late July, a friend hit me up to come to her neighborhood for a barbeque. I was wearing a tank top I had cut from a regular T-shirt, and because I wanted to feel comfortable, I wrapped ACE bandages around my chest to make it super flat. In pictures, I felt I looked so good. It was one of the first times I had felt masculine enough to "pass" as a boy—to have others read me as male solely from my gender expression.

Using ACE bandages to bind can cause serious injury. They would wrap around my ribs, flattening my chest to appear more like pecs, but they wouldn't have any give. I definitely cannot recommend them. There are binders meant for the exact purpose of making a chest appear flatter (I couldn't afford one and I didn't have a debit card).

It's not like I could ask my mom, right?

I had not yet bound around her . . .

Though it was hard, I knew it was time to share some of the words I had learned.

Coming Out

IN EARLY SEPTEMBER, I SAT Mom down on our couch in the living room. Toby was up on the other couch nearby and the cats were wandering about. JT wasn't around because he had already moved to school; I had wanted to wait until he was out of the house to talk to Mom. He had continued to be verbally abusive to me—we didn't get along very well at all—and I didn't want him to know any details about me that he could possibly use against me, especially during such a sensitive time.

When Mom and I sat down to talk, I was prepared. It had been a long time coming and the little signs had shown through. I knew she knew I was going through something . . . but maybe not this. Thinking about my parents' potential desire for a son and a daughter was difficult. That was one of the hardest parts; feeling like I was being selfish. With everything Mom and JT were going through, all I wanted was to be normal. But over the summer, over the past few years—over my entire life, really—waiting to be free and to be my true self had gotten heavier and heavier. I knew if I kept it in any longer, I might drown.

"Mom? Lately, I've been thinking about my identity and who I am and how I relate to this world. Part of that includes my gender, and I've been questioning my gender a lot. I heard about therapy that can be with therapists who know about gender identity and I think that may help me answer some of these questions. Can I go?" I asked, quickly but timidly.

"Of course!" Mom hugged me close, although she seemed cautiously curious. "Was there anyone you had in mind?"

"Not yet, but I've got a short list from someone at church," I replied.

A sense of relief came over me. Before I could react, she spoke up again.

"Call your dad and ask him for permission as well," she said. "I don't want him uninformed about this."

Gritting my teeth, I nodded. It made sense. I had hoped for some more time before talking to Dad, especially since I wasn't seeing him for a little while. But having them both know seemed right and I trusted Mom. She was logical. She was patient. She made the rules.

That night, I picked up the phone to call Dad. I did not want to wait any longer to get the ball rolling. Life or death felt closer than ever; I wanted life.

He picked up after a few rings.

"Hey Goomba, what's up?" he asked.

Cutting straight to the chase, I repeated what I'd said to Mom. I concluded by saying, "and Mom said it was fine. I can go as long as you say it's cool too!"

Dad paused for a moment before saying, "Sure!"

"Really?" I couldn't believe how relaxed he seemed.

"Well you're going to ask questions, yeah? I think it's the right place to do that, with someone who may know some things. That's how you figure life out, you know? You gotta ask questions. So sure, go do it and make sure to ask the *right* questions." He likes to give advice.

"Thanks Dad! Thanks so much! I'm excited to ask these questions!" I couldn't even believe it, to be honest. My dad usually was hesitant, timid about change. Now, he was encouraging it . . . well, maybe he didn't know what was to come, but he was encouraging my exploration of my gender in therapy and that meant the world to me.

Over the next few days, I made some calls to therapists that Ursula, the therapist from church, had recommended. I finally got in touch with one a couple of towns over. I booked the first appointment she had available, on a Saturday morning a little over a month later.

"Hey Mom, can I ask you something?"

It had been a week since I made my therapist appointment. I knew this next step would be a big change, but I wanted to be open with her.

"Sure, sweetie, what is it?" She was sitting on the chair in the living room.

"So, umm, I want to go by a different name to try it out," I said, anxiety building up inside my chest. "And I was thinking the name Skye sounds right. Would it be okay if you tried to call me that instead of Katherine?"

She twisted her face at my comment. "Uhhh. Sure, honey. I can try, but I don't think it will be easy to remember."

"And there's another thing, too," I said.

"What is that?"

"I've been hiding my chest underneath a homemade chest binder so that I look more masculine and flat chested." I felt sweat dripping down my back.

"I noticed." Her words came out too nonchalant for my liking.

"Oh, really?"

"You didn't think I would? Of course! It's not like you were flat chested to begin with."

"Okay." I went upstairs.

Mom didn't seem mad. She knew way more than I had anticipated, and it caught me off guard. The conversation hadn't gone as poorly as I imagined it might, but I definitely felt awkward. I mean, of course she could see I had been playing with my gender. And it was exciting that it was obvious I was binding my chest; it meant I had made some visible progress. I felt relieved, but I also had to talk to Dad. I figured it was like last time; if Mom was going to call me Skye, I better have Dad calling me Skye too.

Up in my bedroom, I called my dad right away.

"Hey Katherine! What's up?" he asked.

It wasn't my usual time to call, so I let him know I had something I wanted to ask him real quick before I went to bed.

"Sure Goomba,[4] what is it?"

"I told Mom, too, by the way, but anyway. I want to try out the name Skye. It's androgynous, and I think it will fit me better."

"Haha, don't tell me about androgyny! I love David Bowie, you know. He is quite androgynous too; you ought to look him up," Dad said.

"Daaaaaad, I know David Bowie," I interrupted.

"Sure, sure. Gotcha. Well, we'll see. Let's see how things go with therapy, okay?" he concluded.

I didn't know what to think, but at least he knew. Maybe it would take him some time.

---

4 Goombas are those villainous sentient mushrooms in Mario that one can stomp on to get coins. My dad has called me Goomba since I was born.

Mom and I had a follow up conversation a few days after the Skye one.

"So as the ball gets rolling, there are some things I must ask you, so I'm prepared . . ." she began.

She went on to explain that she wouldn't financially support me, aside from therapy, and therefore wasn't going to buy me a binder right away. Not the answer I was expecting, to be honest. Binding was important and something I needed to do properly, ASAP. Thankfully, there was a workaround I had read about on on a blog I frequented.

I purchased a gift card at a convenience store so that I could order a binder online. They were expensive—thirty-five dollars on the Under-works site—and I saved for weeks. When I finally had enough money, I asked Amy if I could send it to her house.

"Of course, dude, no worries," she said. She was the best.

The binder arrived after seven days, and I was lucky to grab it from Amy's house that same day. Immediately, I took off my clothes in the bathroom and pulled it on. I looked at myself with a sense of pride in the mirror. As the weeks wore on, I felt it had stretched out or maybe I had gotten a size too big. I had feared binding too tight after my dad had commented my chest looked concave during one of my early trials of binding.

I chose to sew the binder up in half, folding it upon itself to make it tighter. I always liked to sew my clothes anyway.

Mom noticed my new constant, daily binding and offered to buy me a new one after I had complained of the smell. Or maybe she had complained of my smell. Either way, I was stoked she offered, and I chose a half-length binder a size smaller. My first one was designed to go down to cover the hips, but I only wanted it for the chest, hence the folding it up and sewing it.

It felt great to have new binders, knowing I could clean them and have options depending on the event. They were comfortable to wear, I could breathe fine, but by the end of the day, my spine felt achy and my ribs felt fragile. I hoped I wouldn't have to bind for long, but I knew top surgery[5] was a distant possibility. I'd have to be eighteen for that, I had heard.

As I tried on new clothes and was given some by friends and their siblings, I felt confident in my skin. I'd go to the Goodwill with my friends on the weekend in a neighboring town, talking and walking

---

5 Surgical removal of breast tissue to create a masculine chest.

with slushies in the summer heat. I got into flannels and sewing patches onto clothes. All I knew for sure was that I felt awesome looking in the mirror, wearing men's clothing, and feeling like it fit me right.

I'd wear baggier women's clothing too—it felt good. I liked things that didn't cling too tightly to my chest or hips. Skinny jeans and a baggy flannel became my go-to outfit, alongside band T-shirts and baggy jeans with patches I had stitched together.

As I moved through my life, I began to feel more comfortable trying on new things. Chest bound, head high—I was heading home.

Transitioning
Seems Expensive

AFTER COMING OUT AS QUESTIONING, I felt it was time for me to get a job. I was about to turn sixteen and could legally work at some places. I needed a way to make some money so that I could afford transitioning, so that I could afford to move out if I needed to, so that I could get out of my hometown someday.

The freedom I wanted was not going to be free. If my assumptions were correct, I was going to need to save about $875 to see an endocrinologist[6] and have some tests done. Then I'd need approximately $100 to get my first vial of testosterone (aka T). And top surgery—impossibly far away—was an $8,500 savings goal. (These figures ended up being mostly accurate.)

After enjoying some of the summer and moving full speed toward the following school year, I finally felt ready to take the leap of a part-time job. I knew that the local Low Key Mart was hiring. I applied and got a call to come in immediately for an interview. Panicking, I asked Mom what I should wear.

"Dress nicely," she recommended.

Androgynous kid + no formal clothes = doomed.

I went into the interview in a "nice" (qualifications: no holes) pair of black jeans and a tight orange polo shirt. I chose not to bind, as my ID still read F and Katherine. I looked fine enough, I thought, walking

---

6 A doctor who specializes in the endocrine system and can administer hormone replacement therapy.

through the fluorescent lights. The store was huge but felt empty all the time I had been in there. I'd say "sketchy" was what most in town thought about the Mart.

I pushed through the giant rubber doors in the back and veered left into a woman named Kathy's office. One of the lights above was blinking. The interview was short, with not much to note until the ending. It was clear upon walking in there that they were desperate for help and being relatively friendly was good enough for them. Kathy indicated that she liked me and she thought I would fit in; she mentioned I might be the youngest by far. I liked that thought since I got along pretty well with older folks, but it definitely crossed my mind that my androgyny might confuse some folks and I had my fingers crossed for no awkward interactions.

I had this eight-page document in front of me and I flipped through it, scanning the words briefly as she told me about the job responsibilities. Everything seemed doable. Then, on the last page, I saw that they were going to require a drug test before employment. My eyes went wide. Two weeks before the interview, I'd smoked some pot for the second time in my life.

Oh my god, it's exactly like what I learned at D.A.R.E.—one time will ruin your life, oh my god oh my god how could I have done that knowing I wanted a job soon, knowing I need a job to live oh no I'm so screwed oh my god.

Kathy got to the drug testing part, didn't even look up, and told me, "We're going to mark this as complete. Saves us money and time."

Phew. Inside, I was laughing but also so very relieved.

Getting a job that young was so important to me and my personal growth; I feel very thankful that I had such a strong drive to be working. Folding bathroom rugs until nine on a school night was not my favorite, dealing with customers and trying to get them to buy into our "rewards program," which was sketchy as all get-out, mopping up vomit from the bathroom floors. I learned life wasn't going to be easy, but I also learned way more than that.

Within my first month at Low Key Mart, I was ready to switch my nametag from Katherine to Skye. I went up to the customer service desk to ask them if they could print me up another one, and I had it five minutes later, no questions asked. I had already been binding my chest, but no one had seemed to notice or say anything, even though I thought it was quite obvious since my chest had entirely disappeared under my white button-down. I told my boss about my pronouns; no one seemed to have any grievances about calling me by male pronouns.

I do remember a few moments with a couple coworkers where I felt uncomfortable but knew they had no malicious intentions. One day, an older guy who worked in the electronics area approached me.

"When you go for the surgery, do you get to choose how big your penis will be?"

Feeling awkward about this conversation while out on the sales floor in the video game section, I gulped, "Hopefully!"

"Transitioning seems expensive, dude," he said. "I can't even imagine."

Another coworker, Amanda, quizzed me on what it meant if straight girls thought I was hot.

"Since you're still, you know, female, wouldn't that make them gay? Oh my god, like this girlfriend of mine, she saw you the other day and told me 'that boy is soooooooo cute what's his name' and I told her you're Skye but also that you're a trans person, and I don't think she knew what that meant at all but like she still liked you, so is she like, gay now?!"

It could have been a compliment, but I did not know what to say. My face felt hot and, while I was somewhat flattered, I was also caught off guard.

"The other thing is—do you, like, have a penis? I don't think it's a big deal, right?"

At this point, I had no words to defend against these invasive questions. I knew they weren't right and that I shouldn't have to answer them, but I had no way of explaining it that wouldn't play out like:

"Ummmm . . . I don't want to answer that. Sorry."

"Seriously? What's the big deal!"

"Uhhhhh it's personal? I guess?"

"Really? You gotta stop being so sensitive, you know. Everyone is gonna ask that or wonder it."

I wasn't yet able to say, "Hey, that is actually a personal question. I'm not asking you about the size of your genitals or your boyfriend's favorite sexual things; I demand the same respect. And let's be honest— you only need to know what's in my pants if I'm letting you in—and I'm NOT." Or even more simply, "That's an extremely personal question. It's inappropriate to ask anyone, and I know it is simple curiosity fueling your desire for an answer. While I'm also a curious person, I deserve the same respect you have for others' bodies. I've opened up to you about my choice to take hormones later on, but by no means are the steps I've taken in my transition as well as my body as I transition subjects you deserve full access to."

Instead, I stood there with my jaw clenched tight. I mumbled something and moved along. My biggest desire was to disappear, or to have that question disappear. While I remained slightly flattered that a straight girl thought I was attractive, even when I was still eighteen months away from taking my first hormone shot, I began to normalize these occurrences. Invasive questions about my body have never ceased.

As the holiday season rolled around, the store became hectic and busy. One day, I had two visibly queer women in my line and on the way out, they left behind two "Boston Beans"—they were these cute little baked bean figurines. I liked customer service, even when it got awful during the holidays, because of these little moments. I enjoyed most of my time at work, overall. Late nights, restocking the aisles, I felt like I had a purpose. I was working hard, making money, and felt I was moving in the right direction. By winter, I had been promoted to an amazing $6.75 an hour.

Sixteen

THE DAY I TURNED SIXTEEN, I was super excited to get my learner's permit. I wanted to get it as early as possible because I knew I had to drive with adults for six months before I could get my actual license. Looking at the schedules ahead of time, I'd signed up for our school's driver's education course that was in June, less than a month after my birthday.

I'd looked forward to driving for a long time. I could see the independence it offered; the potential for fun adventures with four wheels seemed limitless. In my family, my popop had always driven my nana around, and my dad was usually the default driver when my parents were together. Because of those instances, I thought of driving as a very masculine thing.

Being added onto the car insurance wasn't too difficult. "Wow," Mom said, "it's so much cheaper to have you on here than it was to have JT."

She went on to say something about how male drivers are a higher risk, as are young drivers, so a young male driver is the most dangerous. I smirked. *For once, my sex being female has benefited my life financially.*

Mom's idea was that I could drive everywhere whenever we had to go somewhere together. At first, I was so anxious that I hated my newfound responsibility. Since JT wasn't around, I felt like the "man of the house," and while being the designated driver seemed exciting beforehand, it wasn't so exciting when I was trying to merge onto a highway going 10 mph.

"DO NOT HAVE FEAR OF MERGE!" Mom yelled next to me. "IT'S LIKE A ZIPPER—EVERYONE KEEPS MOVING!"

"JUST GO, KATHERINE! PRESS THE PEDAL DOWN! JUST DO IT!" Overall, she was a great teacher; she still slipped up on my name and pronouns at least once or twice a day, but I promised I'd give her space and time. She was trying.

I finished up my driving classes during the summer and had driven around enough with Mom that I felt confident about the test. Except for parallel parking—that was definitely not my jam. The nice part about living in the suburbs, though, was that I very rarely needed to parallel park. My other weakness was driving in Boston.

Around the time I was learning to drive, Mom ended up having a gigantic cyst grow in her abdomen. I got to drive her to into Boston for appointments at Dana-Farber and Brigham and Women's while it was being monitored and her surgery date was scheduled. In late November, she got the cyst removed.

Once Mom was out of the hospital, I *had* to drive her everywhere. And it was quite snowy out. I became much more confident because now I had to get us to the grocery store every week and get Mom to all her appointments during her recovery, and basically I was the chauffeur for several weeks. With the added experience and improvement in the snow, I was not too nervous scheduling my test for January.

Waiting at the DMV, I worried I might face some type of issue. Although I'd worn my favorite flannel and gone through the trouble of straightening my recently dyed black hair, I didn't feel confident. Going by Skye but having my learner's permit read Katherine definitely left me feeling exposed and I wasn't sure how we would navigate the test with my gender clearly marked F on my papers while I presented as a boy.

The tester was a big, burly guy. He came out to my mom's car and said she could ride in the backseat. That was probably the first and only time she had to be in the back of her own car and I found it so funny. I let him know I went by Skye as a nickname, to cover that up front. He nodded.

The stakes were high, but the test went well (even the parallel parking bit). I walked out of the DMV with my temporary license.

I got in the routine of jogging down to the train station at 5:30 a.m. to pick up Mom's car and get to school in time for a parking spot. Then, I'd have to make sure I was back at the train station by 5:18 p.m. to pick her up. I liked the trouble of doing all of this; I felt independent even though I was still borrowing my mom's car. Some of my friends bought their own cars, but I was too focused on saving my money for top surgery.

A Circle, a Bird

SITTING ON MY BEDROOM FLOOR, I flicked a lighter on. I twirled a needle around in the flame to get the tip hot. Marsh had told me that helped sterilize it. I wrapped it in some sewing thread left over from modifying my worn-out clothes to fit better. Then, I dipped the needle into the ink Sam had bought for me.

I pressed the needle to my ankle, using just enough pressure to break the skin. It was itchy and somewhat painful, but like scratching poison ivy or a sunburn. Gingerly, I attempted to make a circle.

I left about thirty dots in my skin and called it a night. A few weeks later, I reviewed my work and realized I'd need to do many more layers. After a month of working on the circle, I turned it into a male symbol to complete my tattoo. Something felt amiss.

I wanted to add the female symbol and then the trans one, but I took a pause. I wanted to rest in having one part of it complete.

A bird appeared on my thumb. A skylark. A self-portrait I scrawled into my skin with ink.

I never added to the male symbol on my ankle.

Later on, during the summer before my junior year of college, I sat on the floor of my dorm with a girl I loved. She was about to go abroad. And weirdly, she had a bird tattooed behind her ear, her only tattoo.

It symbolized the idea of going back and reclaiming one's past, to understand why and how they came to be who they are today.

She tattooed this bird into my skin. Afterward, I tattooed mine onto her ankle.

Listen Up?

O N SEPTEMBER 4, 2007, I published a note on Facebook and on MySpace. I was transitioning from MySpace to Facebook at the same time as transitioning from female to male. So it went. I addressed the note to all the friends I had thus far on Facebook, but I made sure to block it from family members or adult friends who didn't need to know yet. Most of the people who could see it were classmates from all walks of life. Because I wouldn't see and hang out with everyone right away, I wanted them to know my new name before classes began.

listen up, yo?

hey so
recently i've been thinking
about the whole gender thing
about the whole society thing
about the whole . . . me thing.

and about my name.

so i don't know how many of you are going to totally totally be
*   weirded out or dislike me for this, but it's something i just ask?*
my name is katherine, yes? or kergil. depending on what you call
*   me.*

katherine is a really feminine name . . . and i just don't quite feel the
*   connection with it anymore.*

if you do, now, currently, call me katherine
it would mean the world to me if you tried your hardest to call me
skye.
or kergil, my last name. kergil is unidentifiable, and i don't really
mind it.
but skye is the name i'd prefer to be called over katherine.
cause it's like purgatory between . . . i dunno. any sort of name. it
could go either way and such

i know some of you already talked to me about how you've called
me katherine for aggggggggeeeeeeessssss so it'd be almost impos-
sible to change that.
but like, this would really mean the world to me. if you can't, i
understand and i'll still love you of course

school starts tomorrow, and teachers always ask me "katherine?
do you have a nickname you'd like?" (like katie or something)
and i think i'm going to ask them to call me skye. same for new
people that i meet, i suppose.

i know this seems like wicked strange, but i'm going through a
transition in my life
and it would really mean so so so much, seriously.

(p.s. just cause i prefer to be called by a different name doesn't mean
i'm a different person!)

so peace, love, and hugs as always.

p.p.s. there are also exceptions to those who call me wife or twin
or such. =P

The response to the note was mixed. Most of my friends liked the name
Skye. A few mentioned that they were bound to forget after years of
calling me my other name, but that they would try their best and to
remind them. People continued to echo those sentiments, and that was
totally fine by me. So many people said they loved me and that name
and said they'd do their best. People also joked around. I wanted to
keep it lighthearted and while a lot of my closest friends were taking it

seriously, they also knew I was still the same old person. I was incredibly grateful to see this widespread support before going back to school for my junior year.

Others were less excited. Their response was more "okay" and "I guess I'll try." Most of them were my guy friends; in school soon after, they were quiet around me. It seemed like something had changed between them and me, where they weren't sure how to address me yet.

The thing was: I hadn't straightforwardly announced I was transgender to people. I was still doing an "ease-into-it" situation with those around me. I was trying out male pronouns with some friends, but it wasn't about to be widespread . . . or so I thought.

The first week of school, things were going amazingly well. I went to the counseling office to see if I could get an appointment with the counselor, Rebecca. She was the one who had been helping me out after the frog dissection day.

I was able to see her that same afternoon. As we sat in her office, I found myself fidgeting around in the seat. I was anxious to tell her about the summer and all that was happening; the whole experience was nerve-racking, more than anything.

There were pictures of her family all around. She even had a Polaroid of her dachshund. The space was warm and welcoming and Rebecca gave off a trusting, calming vibe that made me feel ready to open up to her.

"So how was your summer?" she asked.

"It was great, actually," I said. "And I even got a job at the Low Key Mart! So summer has blurred right on into the school year."

"You look a little different, you know?" she said. "Not in a bad way. But like you're happier and less stressed than last year. How are you feeling with this new year starting?"

"Well, that's actually what I wanted to talk to you about . . ." I went on to tell her about my explorations of my gender.

"I am a transgender boy, and it's hard to say that, but it's true."

She didn't display much emotion—she seemed to remain totally neutral. When she spoke, it came from far away; at the same time, it was warm and reassuring.

"Really? You're sure about this?"

"Uhh . . . yeah. Yeah I think so, I mean, I'm about to start therapy for it."

Much to my relief, she chuckled at the situation as I seemed to be trying to justify it.

"No no, it's okay. Well I've got to say, I've never heard of this, but I believe you. And thank you for telling me. Is there something we should do? Is there a name you go by?" There was a reason Rebecca was one of my favorite people in the school. While she didn't understand, she was willing to take my word for it. She was a grown adult; I was some sixteen-year-old high schooler. And she believed me. It made me feel so amazing to know she was on my side.

I talked to her about my new name, about how I had decided on Skye. She offered to come with me to tell my teachers.

"But I don't want to draw attention to it, I don't want to burden anyone," I noted.

"It's no big deal," she cheerily encouraged me. "People go by nicknames or their middle names all the time."

After school, we went around to the teacher's offices announcing my name. I also mentioned that I wanted to be going by he/him. My teachers were surprised but seemed to tolerate the request at first. I mean, I did have Rebecca there and she was letting them know she was available with any questions they might have.

As my teachers began calling me Skye and by he/him, it started to spread to my classmates as well. And I began to feel so much better.

Yes, Skye? After I raised my hand in class.

Oh, haha, he's just being silly. A comment after school.

It wasn't all perfect; my math teacher and a few others seemed to have difficulty adjusting. They'd sometimes forget, or correct themselves. But my friends were like that, too. And I was blessed to have allies. Amy was one of my biggest allies when I was first coming out. She instantly started correcting people for me.

"Hey Katherine, what's up?" Ryan came out of nowhere.

"You mean *Skye*, right?" Amy interjected before I could react.

Ryan turned red. "Oh sorry! I'm so sorry!"

"It's okay"—I lowered my voice—"but yeah, call me Skye, please."

"I just forgot, my bad," he went on.

This happened so often. Amy was also great about helping with pronouns, which can be exhausting to correct over and over again. Slowly, most of my closest female friends began to regularly call me Skye and he/him. I felt affirmed every time that they did.

Unfortunately, some of my guy friends were struggling.

"I mean, I don't know that I can call you Skye, like I'll still call you Kergil, but Skye's too weird for me," one guy confessed.

"It's okay, dude. Kergil is fine, that works. Don't worry about it for now," I trailed off. It was still a letdown.

Another friend explained to me why he wasn't getting better at respecting my pronouns.

"You still look like Katherine, you know? Like you're still the same person, so I can't see you as a guy."

I hadn't made any physical changes other than binding. But I knew, by then, that I likely wanted to start hormones. It wasn't going to happen until I was eighteen, it seemed. That was far away.

"I get it, man. But you'll see someday, and it'd be good to try to start now if you can," I said.

"I dunno, dude. We'll see, I guess," he replied.

Sometimes, I'd hear those same guy friends talking about it behind my back. Little comments about it being weird, but them still loving me. One time, it went too far.

"You're pretty as a girl—you'd make an ugly guy," one of them remarked.

I stopped dead in my tracks and looked at him with total confusion.

"Well, you like girls, right? So of course I'll be an ugly guy to you. I don't care if I'm the ugliest guy in the world, okay? This isn't about YOU or what YOU want or what YOU see." I stormed off.

Within a couple of weeks at school, people began to ask me what bathroom I was using. I had been using the women's most of the time, but had once or twice used the men's room. My friends supported using the women's for now, since there weren't any gender-neutral ones.

Sam mused, "Yeah, like if a guy was in the girls' bathroom, he wouldn't get beaten up because the girls would run out."

"If a feminine guy or a girly looking one was in the men's, he might totally get beat up," Marsh added.

My ability to choose didn't last long. I was called down to the counseling center one day. Another teacher, someone I didn't know, was in the room. Rebecca sat me down and told me that some parents had called in.

"They were asking about a boy, potentially, who has been using the girls' bathrooms. Said something about it making their daughters uncomfortable. It was a few people, but I wanted to ask if this was maybe you. And it's totally understandable if it is; it's your right to use that bathroom," she said.

"Yeah. I've felt safer in there, you know? The boys' room can be intimidating. But it's not like there's another option, right? Where else would I even go?" I felt so trapped in that moment.

"We will work on that, don't even worry," she said calmly. "For now, keep doing as you are. We've informed the principal of the situation."

"Oh, wait, really? I mean, okay. Is it all good?" I was anxious.

"Yeah! Absolutely. She totally understands. You'll be fine," Rebecca concluded.

Leaving, I was still uncertain about which bathroom I should actually be using. I started going into the men's more, knowing I'd be using it full time one day. I didn't drink too much water after that because I preferred not to have to deal with it. But when I did, I'd duck in and beeline to one of the few stalls. Usually, no one came in while I was in there, so it worked out fine. A few times, I had to stay in the stall while someone used a urinal and wait until they left. Going in the middle of class time when no one was in the hallways helped make me feel better about not interacting with anyone.

As I darted out the door, I'd glance to make sure no one had seen me. Inevitably, a few times, I was seen. No one said anything. It only seemed to matter if I was in the women's room. Funny.

Sitting in the stalls, I'd hover and try to make it sound like I was peeing from a distance—but only if someone else was in the room. Otherwise, I'd try to get in and out of there as quick as possible. Rushing to the faucet and out the door in seconds. It was like a race to me. Also, forget pooping. That wasn't going to happen at school ever. I'd be trapped. No way.

Within a week or two, Rebecca got back to me with what was going to happen.

"So the school has thought it over and decided that you can use the nurse's bathroom," she explained. "They'll be taking the gendered signs off of them so that they'll be usable by anyone regardless of gender. Does that sound good to you?"

She had been working with leaders of the GSA. But the faculty leaders weren't too happy with this solution, I came to find out later. And the reason was pretty darn obvious.

The school was built in a linear way so that the main hallway was over a quarter mile long. The nurse's office was almost in the middle of it, but from upstairs on the second floor, it would easily be a five-minute journey every time I needed to go there. Plus, there were two of them and technically they were meant for kids that were sick. Having to go through the nurse's office all the time wasn't something the other kids had to do. Nor did they have to travel more than thirty seconds down a hallway to find a bathroom.

I accepted it, though, because I didn't have any other choice. And, in reality, I was lucky to have anywhere to pee. Other schools, I had heard, didn't have *any* accommodations. They left it up in the air, like when I'd been in limbo for a few weeks. I could've been like that for forever; so I was thankful for the option, but also pretty impressed with my school. There were no laws protecting transgender students in bathrooms, but my school had at least done one small thing to help me out.

They took the gendered signs off the bathrooms, but didn't repaint them. One was blue and the other one was pink. I usually used the blue one out of comfort, but occasionally I would venture into the pink one, feeling rebellious.

The phone calls to the school about where I was peeing stopped.

I was inconvenienced, sure. But most of all, I realized existing in public would not always be easy.

Gender Therapy

the first meeting went so well
with a gender therapist

i'm finally going somewhere
and it excites me

O N NOVEMBER 3, 2007, I had my first appointment with Julie, the therapist Ursula from church had recommended. Our first appointment involved going over various parts of my feelings, life, and history. She focused on my family and my relationship with them and others, but not so much about my gender specifically.

In our weekly sessions, we talked about my moods, which tended to range from extremely hyper and happy to more sad and anxious. She wasn't too concerned about the fluctuation. A lot of teens experience a range of emotions, she explained, and especially with all I had on my plate, I should allow myself to feel that range of emotions. She was speaking about my gender identity, going to college, my mom's cancer, my parents' divorce, my brother going to college, my dad living far away, my friendships, my teachers, my school year. Basically, she figured I had a lot on my plate. I guess I did.

Sometimes, I felt she was focusing too much on my dreams. Like overanalyzing my dreams, which were often vivid and crazy. But I wanted to talk about my reality and my struggles with my gender. I wanted her to be curious about that and not my dream symbols. The constant focus on dreams and reading into their meaning all too much made the sessions feel unproductive. I started to wonder if she'd ever actually had any other transgender clients or clients questioning their genders like I was.

So, one day, I voiced my concern.

It took me a long while to get the courage, because although therapy was supposed to be a mutually respectful situation, I still felt like she had all the power. Like I had to impress her or follow her lead, rather than the other way around. Therapy was new to me, like gender identity. I was still figuring it all out.

Julie told me I was, indeed, one of her first gender-questioning clients. I knew then that I wanted someone who specialized in gender, but I didn't know of any other therapists and there wasn't any info I could find online. Julie and I kept talking about my dreams, and I started to feel like I wasn't getting anywhere. Therapy went from exciting to frustrating, fast.

I began to feel lost and hopeless with it, but I kept going. I had no other choice.

Gym Class

IN MIDDLE SCHOOL, WE HAD started changing for gym in large locker rooms. Back then, I found myself feeling extremely uncomfortable in the girl's locker room, even though I "fit into the mold." No one could likely tell how awkward I felt there.

Other girls could chat about their bodies or their clothes or shaving their legs and armpits or whatever. I had finally figured out why Mom had offered to buy me that razor; eventually, I went to the pharmacy and got myself my own pack to shave my legs with. I shaved my armpits, too, since changing in front of others meant they would be exposed.

In the locker room, talk sometimes turned to bra size. I wasn't even sure what size I was; I preferred sports bras or camisole shirts so I didn't have to deal. I finally did get one bra, reluctantly.

But still. I didn't want to be around others discussing that. I didn't feel like I fit in with the girls and while they would chat amongst themselves, I felt guilty when I looked at them in the locker room. Like I shouldn't be there.

In my sophomore year, we had played water polo in gym class and I loved it; however, when changing in the locker rooms for swimming, I felt just as uncomfortable. Like I shouldn't be in there with the girls and have access to this private, girls-only space. But by that time, I did have a hunch as to the reason why I felt like an outsider.

When junior year rolled through, I still had to fulfill the physical education class requirement. But with my new nurse's bathroom situation and no real talk of what would happen at gym for me, I felt exposed. I felt like there was no way it would work out.

The first day I had PE, I went to change in the nurse's office like expected. I carried my clothes and backpack down the hallway to get to gym class. On the way there, I bumped into a few guys I'd never seen before.

One of them shoved me pretty violently up against the wall.

"Where you going, faggot?" another guy behind me said.

The two of them burst out laughing. As I turned around, they stopped.

"Ummm . . . I'm a girl." I stammered.

They looked confused for a millisecond.

The guy who had pushed me grunted, "What? Uh, okay," and then took off down the hallway with his friend.

I had dropped my clothes on the ground, so I picked those up and looked around. Nobody was in sight, which was pretty odd for the gym hallway, except that I was slightly late because of the walk from the nurse's office to there. Damn.

I had "admitted" I was a girl, which wasn't true. It felt gross on my tongue. It was a ridiculous excuse to deescalate a situation; in that moment, I needed to use it. I understood that, but still felt defeated and weird. I felt too ashamed, and truthfully I am terrible with faces. I wouldn't have recognized them in a lineup, which was awful. I didn't want to tell anyone about it and debated whether or not I should. I decided after gym class. I wasn't going to tell anyone except Rebecca.

When I told her about the incident, she let me know she took it very seriously. I informed her I didn't want anything big to come of it. I didn't like the idea of drawing attention to myself and having to go through that, especially so soon into the year. She understood.

"The other thing is that it took me so long to walk from the nurse's office down there that I was late," I pointed out.

"Why were you at the nurse's office before?" she asked.

"Because that's where I was told I had to change?" I said, confused.

"Oh! Right, I'm sorry I forgot. That makes sense. Darn, well, that is awfully inconvenient. How has gym been otherwise?" she asked.

"It's been okay. I don't know if it's working out though, the whole being transgender in a very gendered gym class situation. I mean, I can deal with it but I don't enjoy the isolation, I guess."

"You know, I heard about night gym that some students do. I can find out some more info if you'd like," she offered.

"My brother totally did night gym! It's like some nights in the evening, right? In the weight room in the back?"

The idea excited me. I'd have the freedom to lift weights or do cardio. Plus, I could drive to gym in the clothes I was working out in and not have to worry about changing. And even so, the weight room had two single-stall bathrooms in it. One for men and one for women, but I would be safe in a single stall regardless.

"Great! I'll look into it. I don't think it's even started for this semester yet, so if there's space, we could get you in. I'll let you know!" Rebecca was happy to have found a solution. "Also, I will keep you updated about the incident today. I respect your wishes, but I will have to pass the info along to a few other people. I want to make sure you feel okay and you feel safe."

"I do." I meant it. "I don't want it to be a bigger deal than it is. Night gym sounds fantastic, though!"

I was happy when night gym started. I didn't have my license yet, so Mom had to drive me there and back unless I could get a ride, but I didn't know anyone taking it yet. After she dropped me off, I walked into the back entrance of the gym, where the small weight room was.

There were a few other guys in the hallway. They were silent and seemed intimidating. But as I stood there waiting with them, a queerish-looking girl showed up. *Score.*

"You can call me Pal, but that isn't my real name," she told me.

"You can call me Skye, but that isn't my technically real name either, although I will legally change it."

I hadn't recognized her because she was a year ahead of me. I found out she lived in my general neighborhood, too. Turns out she knew a couple of my friends who we overlapped with, mainly because I'd played shows and gigs with upperclassmen when I was an underclassman. It was awesome getting to talk with her as it definitely eased my tensions around the whole ordeal.

A few weeks into night gym, someone was waiting to pick her up.

"Have you met my friend Rex?" She introduced me to this girl who she kissed on the lips. "We aren't dating but we basically are."

"Hi," I looked at Rex. She was beautiful, with long brown hair.

"Heya." She smiled and winked at me. It was weird, for sure. I thought maybe I liked her, but figured she was actually dating Pal. Rex, Pal, and I would often hang out at Pal's car after night gym. Pal began giving me rides home, too.

After night gym started, I began to feel like I was getting stronger from lifting weights. I felt productive, like my body was moving in the right direction. I had dysphoria around my thighs, hips, and chest, but as I began to gain strength, things were shifting. I figured any type of muscle gain and fat loss could assist in uniting my mind and my body. Fewer curves to focus on and more determination to move my body in the direction I wanted to go.

The release of exercise eased the tensions I felt building up in me at times during the school day. I looked forward to gym at night. I didn't miss being around my classmates, though I realized my enthusiasm about night gym was unusual. The other people attending were not happy to be there. They ranged from not having time in their school day schedules due to failing classes to being absent from day gym too many times. Me? I was just transgender, my own individual delinquent of the binary system.

Yeah, that's dramatic. But that's also being a sixteen-year-old.

Parental Involvement

O NE DAY, REX KISSED ME by my locker. It came out of the blue. "I've liked you for a year, by the way. And Pal was joking about she and I dating," she said, giggling. "I can't believe you fell for it."

I must have looked like a deer in the headlights. She was a grade ahead of me, talented at music, and intimidating.

After that, we were dating. A month later, she even gave me a promise ring. She supported my transgender identity, talking about how exciting it would be once I began hormones and hoping she'd be around for that journey. I met a bunch of her friends and she seemed to get along well with mine. Honestly, it felt like something out of a movie at first—a bit of sneaking around (her parents didn't know her sexual orientation), lots of flirty texting, note passing between classes, making mix CDs. Sometimes I'd get a text asking me to sneak over to her house. I had to be careful to avoid letting any neighbors seeing me—they always seemed to be out and about and could potentially tell her parents they saw me going into their home. The paranoia made it almost more fun. Sneaking kisses in her bedroom and then having to run out the door was exciting. I liked the rush of it at first, but over time I realized it was exhausting. And it made our relationship seem less legitimate.

Because of my first relationship, I had difficulty trusting Rex at first. And she was an extremely flirty person. Added on top of us being somewhat sneaky about our relationship, I felt it would be easy for her to not tell people about us. Our lives weren't intertwined immensely, like Ashley and I had been for a while, so I did get insecure at times. Plus, with therapy not going that well, I was feeling stagnated in my process. I was barely making any money at work, slogging along toward my future transition expenses, no big exciting plans beside that. But she was a senior and planning her trip off to college. It was an exciting time for her, lots of firsts and lasts as high school wrapped up.

I tried to measure up to her standards and wondered if I could. She told me about her parents, both therapists, and how they weren't tolerant of her bisexuality but seemed to accept me so far. She wanted me and my mom to come over and meet them.

When we did, I was incredibly nervous. They knew for sure that Rex and I were a thing. But at the dinner, they didn't seem to take it too seriously. They mainly chatted about psychology and the conversation grew tense at some times. Mom sat there awkwardly. It was also the first time that I'd been in her house with her parents there.

I felt bad for abandoning Mom upstairs, but Rex and I snuck downstairs to play some music and escape her parents' rambling argument about something or another.

"I'm sorry about them," she said. "They can be so overwhelming. Now you see what I deal with every day."

"Yeah, yikes. I hope my mom's okay. I feel like your parents could be nice but they seem to point out everybody's flaws . . . like diagnosing every action."

"Something about therapists, you know?"

"Haha, yeah. I'm looking for a new one . . . but obviously not your parents." I laughed.

"Sometimes I wish you were able to have started your physical transition already. They wouldn't have even known or cared if they had just met you as a boy," she mused.

"Well, I mean, they did meet me as a boy. Like, I was a guy when I first met them at school a couple months ago," I said, defensive.

"You know what I mean though. If they knew you as the guy you are, if they could see that, they wouldn't have any problems with us. Heck, you'd probably even be able to sleep over like my last boyfriend," she said.

"Really? And your ex-girlfriend slept over too?" I asked. She had dated a girl for like a month.

"Well yeah, but they didn't know about us and thought we were friends."

"Ahhh yeah, I did that with Ashley," I recalled.

"Well, I wish they were okay with you. I adore every bit of you, especially the parts they seem to hate. You are a real boy to me, I couldn't see you any other way." Her words warmed my heart.

We ended up making out in the basement but then we heard voices and remembered our parents upstairs. Running up, I felt bad I hadn't rescued my mom from the awkwardness sooner.

"That was odd," Mom remarked in the car. "Strange parents, indeed."

"Yeah. I think you get an idea of the whole picture now . . ." I trailed off.

On Birds and Bodies

Song lyrics, written 2007, released 2010 under the name Lentils and Dirt

Yesterday, I found out that my bones are hollow—
When did they plan on telling me that?
So today, for the first time, I'm going to try to fly—
Don't test me now.

And my body says,
"You can't do like you used to, boy,
no, you can't do like you used to."

What part of "I need this to survive"
Did you not understand? Did you not understand?
It's hard enough to say "I am alive,"
Did you not understand? Did you not understand?

Tomorrow, I'll be found eleven miles west,
In the grass, when did they plan on telling me that?
So for now, I'll just leave my world behind
I'll just leave my wife behind, yeah.

And my body says,
"You can't do like you used to, boy,
no, you can't do like you used to."

What part of "I need this to survive"
Did you not understand? Did you not understand?

It's hard enough to say "I am alive,"
Did you not understand? Did you not understand?

I felt like I owned this land
but now I'm not all I could be
now that I know what I could have been.
I feel like I am whole again,
with solid bones and ripped up skin,
this is all that I've ever been.

(This is all I've ever been.)

So what part of "I need this to survive"
Did you not understand? Did you not understand?
It's hard enough to say "I am alive,"
Did you not understand? Did you not understand?

Full Speed Ahead

SOMETHING MARVELOUS HAPPENED IN APRIL. A friend in one of my English classes came up to me. She started gushing about her boyfriend and told me he and I should be friends. Since Bianca was such a wonderful human, I trusted her judgment completely. Then she informed me that he was a trans guy.

"What!?" I exclaimed, super excited to hear this.

"Yeah! He's a freshman this year, so maybe that's why you hadn't met him yet but he is such a sweetheart!" she told me.

"That's so cool! I want to meet him!" I beamed.

"You will! I'll definitely introduce you two, I can't wait!" she responded.

We settled on meeting up in the common area after school the next day.

We hadn't considered that it was the Day of Silence and so I was committed to not speaking. Bianca had gestured to me that she still wanted me to meet him. She wrote down that his name was Aiden. We walked together after our English class down to the commons by the theatre. She pointed out her boyfriend and he walked on over, but he was also participating in being silent.

"I'll try to translate for you guys but basically I wanted you to see each other so you know who one another is!"

Aiden and I both smiled and wordlessly decided we would hug. I loved hugs. Even while binding, hugs felt good from friends and gave me a lot of comfort. When I hugged Aiden, I felt his binder underneath his shirt. While he appeared to already be on hormones, with facial hair sprouting on his cheeks and upper lip, it was nice to know we shared a similar plight of binding on a daily basis.

Since we couldn't talk, we planned through Bianca to hang out the next day. When we did, it was profoundly life changing. Unlike with Kayden, I felt comfortable talking to Aiden. He was smart, funny, and into sports like I was. He had been on hormones for a while, maybe even puberty blockers,[7] since he had started so young. I didn't ask, but he definitely had been through most of male puberty by the time I met him. Not going to lie—I was a little bit envious of his progress and how masculine he was. He looked older than me, even though he was two years younger. He was on his way to a full beard!

"Who are you seeing for therapy?" he asked one day in the cafeteria.

"Oh, this woman named Julie that this lady from my church recommended. She has no idea about trans stuff though. It's bumming me out." I felt my shoulders droop.

"Dude, you should see my therapist!" He seemed so happy to be helping me. "Her name is Rachel and she's awesome. She referred me to my endocrinologist, I mean, my hormone doctor, so I could start on testosterone! She knows what's up about that stuff. I think you'd like her."

He gave me her phone number and I called her that afternoon. We set up an appointment in June, a couple months away. I was used to waiting lists by then.

I thanked Aiden for the info—he shared so much knowledge with me that I am forever thankful for. After that, we didn't cross paths too often, but when we did, we would update on what was going on. A head nod and a smile in the hallway. He was, at that time, what a lot of people call "stealth."

Stealth meant that he didn't tell others he was transgender. He wasn't a stealth fighter pilot, no. He existed as if he had always been a guy. He completely "passed" as a guy—a word used to signify being recognized as your gender out in public.

Even though he had gone to middle school with the majority of his classmates, he was still starting anew as himself. I respected that. Over time, as he explained it to me, I analyzed my own thoughts about it. Maybe I also wanted to be stealth someday . . . to no longer have to

---

7 Puberty blockers are used, often pre-puberty, to block hormones that come with puberty. If I had been pre-puberty, around 11–12 years old, my doctor might have put me on blockers. Once I had gone through puberty, it didn't make sense to try to block estrogen, which had already done its job.

announce my gender verbally or look over my shoulder when running into a public bathroom. At the time, that's what I imagined it was like.

And with my upcoming appointment with Rachel, I was feeling more and more like that day would be possible. I knew my parents wouldn't consent to me starting hormones and that I'd have to pay for it on my own. Mom had made that clear.

At the same time, I was quite overwhelmed with schoolwork. I was falling behind in my classes, one of which was peer mentoring. I loved peer mentoring; I got to be a "big brother" type figure to a soft-spoken and interesting middle school kid.

One time, he tilted his head at me. "When do you know you're a man and not a boy anymore?"

"I'm not sure, you know?" I tried to come up with a good answer on the spot. "It depends what you have been through and how you see yourself, I suppose."

"Is it when you know your purpose? Like life purpose? What you're here for and all that?" he inquired.

"Sure! That could definitely be it."

While he was often silent, it was wonderful getting to mentor him. He may have known I was transgender, he may have not. He seemed to think of me as an older guy. I had been passing as a boy more often than not and feeling incredibly confident in that.

In Spanish class, I was getting closer to a girl named Winnie. She had glasses and was in chorus; we had enough to talk about at the beginning, but as we got to know one another, we began to realize we had a lot in common. A friendly upperclassman named Jason was also in our class and together we formed this triad. Our senses of humor all meshed perfectly.

"I have something I want to share with you guys," Winnie said one day. She sounded timid.

"What's up?" Jason sprung up, eyes wide.

She took a nervous glance around and avoided eye contact with us. "I think I'm bisexual."

"That's awesome!" we both responded.

It took me a moment to register that she had come out to us and trusted us with that information. Imagining how it must have felt like a load off her chest, I felt inspired to share my own truth. I leapt for it.

"I think I'm transgender, guys." I sank into a feeling of relief.

"Really? That's wonderful! What can we do to help?" They both seemed somewhat surprised, but maybe not. It was wonderful. While most of my classmates were questioning my appearance, there hadn't been many I'd flat-out told. I felt like I owned it in that moment.

After that, Winnie and I grew closer together. During the same time, she had met Amy, and before long, Amy and Winnie were getting along wonderfully. One day, Amy asked her out and my two close friends became a couple!

Around that time, things with Rex had begun getting intimate, but I wasn't able to open up to her. We got to sleep over at a friend's house together. We had played music with our friends all night, then wandered into the field and smoked some pot, and giggled as we fell asleep. Rex and I had most of the pull-out bed to ourselves.

We were kissing and as one thing led to another, I began touching her chest. She had her hand on my collarbone. My binder was digging into my armpits like it often did, but it didn't bother me this time. I was too distracted by the moment. And in that moment, I wanted to show her I trusted her.

I put my hand on top of her hand and placed her hand over my heart, in the middle of my chest, toward the top. I led her hand over the seams of my binder and stopped in the middle of my chest. I heard her breathing and for a moment thought she was crying. I think she might have been. I was.

Silent, trying not to make any sounds at all because our friends were nearby, it was one of my most vulnerable moments. No, I wasn't naked. No, we never had sex. But at that moment, I felt I showed her I trusted her. And she trusted me.

The next few weeks were blissful, like a movie again. She wrote me love poems and songs. She told me that she always wanted to be with me, even when she was planning to go off to college, even when her parents almost entirely disapproved.

Slowly, that bliss dissolved. Rex became irritable with me and I could tell something was up. She had been moodier than usual but I wondered if it had been because of my moods, too. I had been reclusive, I'll admit. I had been staying up late writing in my journal, frustrated about the lack of progress as I awaited a new therapist. I acknowledged how thankful I was, but I also still felt like my family wasn't taking me seriously. It had been announced to them, sure, and they were trying to call me Skye, sure, but they still seemed to assume it was temporary.

This sent me into a depression. I'd always been a hyper, social kid. All of a sudden, I was feeling apathetic. I didn't want to be around others and I didn't feel understood by anyone. I had started attending a queer youth group in Boston and was making some rad friends that were helping me feel better and more a part of a community, but at night, I felt so alone. I was tired of waiting. I'd been waiting my whole life. And I worried that even at eighteen, I might not get testosterone instantly. Thinking about the future began to give me anxiety.

I went for a walk with Pal one night in my neighborhood. I definitely needed it, even if it was midnight on a school night.

"Do you ever feel like you're the only one who will truly ever get it? Like even if someone else got it, they probably wouldn't see it the same as you do?" She gazed up at the moon.

"We probably all see colors differently. I think about that a lot, actually. No one will ever be with you in your head. You've got to be okay trusting someone from the outside in. Once you know one another, you'll know how the other person thinks, even if that's not necessarily how you think yourself," I replied.

"Sometimes I feel like I'm like everyone else, but then I wonder why no one gets me. No one gets it, except Tim, I guess."

Tim was her current fling—he was an androgynous fella. I didn't know too much about him except he had lots of tattoos.

"Yeah. I feel like that about Rex, I think," I thought aloud.

"You think?"

"I mean, I know. Like, she understands me. But I still feel like something's up. I don't know. Prom is coming up and I'm excited for that at least," I mumbled.

"Dude, it'll be okay. I'll be at prom, too, actually. I decided to go to that shit, haha. We can kick it there at least," Pal laughed.

I was glad to know she'd be there.

Prom was sneaking up quickly. As a junior, I needed a senior date to be able to attend. Thankfully, a few of my friends also had senior dates, so I wouldn't be alone.

When I had talked to Mom about prom, she suggested I rent a tuxedo. I figured that would be the best option. But then, one of my close friends from another school invited me to her prom, which meant two tuxedo rentals that year alone. Mom figured it would be a better bet to buy me a tuxedo.

"Why not? It'll save us money," she said.

"Yeah, I guess you're right. But the important thing is to match, like, I should have a yellow vest and tie if she's wearing yellow. And what if next year my date wears green or something? Ahhhh."

"Well, you could get a neutral vest and accent it with something else small, like a pocket square," she suggested, "Silver would look nice."

"Silver? That sounds awesome, actually." I began to picture it in my head.

We went to the mall to try to find one that would fit. Men's clothing still tended to be too big on me; I had a hard time finding shirts or pants small enough for my frame and often ended up having to shop in the boys' section.

At the suit shop, the salesman greeted Mom and me. He saw me as a boy, too—I was being seen as a boy almost one hundred percent of the time, even if inside, I was feeling dysphoric as all get out.

"Alrighty, son, so what are we looking for?" he asked.

"Well, I'm going to prom with my girlfriend this year and it's likely I'm going next year, too, so we figured buying it would be easier than renting!" I straightened my posture, getting excited to try on a tux.

"Ah, a bit of a player are we?" he chimed in, laughing.

I felt uncomfortable, though I knew it was intended as a compliment in some weird masculine world. As he began showing me options for tuxedos, it became apparent that I'd have to make some choices. I'm not the most decisive person, but with these options, I also had no real language to distinguish them from each other.

It's not that my dad had never taught me about menswear. It's that I was never interested and never asked questions about ties and suits and watches and shoes and socks and nice things. Being well-dressed was never one of my priorities.

We selected a vest, bowtie, regular tie, and pocket square, all in matching silver. And finally, with Mom's help, I settled on a plain black tuxedo. The smallest size they had still left me swimming in the shoulders and pants. While sizing me up, the salesman had noticed, but attempted to dispel any of my worries.

"Ah, no worries son! You're clearly still growing, you'll grow right on into it!" he assured me.

I laughed to myself at his comment, knowing full well that the second puberty I was heading toward wasn't going to make me taller. My pants would still be trailing the ground even after starting hormones—it's a myth that testosterone therapy makes people taller once they've been through puberty the first time around.

Prom rolled around in May. I was a month away from my first appointment with Rachel. I felt confident in my gender identity, confident wearing my tuxedo, and confident that Rex and I would have a great time.

In the end, I'm not so sure we did. She spent a good chunk of time with her senior friends and dancing with some of them, but we also had our moments dancing together like a hetero-seeming couple in the middle of the dance floor. A few of my friends were also there as dates of other people so that was nice. At one point, I needed to use the bathroom and my friend Clare came with me.

In my tux, and identifying as male, using the men's made the most sense. But I was still surrounded by people I went to school with—the same people who may have had an issue with me using the bathrooms there. Still, it was unlikely (though the thought crossed my mind) that I could get in trouble.

I ended up doing my usual routine of beelining to the stall and getting out of there are quickly as possible. I was so quick, I had to wait a little bit for Clare to be done. When she came back, I thanked her for coming with me. She cracked a joke about peeing at the speed of light and we went back to the dance floor to find our dates.

As the night came to a close, Rex kept kissing me and telling me how handsome I was. I felt more masculine than ever; even in pictures, I looked flat chested and like a man, not like an androgynous girl as I had in the prior years. It was incredibly affirming. After feeling like I stuck out for so long, I wanted to appear "hetero" and "straight" and "normal." I wanted to fit in.

Back at her neighborhood, we hung out in my mom's car before I had to drive home. We talked a bit about the night.

"Pal looked happy," she said, "like happier than she was last week, but I still wonder if she and Tim are going to break up."

"Why are you bringing that up?" I asked. A pit formed in my stomach.

"Nothing, nothing! It's just like, the end, you know? I'm reflecting. I'm sorry, I do want to be here with you in this present moment." She kissed me.

I shrugged in my seat and told her I probably needed to head home.

"I wish you could stay over, but we both know that's impossible," she sighed.

"Yeah . . . me too," was all I could say.

"Are you mad at me?"

"No no, tonight was fun," I said. "I have a lot on my mind."

It was a half-truth. I felt weird about her comments about other guys and how she had ignored me for much of the night. I wanted to be happy, but part of me felt like something was missing. Something wasn't being brought up. Feeling confused was one of my least favorite emotions.

I got home and JT was there with a couple of friends. They were playing loud music in the basement. I brought Tiger up to my room, plopped him onto my bed, and climbed out the window that went out on the rooftop above the garage. Sitting out there, I looked up at the stars.

I'm a real boy, I thought.
It will all be okay.
I'll make it to my dreams.
Maybe I need to be alone to really see what those are.
Does Rex really love me?
Do I really love her?
Who am I?
What am I?

JT was home a lot after dropping out of college. And although he sometimes did talk to me, he wasn't too happy with me going by Skye and being his brother. He didn't accept it for quite some time.

I felt bad because he hadn't been around that much when I was first coming out. I worried that was the reason that he was having a hard time dealing with it. Like he had been left out and would have to catch up.

Being at home with him wasn't very fun, though. I tried to be out of the house as much as possible and ended up at friends' houses a lot. I felt safer and more like myself when I surrounded myself with people who at least respected my name and pronouns.

With the strain at home, however, and the strain with Rex's family at home, our relationship was beginning to become difficult. I could feel it in our conversations on the phone at night, she was living in the future and not so much with us in the present. And I didn't blame her; so was I.

A few weeks before I had my first gender therapy appointment, Rex and I were hanging out at her place without her parents around. She had seemed off all night and finally came out with what she needed to say, right as she was ushering me out the front door.

"I don't think we should be together any more, Skye," she said, beginning to choke up.

"Wait, what? Why? What do you mean?" I felt like I was falling.

"You know, I don't think this will work out when I go to college. There's a lot of life ahead of me, and I love you, but I don't think we are meant to be together right now."

She was bawling. I hadn't thought about being with her forever, like I had at times with Ashley, but in the whirlwind of our relationship, it felt more meaningful than something one could shrug and give up on.

"But you aren't leaving for college for another three months."

"Well, yeah, yeah I guess I mean that is true, you're right," she said, stumbling through her words.

I refused to leave without clarity. *Is there someone else? Is this seriously about college? Did I do something?*

I could tell from the look in her eyes—dark, but also compassionate—that she didn't want to talk about what was on her mind.

"Honestly, I think being transgender is a mental disorder. I don't think you'll ever be happy and not even with the steps you've decided to take to transition, if those ever happen. I think you'll always be unhappy and miserable with your body, and I don't want to be with someone like that."

"You really think that? I'm about to start actual gender therapy, though, which may help lots," I tried to say, but who knows what words came out. I was in disbelief.

I thought about defending myself for a moment, but what she announced couldn't be unheard. And I knew fighting her "realization" would do nothing to prove I wasn't some sick, mentally disturbed person.

Driving home, I slammed my hands on the steering wheel out of frustration. *Why again? Why me? Just because I'm transgender? She knew that! She knew the ENTIRE time that I was trans! How could she change her mind? Was it her parents? She thinks I'll always be unhappy? What if I'm always unhappy? Oh my god what if I am really sick? What if people have been lying to me that they accept and love me even with me being transgender? Are people waiting around for me to change my mind?*

My trust flew out the window and my self-esteem plummeted. I desperately wanted to erase Rex from my life. I had been building up my identity, careful to share it with those I could trust and keep close to me—only to have a person I thought I truly *loved* doubt me.

Thankfully, I had spring break coming up and therapy pretty soon after Rex dumped me. And my new therapist? Absolutely worth the wait.

2008

I T WAS 2008, OVER EIGHT years after the world was supposed to end at the turn of the century.

I borrowed the car and drove up Interstate 495 on a rainy June afternoon. While I felt optimistic, I didn't know what to expect. I was nervous, worn down. Ready to start something while being prepared for it to stop suddenly.

It wasn't a waste of time with the last therapist, I kept reminding myself, *she helped me during the time I was waiting to get here . . . I think . . . hopefully this is finally the right spot . . .*

I felt ready to move forward with some physical or legal steps in my transition. Socially, I'd stagnated. I was seen as a boy as much as I could be seen as such. At least, many people treated me with respect by using he/him pronouns and calling me Skye. I'd been trying to treat myself with respect, but dealing with my body was a battle I fought daily.

I was fortunate to blossom in a community that, while not necessarily ready for transgender people, was willing to learn. As senior year swiftly approached, the future seemed less certain. But I knew full well that I wanted to be on testosterone and Rachel seemed to be the one who could get me there.

Rachel practiced therapy right out of her house. I entered the small office space behind her garage. Her shelves were full of books dealing with gender, depression, and being a teenager. She was a bright, warm person, and I instantly felt comfortable around her, which was a huge relief. She began by asking me a bunch of questions about my past, including my past experiences with therapy, and what had led me to her that day.

"I haven't felt like my previous therapists were knowledgeable about gender. And it was pretty discouraging to have to educate them, you know?" I said.

"That's understandable. And in many ways, therapists who don't have the right training for your issue may not be able to effectively help you, although they can, of course, help in other ways. I want to let you know I've had dozens of trans clients, ranging from pre-teen to adults, and that therapy is a conversation about what's going on, not a checklist of criteria to fit a certain mold." She was super calming and friendly.

She asked me questions about my identity and how the past year had been. I mentioned the slow progress with my parents, noting that I wanted to fully come out to them again once I knew what my future was looking like. She asked what I meant by that.

"You know, I was questioning my gender for a long time, and my friends know I identify as a trans man now, but I'm not sure my parents fully understand that I am who I am—like they think it's a phase. And I worry a lot about that, that maybe they'll never believe me."

Rachel let me know that I could bring my parents to therapy, if I ever wanted. I hated the thought at first; the idea of my parents joining me and another person in this formal capacity to talk about my gender identity seemed daunting. After a few more sessions with Rachel, I thought she understood me and what I was going through. Better than any other adult I had yet to meet.

I wished I had met her first. Nowadays, there are resources online to find gender therapists or therapists that are familiar with transition or gender variance. Finding a knowledgeable and helpful person first is ideal!

I decided to ask my mom and dad if they would like to come into therapy with me, but before I did, I sat Mom down to fully come out to her.

"Mom, I wanted to let you know, after seeing Rachel for these past few months, I've realized I am a transgender man. I believe I am your son, and I have had these feelings for a long, long time. I never knew what they were, and puberty totally messed everything up for me. I want to physically transition to be male." Sitting on our blue leather couch, I nervously rubbed my hands against my knees.

"Oh . . ." Mom got quiet.

"You can come to therapy with me, actually, I want you to if that's okay!" I suggested. "There are other people like me and it's possible for me to be happy and feel like myself finally."

"It's not that, it's just"—she started crying—"I can't financially support any of this, this choice. The world is going to be so much harder if you choose this path. What if you can't even go to college? Or find a job? Or a loved one? It's going to make your life so very, very hard."

I felt like I had broken her heart. I asked her real quick about the financial support part of her statement, and she said she simply wouldn't pay for testosterone, surgery, or anything else that reinforced "this idea I had." My therapy sessions, thankfully, she was willing to still cover. Even though it was the second time I had heard it, it was heartbreaking for me, and I got super angry as I walked up to my bedroom, feeling again like the world was out to get me. That I'd never be happy. That of course these suicide rates are so high—look at what we deal with!

I punched my pillow and then picked up my guitar.

After playing around for an hour, I took a deep breath and kept moving.

I called my dad to let him know the fact that I was, after all, a transgender boy. A year of asking questions and discovering myself seemed like it would be reassuring for my dad. He liked to know things had been thought through. I hoped that was what he would garner from the conversation. When I called him, it was late and he sounded tired.

"Hey Dad, there's something I should tell you. Oh, and Mom knows, too, by the way, I just told her so I'm telling you right after so you both know at the same time. You know how I've been in therapy? Yeah, so I have learned a whole lot and had a lot of questions answered and feel like I need to tell you that I identify as a boy . . ." I took a breath.

"Hold on, can you slow down a moment?" Dad asked. He sounded more awake now.

"Yeah, sorry," I said, getting nervous.

"So you are saying therapy has helped and you realize now you are a man? Like you're a boy?" he asked.

"Ummmm . . . yeah! That's how I've felt for a long time, I just didn't know other people felt like me." I tried to sound confident, but could tell my voice was shaking.

Dad was silent for a moment, but like me, he's a talker.

"Huh," he continued, somewhat chuckling, "well, why can't you be a normal lesbian?"

"Dad, I never said I was a lesbian."

"Oh, well, I mean, you began dating girls, you know, and there seem to be women who look like men but are still women, you can still be you but be a woman, you know." He was calm, but I was getting more upset.

"That would be a fine option if I was a woman, Dad. I do not identify as a woman. I'm a boy, and I've known this for a long time." I tried to be as clear as possible

Dad continued musing about gender and sexual orientation, conflating the two. We had a long road ahead.

By September of my junior year of high school, I was ready to have my parents to come to therapy with me. I felt Rachel truly heard my thoughts, understood them, and as an adult, I thought she could help me translate my identity and needs to my parents. They would come separately; I had Mom come first since we lived together.

Sitting on Rachel's light yellow couch with Mom, my heartbeat was much slower than it had been when sitting on our blue couch at home. In front of us was Rachel, sitting tall with her notebook and hands on her lap, smiling and ready to go.

The time was spent as a mediated conversation; I let Mom know that after these past few years, and the four months with Rachel, I was definitely ready to take steps towards physically transitioning. Mom expressed her concerns, much like she had the first time. Rachel reassured her that she had helped other young adults begin their transitions in this world and that the benefits of transition seem to greatly outweigh the concerns of society's rejection.

"Otherwise," she explained, "instead of society harming a transgender person, that individual may turn on themselves, no longer feeling capable of being seen. While some may think of this as a choice, it's important to know that, like sexual orientation, it's not. The most recent studies show that family acceptance has the largest impact on the health and well-being of a transgender child."

"I love her—I mean, him," Mom said, "and I cannot bear the thought of this world treating him like he's not human and not worth loving and not worth being given a chance when he has so much to give to this world."

"Well, I won't have a chance to exist in this world if I can't exist as myself. I can't keep pretending this will go away or I'll wake up tomorrow with my mind changed. It's like I wake up every single morning and I'm a butterfly but everyone sees me as a caterpillar. So I spend all day being seen as a caterpillar and no matter how many times I explain that I'm a butterfly, they only see caterpillar. And sure, I see caterpillar with my eyes open in front of the mirror, but with my eyes closed, I know I am a butterfly. It hasn't changed in years, and I hope to begin this journey with you, Mom, around Acton—not off at school coming home from winter break as an entirely different person!"

"It sounds like what Skye is saying is that he wants a chance to be truly seen as himself. Before he heads off to college, in a safe place, he wishes to see if this is right and to be around you, his friends, and his supportive school while he takes a big step," Rachel chimed in.

Mom and I went over some of the potential effects of testosterone with Rachel. She let us know she often referred youth to Dr. Spack, an endocrinologist at Boston Children's Hospital, and that contacting him ahead of time might be a good idea as their gender clinic often had a wait.

On the drive home, I wanted to ask Mom for guaranteed permission we could contact him. I was excited knowing this option was presented and that Rachel would be willing to write my referral letter already. Instead, I kept to myself. I felt both sad and excited. I didn't know what to say. As the sun set on our ride home, Mom asked what we should have for dinner.

"Ravioli?" I asked.

"Sounds good to me!" She smiled. "And I think this went well, Skye. I'm glad I got to meet Rachel. I can see why you like her so much."

"I'm so happy I found her." I smiled. "Did I ever tell you that it was a trans guy at school, Aiden, who gave me her info? He's already on T. He's so happy, Mom, you can't even believe it."

Mom seemed pensive. "Oh, well that's nice. We'll talk more about what she suggested after you and your dad have your conversation with her. I don't want to jump to any conclusions without Dad being included. You know how he would feel about that. Right now, though, I feel much, much better about this whole situation."

And so did I.

Dad met me at Rachel's house the next week. Back-to-back parental sessions; not ideal, but I desperately wanted everyone on the same page.

I don't remember too much of the conversation. Dad was quieter than Mom, mainly listening and then expressing some concerns. I felt comfortable during the hour, but it didn't feel as concretely productive as the one with Mom felt.

Afterwards, we went out to a late breakfast, our favorite meal together.

"Your therapist seemed nice," he said. "But this whole thing is still weird for me, Katherine . . . I mean, Skye. It's a slow process. I like that it is a slow process, and it should stay a slow process. You have so much life ahead of you; let us take our time here."

"Oh yeah. Yeah, yeah, yep. Yeah. Totally," I sipped my coffee. "There's no need to rush, but I think I don't want to wait much longer. I want to go to college and have this behind me."

He raised his eyebrows and then we talked about the weather.

"I love you no matter what, Goomba." He hugged me goodbye.

A few weeks later, Mom asked if I was going to get the information about contacting Dr. Spack. As I drove to therapy, I felt eager to ask Rachel about it.

"How was your week?" she asked.

"I feel worried but I'm so excited. I'm feeling more optimistic than I have in so long. I feel like I can see the light now, and I know full well how much testosterone will help me. I mean, I have an open mind, like I know there are the side effects that may be difficult to manage or pose their own risks, and then superficial stuff like going bald eventually, probably, I mean, look at my dad . . ." I had a lot to say.

At the end of the session, she offered to write me a referral letter, diagnosing me with Gender Identity Disorder (GID)—at the time, the diagnosis a gender therapist had to give to satisfy requirements to begin hormone replacement therapy (HRT). For folks going from female to male, options included puberty blockers (but I was already post puberty), estrogen blockers (usually not necessary because estrogen is a weaker hormone than testosterone), and testosterone. That's what I learned from what I had read online and what Rachel had mentioned.

"So I'll be faxing this letter to Dr. Spack's office today, perhaps give them a call tomorrow to make sure they got it," she said, smiling.

"That's it?" I asked, reflecting on all of the time I had spent in her office hoping for this day.

"They may have some questions for you, but yes. That's it!"

It was the end of September. I called Boston Children's Hospital on my lunch break at school and got their next available appointment for January 21, 2009 at nine in the morning.

Have You Hugged Your Kid Today?

URRICANE KATRINA HIT IN AUGUST of 2005. It took a few years to organize, but my congregation sent our youth group down on a trip to New Orleans to help a church during spring break of 2008. I hadn't traveled much—just a few family trips to visit relatives and a couple of chorus trips to big old churches. Eagerly, I helped raise funds so I could attend.

This church had sat under water for weeks and it showed. The sanctuary looked abandoned, with pews full of water damage and the paint peeling off every surface. Lights didn't work in many rooms. They put us up in bunk beds upstairs. I stayed in a coed room, peeling my binder off late at night as I slept in a giant pile of my own clothes.

There was a girl from another youth group who I overheard calling me "dreamy." I kept laughing and laughing at the thought. She didn't know I was transgender, thinking I was any other cute teenage boy, and it was flattering. Hank and I kept poking fun at the flirty comments this girl kept making to my face and behind my back.

I spent the week helping paint the fence of a social services center. On our second night there, we went to a coffee house that had poetry slams every week. I felt inspired, listening to others who got up on stage. Grabbing a sharpie, I began scribbling some words on a napkin, inspired by the incredible trip.

When it was my turn, I stood up at the mic and read from the napkin. My high-pitched voice shook . . . but with each word, I gained confidence. Looking out at some of my best church friends, especially

Hank, I felt solid. I felt recognized. I felt creative and inspired for the first time in a long time.

Although the sharpie bled out and my handwriting isn't very clear, I still have the napkin.

Once, I was brought in for disorderly conduct,
I guess I just hadn't watered my plant enough
And the police officer asked me if I knew how to make origami,
So I built her an airplane and flew out of that place.
With dirt stuck in my toes
(likely due to my bare feet,
my rusty, bare feet, mind you)
I began to piece together that maybe
The alleged "free underground"
Was a secret mafia I wanted to join, cause
I have better things to do than sit around and sniff glue, mate.
So I climbed onto my bike
And ended up behind an old van,
Where a bumper sticker screamed at me
HAVE YOU HUGGED YOUR KID TODAY?
Hell yeah.

On our last night there, I fell asleep next to one of my new friends, Veronika. She was in my youth group but we hadn't really connected before. We had stayed up late talking in a sanctuary room full of several organs, a piano, and a lot of couches. I woke up moments before having to leave for my flight, leaving a puddle of drool on her arm.

I missed my flight, twice. I fell asleep at the gate, twice, from having stayed up so late with Veronika. In a twist of events, I ended up in a first class seat . . . right next to Veronika. I had my CD player and a booklet full of mix CDs; Veronika had a headphone splitter. We spent the flight listening to songs I loved. As the plane landed, she put her number in my phone.

I was thankful for the gesture but simultaneously I felt this intimate moment slip away. In just a few days, I felt closer to Veronika than I did to most folks in my life. She hugged me goodbye and gave me one of her flannel shirts (which I didn't wash for weeks since it smelled like her and that trip).

Soon after, she gave me a mix CD—some of the songs on it were super romantic-seeming, but I didn't want to get my hopes up too high that she was interested in me. She was way out of my league, too beautiful to date a fool like me. She was pansexual, a word I hadn't known yet.

"It's like bisexual, except that bisexual implies an attraction to the two binary genders. Pansexual is less about gender, actually it has nothing to do with gender or sex, it's about being attracted to a person because of their personality," she taught me.

Veronika lived in a nearby town. When I went to visit her a month after New Orleans, she had broken up with her long-term girlfriend. We went for a long walk in the woods and I found myself seeing her with new eyes. A month or so after that, I asked her to be my girlfriend.

She kissed me and said, "I think that's a yes."

I wrote a million songs about that moment.

Bathroom Bouncer

ITWAS OCTOBER OF 2008 and, being young queer folks, my best friends and I *had* to go see Tegan and Sara when they came to town. Amy, Winnie, and I got dropped off before doors opened so we could get up to the front of the general admission area. I was wearing my white Social Distortion shirt over a black Under Armour shirt that I wore over my binder to even out any bumps. I was layered. I wore my usual black skinny jeans and looked a lot like many of the other androgynous people around. I wondered how many of them were trans guys or trans girls or part of the trans community, but I didn't see any trans flag patches. Lots of rainbow ones, at least.

Super stoked to hear T&S live, I sang along to almost every song. And although I usually tried to avoid drinking much water in public spaces, I had to stay hydrated to keep enjoying singing. So I drank plenty of water throughout the first part of their set and, disappointed to forfeit our spot close to the band, I finally relented to needing to pee.

The bathrooms were down a short hallway with the men's on the left and the women's on the right. As Amy and I navigated through the bodies crammed together, waiting for beer at the bar, I could see the situation ahead. Since many men's bathrooms don't have stalls, or have stalls with no door on them, or have one stall that is constantly in use, or have stalls with doors but no locking mechanism, I had become pretty conscious about bathroom choices.

In this situation, I felt apprehensive about the men at the show and the men near the bathroom, even if in a crowd of randomly selected folks, I would imagine I would be seen as a young boy. In the context of this crowd, however, I could easily be read as a butch lesbian, as a girl, as an androgynous girl, as a trans man or anything else.

After quickly weighing the pros and cons, I informed Amy that I'd go with her to the women's bathroom. I figured that was the safest bet—if anyone asked, I could easily speak and explain the situation, whereas a hyper masculine space might prove more aggressive. While I hated my high voice, I knew I could use it to clear up any problems in the women's room.

There were at least four or five girls in the bathroom. Though no one even looked at us, I felt uncomfortable. I beelined right to a stall like I normally would regardless of which gendered bathroom it was. I did my business quickly, exited the stall, and was happy to see Amy was washing her hands at the same time.

Happy, that is, until this figure appeared, blocking the exit of the bathroom.

She could have been a very large butch lesbian, she could have been trans like myself, she could have been a very intimidating, straight woman—she could have been whatever she wanted. But let me say this—she was big, overbearing, and *waaaaaaaaaaaaaay* more masculine than I will ever be. I'm talking military buzzed haircut, huge baggy pants, boots, black muscle shirt, chest that looked like pecs, big bushy eyebrows. She glared down at me. She was not happy.

"Excuse me, you can't be in here," she practically yelled at me as she pointed to her employee nametag.

"Uh . . . Umm . . . what?" I mumbled.

Then I heard Amy's voice, much louder than mine, as she took a step toward this woman, pointing her finger at her and saying, "What are you, like, a bathroom bouncer?!"

The look on the woman's face was somewhat confused and before she could respond, we were squeezing past her, out into the hallway, out of that bathroom.

"JESUS! Seriously? She looked more like a man than you do, no offense, Sky, you know what I mean. So what the hell. What was her beef?"

"Maybe she was a security guard?" I responded, shaken from the confrontation.

"Well, if a girl in that bathroom called in security because they were worried about a man in the girls' bathroom, they shouldn't be sending a woman who looks more like a man than anyone else here to confront the situation," Amy said.

She was right. If the fear was of having a man or a masculine presence in the girls' bathroom, this security guard (or whatever the role is called for working the patrol of gendered bathrooms) likely would have intimidated the women in the bathroom more than I did.

But what baffled me most of all was how quickly the situation escalated. I wasn't standing around in the bathroom—I was probably visible in the communal bathroom space for less than thirty seconds before someone's alarm had gone off.

While I could have been honored that *wow I passed so well for a man even pre-T and even while not going above and beyond to pass*, I was more bothered by the policing of a very queer space. There were others that looked practically identical to me in gender expression. Why did I get singled out?

Why couldn't I use the bathroom in peace? Why couldn't I enter a bathroom that corresponded with the sex my birth certificate without causing a disturbance? Why couldn't I enter a bathroom that corresponded with my gender identity without worrying about my safety? Why weren't there any options for those who drift in between, those who aren't seen, those who don't have a gender?

I learned my lesson. When in public, I should fear harassment in gendered bathrooms. And although that was a decade ago, we are still facing these same issues today. Laws prohibit transgender people from using public accommodations that are gendered; the fear rhetoric around what a transgender person may be doing inside the bathroom (preying on children, something sinister, something else ridiculous) perpetuates this problem throughout the US. Transgender people all can be subjected to persecution for merely needing to pee.

What transgender people do inside bathrooms—check themselves out in the mirror, use the toilet, put on makeup, wash their hands—is no different from what cisgender[8] people do inside bathrooms.

Someone who is planning on doing something illegal is going to do it regardless if the symbol on the door is wearing pants or is wearing a skirt or is gender neutral.

---

8 Describes people who are not transgender or gender-nonconforming (such as my brother, who was born male and identifies as a man).

Getting Accepted
into College:
A Casual Miracle

D AYS FELT LIKE WEEKS, WEEKS felt like months, months felt like years as I waited for my endocrinologist appointment with Dr. Spack. Thankfully, it was also the fall of senior year, and it was also time to make some huge decisions about my future. I had sat pretty darn still during SAT testing and done all right. Schools began sending me pamphlets over the summer; Mom and I planned a long list of tours, some of which rolled over into the fall so we could see students on campus.

I toured several local colleges, including some random ones that had offered me scholarships, but the farthest Mom and I went was the Pittsburgh area because I didn't want to have to fly to or from school. I fell in love with Skidmore College; it was the third on our long tour. The reasons I liked it had nothing to do with academics. I loved the campus, the weeping willow trees. I loved the people I met on my tour and the staff I was introduced to. I loved their slogan: Creative Thought Matters. Later on, basically all throughout college, whenever my friends and I would do something mildly DIY or quirky, we would chant "CTM! CTM!"

Oh, and I liked that their application had a separate box to select and write in my own gender. And they also had a line underneath legal name. It looked like this:

Preferred name: _____

All right, all right. I wasn't that chill. I was smitten. Out of the seven colleges I had picked up applications for, Skidmore was the only one with space for preferred name. My googling led me to believe very few schools had this in practice in 2008. Because of this, I knew I wanted to eventually educate other schools and explain, among other things, the importance of inclusive language on applications.

Simply because of the inclusivity, the offer of gender neutral bathrooms on campus, and the statement that they already had gender neutral housing in place—I was sold. I knew I could be myself at Skidmore without needing to pave the path like I had to do many times throughout high school. They had things set up. I could attend without creating special circumstances. Yes!

However, I knew Skidmore would be a challenge to get into—my grades were teetering on the lower end of what they would accept. Because of that, I chose to do an in-person interview at their admissions office in the fall, a few months after I had toured and fallen in love.

The man who interviewed me was young, black, and dressed with a very dapper bow tie. He had a warmth to him that felt inclusive. I beamed, realizing my instinct was right from the papers I had read and the tour I had been on and the vibe I had gotten.

I explained that I am transgender, and that my goal was to attend college as the man I've known myself to be and to get my Bachelor of Science in Studio Art. It sounded like that would definitely be possible at Skidmore. I also mentioned that a reason my grades had begun to dip later on in junior year was due to the struggles I was having with support from my family and feeling lost with how to be my true self.

"I understand. I came out as gay in college and found it to be such a safe space." He smiled, remembering.

That was such a small part of our conversation; we mused about the origin of ideas, what one truly owns, and what creativity is. The moment I remember crystal clear was my knee-jerk (and very cliché, let's not even lie) reaction to this question:

"What does it mean to you when someone says, 'Think outside of the box'?" He tilted his head at me as he crossed his legs and pushed up his glasses.

"What do you mean 'outside of the box?' Why is there even a box?" I said.

He smiled. I let out a sigh of relief.

I applied early decision to Skidmore; my understanding was that if I was accepted into Skidmore, I was locked in. In theory, I could pay a fee and no longer be locked in, but I wasn't worried about that. If I was going to college, I wanted to go to Skidmore. I had looked at so many schools that outwardly appeared awesome, but they didn't have inclusive language on their application.

I was exhausted by having to fight to simply use a bathroom. I couldn't picture myself anywhere less than safe for and inclusive of LGBTQ people.

Seven weeks later, I received a huge envelope in the mail. As I was holding the envelope in my hand, my neighbor Sayad came out of his house to check his mail as well and smiled as I looked at him with huge eyes.

"I think this is it!" I exclaimed. I had kept him updated on my college process while he had been teaching me how to drum in exchange for me babysitting his kids. I loved my neighborhood.

"Oh goodness! Open it!" he said.

I pulled the envelope apart to reveal a large folder. It looked like all of Skidmore's other marketing on it, except in red, yellow, and green amongst the black on black letters it read:

"Yes!"

Sayad yelled out in joy and hugged me. "I'm so happy for you, Skye! I knew you could do it!"

Tears started welling up in my eyes. I finally felt like I had a future ahead of me.

Early decisions had come just before the Christmas holiday, which was fantastic timing. I was able to share my excitement with all of my friends before holiday break. Some of my friends had also received acceptance letters too; it ended up being a pretty bittersweet time. Both celebrating the joy of our future independence, lives, and studies as well as realizing that this inevitably meant we would no longer see one another every day.

A lot of things were about to change as high school came to an end.

"I'm an Obama Baby!"

ON JANUARY 20, 2009, PRESIDENT Barack Obama took the oath of office. When I got home from school that day, I wrote in my journal.

12
twelve hours . . .

nervous
scared
anxious
but more than anything,
ready.

The day after Obama's inauguration, I missed school for the first time in my life. I had never been sick enough to stay home, never left early for a vacation—I had been to school every day that school had been offered.

I made an exception that day, January 21, 2009. I was going to see the endocrinologist in Boston. I was going to start testosterone.

We left early in the morning; the sun hadn't risen but I was used to getting up early. I had hardly slept the night before. The excitement, anxiety, and overwhelming disbelief that this was truly happening had kept me up.

My mom was getting her cancer treatments in the same medical area as Boston Children's Hospital. I recognized the area from having driven Mom to her appointments. Very medical-y. Very nice, though.

We parked at Dana Farber, where she had a pass, and walked over to the Children's Hospital. I was seventeen and a half years old and waiting in a starfish and dinosaur–themed lobby. There were tiny tables with stacks of coloring books. Mom and I squeezed into the little kid's chairs and started coloring.

"What do you mean they don't have red!" She was trying to color in a rainbow (a lot of the crayons were missing).

I heard my name get called and my palms began to sweat. I had counted down to this day. What if something went wrong? Something was always going wrong.

But I passed the initial tests; my blood pressure was fine, my heart rate was normal, and my weight was healthy. Dr. Spack came out to get me. I asked if Mom could come, too, and he gestured her to follow.

He was older than my parents but younger than my grandpa, I estimated. He made a lot of jokes. He was bald, with a short white beard and a kind face. As we walked down the hallways, the colorful walls dotted with children's cartoon images, I felt relaxed. My hands uncurled from each other and I had a spring in my step as we entered the exam room. My mind felt calm, my heart at the right pace, and I smiled as I looked at him pulling up my chart. The letters hadn't changed; they read: Katherine Kergil and F.

But there I was, Skye Kergil and FTM in reality, just not on paper.

Mom and I sat on chairs as he asked us questions about my history, my feelings, why I was there. He began explaining the effects of testosterone, slowly so Mom and I could take it all in. I had looked it up lots ahead of time; there were some websites dedicated to explaining the benefits and risks of the physical FTM transition.

We both had a lot of questions for Dr. Spack. Mainly, I wanted to know about how the testosterone would be administered; everything I read online indicated it would be through a several inch–long needle into muscle in the thigh. Intramuscular. The word was long, exciting, and terrifying. I wasn't fond of needles.

The needle Dr. Spack showed me was smaller than I had imagined.

"Injecting it subcutaneously, or below the skin and into fat, shows the same absorption rate as intramuscular without the risk," he explained. "Instead of being two inches long, the needle is about one inch and the injection site can vary. You can do it into your side buttock, which is where you will start out, but you can also do it in any area that you can grab a fistful of fat. I would recommend the buttocks and thighs, simply because they are furthest from organs. The half-life is about ten to twelve days, so for the first month I would have you doing your shot every other week. After that first month, we'll do another blood test and you'll be injecting once a week."

My mouth dropped open. He was talking as if this were happening. It really was happening.

"Since you're under eighteen, you need both parents' permission. You know this, yes?"

I nodded as I gestured to my mom. Again, nervous, but feeling like so far, we had had so much good luck. I gathered my thoughts but then Mom jumped in.

"I am comfortable with him beginning his physical transition. He has a supportive friend group and school, and this might make him feel more comfortable before he goes off to college."

"And his father?" He raised an eyebrow.

Mom turned to me. I looked down at the ground briefly and then back up at the doctor.

"He is okay with it, he knows I'm transgender," I said.

"But starting hormones as an minor requires express permission from both parents." He was firm.

"We could call my dad?" I was about half confident that my dad would say it was okay.

When we got him on the phone, Dad confirmed that he understood my wishes and was willing to accept it since my mom was willing to accept it. I was so thankful—at least he had deferred to Mom's good judgment. He said he hoped it would help, although he worried I would regret it. I understood.

"Okay," Dr. Spack declared, "I am going to start you on 50mg every other week, like I mentioned, and then I'll have you get some blood work done before March.

"Will I be able to learn how to inject it here today?" I asked.

"Sure, if you have the prescription filled, I can show you what to do. Let me fill it out now and also another one for the syringes and needles. You'll be using the same needle to draw the testosterone out of the vial and to inject."

"We'll try to fill this downstairs and be right back!" I practically ran out the door.

As we got in the elevator, I marveled, "I can't believe it! Thanks so much, Mom!"

When we dropped the prescription off at the pharmacy, the pharmacist instructed us to wait while she made sure they had it. The copayment through my insurance was going to be $20 but without it, it was $87. Insurance takes some time to process.

Mom and I waited around some art installations meant for kids. Big contraptions of balls falling through railings and assorted obstacles. A combination of science and simplicity. Turns out, they had the vial in stock and got the syringes ready. Thanks to some lucky stars, after about an hour, we were back upstairs waiting for Dr. Spack. A nurse led us down to his room, where he was busy typing away on the computer.

"So we're ready! Great! Okay, first things first, let's see what size vial they gave you. Sometimes they'll try to give you some small 2ml vial. Make sure you refuse it and get the 10ml I've prescribed. The smaller ones are flimsy and you can never get all the fluid out! So, what you need to do first is place this under your armpit for a few minutes, until it's warmed to your body temperature. This will make it easier for the injection to absorb."

I thought I was listening but I think I was imagining rainbows, vials of testosterone, syringes, me with a beard, a deep voice . . . all floating around in my head. Daydreaming, as usual.

I held the vial in my armpit and unwrapped one of the syringes. As I drew the thick, yellowish clear substance from the vial, Dr. Spack showed me how to get the bubbles out, as one wouldn't want to inject a bubble. What was left was such a small amount of T, in my uneducated opinion, but so cool that it must be so powerful!

He showed me how to grab my thigh fat to inject at an angle. As I counted down "3 . . . 2 . . . 1 . . ." I hesitated as I tried to stab myself real fast. I pulled the needle back out by accident.

"No, no you need to leave it in!" He flailed his arms around.

"Okay! Okay!" I tried a second time, but again, I pulled the needle back out without pressing the plunger to inject the fluid.

"Look, you gotta leave it in!" he said. "Every time you puncture the skin it's wearing the needle down, so you could accidentally hurt yourself."

"Of course, of course! Sorry, I'm trying to leave it in, I've never done this before, ahhh!"

Mom knew exactly what to say. "Skye, if you don't do it now, we're going to have to come back here to have them inject it for you, and you won't be starting hormones today or anytime soon."

"OKAY! WE ARE DOING THIS!" I exclaimed and stabbed the syringe in. Holding it into my side butt fat, I pushed the plunger, injecting testosterone into my body.

Within milliseconds, placebo effect took hold. I felt I had more energy instantly. I felt confident and happy. I was practically bouncing up and down. I felt changed, excited, and so very, very content.

Dr. Spack outlined my future appointments and blood tests to keep track of testosterone's effects on my body. He wanted me to call if any unusual side effects occurred, but he had given me a good outline of what to expect. Plus, I'd be going back in a month for bloodwork, so not too much could go wrong.

The general gist of changes to come would be similar to what cis-men went through at puberty, without the massive vertical growth spurt. I was looking forward to my period stopping, my voice dropping, my skin becoming rougher in texture, facial and body hair sprouting, an increase in muscle, body fat shifting around, an increase in sex drive and my hairline becoming a bit more "masculinized" (less hair, more widow's peak).

I was well aware that I could not pick or choose changes and that the effects T would have on me would be largely dependent on genetics and other factors. I wouldn't magically get muscle—I knew I would have to continue working out to get toned and bulk up. Body fat and bone structure would take a while to shift, if at all, and it likely would be very slight. I knew I would eventually go bald—that was in my genetics. I might have mood swings. I might never get facial hair. I might get bad acne. I might have increased cholesterol. I might gain fifteen to thirty pounds in the first year, and it wouldn't magically be a six pack. I had to accept everything, the good and the bad, when I injected testosterone.

Some changes are permanent, like voice dropping and genitalia changing (the clitoris can grow up to a few inches or more, much like how it grows into a penis in the womb once testosterone levels increase). Facial hair growing in wouldn't go away if I stopped testosterone, so should I decide the effects were not helpful to me or, worst case, wrong for me, I would have irreversible "damage" and have to shave my face daily to "pass as a woman." I didn't mention this to Mom, though. She thought it was all fairly reversible for a few months.

Going to the gym prior to and while beginning testosterone helped me immensely. There is a lot that testosterone won't change. Learning to exercise as a form of self-care was valuable. And I had to learn to love my pointy nose, my "feminine" lips, and my long eyelashes. I'd be carrying them with me for life.

The changes T could bring to me would hopefully allow me to better accept that which I could not change.

Day One–January 21

ON THE DRIVE HOME AFTER my first shot of testosterone, Mom let me know that I could stay home from school for the rest of the day since I had taken it off. But we were home by eleven in the morning and I was energized. I packed my bag to head to school.

She looked at me with wide eyes, like "What kid wants to go back to school when they could have the day off?" but agreed that that was fine. It was my choice.

When I got home, I ran up to my bedroom to store the T vial and syringes in a safe spot, away from the cats and Toby. I kissed Tiger and told him that I'd still be the same person but to get ready for some big changes. "I'll always be your parent, you know that."

I flipped open my MacBook and hit the record button on the built-in app that came with my computer. The webcam wasn't the best quality, but this was the only device besides my digital camera that I could record on. Plus, I didn't care about seeing my face nearly as much as I cared about my voice. I wanted to make sure I knew what my voice sounded like pre-testosterone so that I could compare.

I looked into the camera and spoke; I hadn't planned anything.

Hi, ok, so this is my first video where I'm actually talking . . . um yeah. So it's January twenty-first, it's like, noon, and this morning I went to the endocrinologist in Boston, Dr. Spack. He was late and Mom was all frustrated, but he wrote my prescription for testosterone in like two hours, and so my mom was all like, "Woah, I didn't know this was happening so fast!"

And I was like, "Woah, I didn't know this was happening so fast!"

But, um, so she was all like, "Yeah so I want to see how he does the shot because I don't want you doing it by yourself."

151

And I was like, "Okay, whatever, I don't care so long as I get to shoot myself up with man today!"

I talked through the process for another minute, then slammed my laptop shut and ran downstairs to head off to school. I couldn't wait to tell all my friends about my morning. I galloped up and down the hallway at school, waiting for the class period to end.

I couldn't believe how free I felt and when I bumped into Amy right as the bell between periods rang, I couldn't wait to share my joy with her!

"Wait, didn't you have the doctor today?" Amy asked. She knew how anxious I had been. "Did it not happen? What's going on?"

"It did! I started!" I couldn't contain myself. "I did my first shot today at the doctor's office!"

My closest friends gathered around. I was ecstatic and they seemed stoked too.

"Do you feel any different?" Winnie was genuinely curious.

"I think so! My neck feels itchy." I kept giggling.

My voice gets higher when I'm more energetic, but I didn't care. I knew that was changing. That was the one thing that would definitely change. I didn't know how low it could go, but I couldn't wait to find out.

YouTube and Community

IN THE WEEKS AFTER MY day one, I continued to record daily clips of my voice on my laptop. By recording myself at multiple times a day, I figured I could capture the exact moment when it dropped. While I was awaiting the big drop, I rambled on in my videos, noting what else was going on.

The first change I noticed was the hot flashes. I started to get hot at night, and then all the time. I had heard it could take months before my period stopped, but it stopped immediately. As the weeks went by, changes slowly became a part of my day-to-day life. I had a sore throat for three months before my voice had a huge crack and dropped. I couldn't sing well for several years, though, as it was adjusting. My thigh fat began to shift toward my belly; so did my arm fat, hip fat, and, basically all of my fat. Fat I didn't know existed on my body slowly migrated to my belly and to my belly alone. Spack had warned of that—men are "apple" shaped and women are "pear" shaped and that being a "pear" is actually healthier than being an "apple" due to issues involving our vital organs being surrounded by fat.

I started getting headaches more often. I had less fluctuation in moods after missing several periods. I had increased energy within a few weeks, and sometimes would feel a lack of energy the day before my shot. My libido rose up to the highest it had ever been, uncomfortably high at times due to my lack of overall sexual drive and the dysphoria I had about what was between my legs.

I grew into thicker skin (seriously!). Muscles began to come toward the surface more easily. I was hungry all the time. I started eating nearly twice as much and didn't gain any weight. My friends and family began commenting on my voice and other changes they noticed over time, like how I had started to smell like a gross teenage boy and how much acne I was getting.

I'd listen to my "day one" voice and compare to how I sounded as my voice changed. Documenting my voice was so important to me; I was incredibly thankful I recorded it before T kicked in. However, around a month into recording clips, I hit the record button and got an error message:

There is not enough space available to record video.

I couldn't afford an external hard drive and didn't have any USB sticks. Online storage was still in its infancy, every site charging a fee to store those precious gigabytes. Except YouTube.

I had just heard of YouTube in the past year—our teachers would sometimes have us upload class videos there. It was so new that they had to hand out a page-long document explaining how to create an account, how to upload a video, and how to bring the link into school.

One time, when following those instructions, I accidentally deleted a class project video from my computer. Panicking, I went onto YouTube and found out I could download it back onto my computer after having uploaded it. Amazing!

So when my MacBook ran out of space, I thought to put my videos on YouTube. Not wanting them linked to the account I used for school projects, I needed to come up with another username.

Skylar made sense. But it was taken. Skylark? Taken. Skylarkergil? Too identifiable as me. Skylarkybirdybird? Available, but I'd never remember how many birdy birds I had on it. Skylarkyellow? Looked like Skylarky—bleh! *Birds. Yellow. What else do I love?*

My favorite number is eleven, so Skylarkeleven? Available. I clicked "go," entered some more info, and had my day one video uploading in a matter of moments.

I gave it a quick title, published it without any tags or much info, and left it up online. I deleted it from my computer, making space to record my next clip. I repeated this process about every week.

As I began plopping all of my journal-like entries online, people began watching them. I had no idea how they had found me, but they were all seemingly supportive. A couple of comments here and there. Some words of encouragement.

I felt a little paranoid about my peers stumbling upon them. They were intimate and I discussed things I didn't even want my parents to know. I hadn't told any of my friends or family about my videos online out of fear they would seek them out.

But the comments kept me going. People were curious or in need of advice and information. I made an email account and a Tumblr to go with the YouTube account and began chatting with so many young folks across the world. I started watching a few other YouTubers' videos. Tyler Oakley was one of the first people I watched regularly online once I started uploading; he was hilarious and his viewers were so sweet. Through some of the comments on his channel and through the search bar, I found other trans people—mainly trans women. It was eye opening to learn about the different struggles they faced. There were a few trans guys, but they had all slowed or stopped vlogging[9] after top surgery. It seemed like they gotten to a point where they felt their transition was complete and then moved on with life. I watched as many trans-related videos as I could find. It helped me feel less alone to hear more stories, even if a lot of the people sharing them were struggling or sad at the moment.

I vlogged happy moments, I vlogged sad moments, I was open about some things and tight-lipped about others. I began speaking into my camera as if there might be someone listening—talking about physical changes that I might not have talked about if I had been keeping it for myself—and it was helpful and challenging.

YouTube gave me a community when I needed one. It was accessible at my fingertips; many stories being shared simultaneously. We were living, breathing transgender human beings.

---

9 Online video blogging, often hosted on YouTube.

As Our Lives Change, Come Whatever

B Y THE END OF HIGH school, everyone around me referred to me using male pronouns and my correct name. I had switched Skye to Skylar on Facebook, noting that folks could still call me Sky. No one seemed to notice or mind, as it seemed like a natural progression toward my legal name change. I also added that my middle name would be Tucker, to which a lot of folks raised an eyebrow, as there was already Tucker in our school.

When I had come out as Skye, I thought of it as a transitional name. Something for folks to adjust to. Tucker was the name I would have chosen for myself the second time around. But since it had been such a challenge to get people to call me Skye consistently, I figured it'd be easier to keep it.

As I neared graduating, I wondered if I should mention that I'd sent in a petition for a name change to the Massachusetts State Court, but hadn't heard back yet. Rebecca informed me about the principal's decision regarding my diploma.

"You just need to go into the office and write down the correct spelling for your name or nickname, whatever you choose!"

"Seriously? It's that easy? I don't even have the date for my legal name change yet!" I was ecstatic.

"Of course!" she replied, gesturing toward the door, suggesting I might as well go get it done right then.

I walked into the principal's office to find a yellow pad of notepaper on a small table. It read "Diploma Name Correction" and had about five names already on there to be fixed. I wrote mine down as Katherine Elizabeth Kergil corrected to Skylar Tucker Kergil. It felt simple, almost too simple. I glanced at the rest of the sheet. Some were simply nicknames, but a few were clear misspellings or for people who went by their middle names. Everything was working out and I simply couldn't believe it.

Except one thing. The yearbook had my name as Katherine. I had been explicitly promised that it would be Skylar and not to worry for a single moment. When Amy flipped open to my page, I thought she was going to march right up to the yearbook office.

"What? They promised! They swore you'd be Skylar in this and that was like six months ago. What the heck?" She was livid.

"Oh no, what do I do?" I said, feeling miserable. Amy hugged me. My whole high school experience would be inextricably tied to this name because of one small, careless mistake.

I felt like I might cry. *Wow*, I thought, *this is a slap in the face.*

While I knew I couldn't totally shed Katherine from me, it was hard to be constantly surrounded by the name. My brother used it against me, as a way of putting me down. Others would slip up. I felt so far removed from Katherine. I was Skylar, damn it.

Seeing my senior picture with that name underneath it, it simply didn't correlate. I took a deep breath and decided. I'd accept that that was who I had been once upon a time, but I was no longer Katherine and I would never show the yearbook to anyone.

On graduation day, dressed in blue and gold, I lined up in a field with my best friends around me. I held my breath. As my name was about to be called, I panicked, certain there was no way this would go right. Then they called out Skylar Tucker Kergil. I accepted my diploma, shaking hands with the principal, who smiled back at me.

I graduated, at once afraid to leave high school and ready for the next chapter of my life. Surrounded by the people I had known longest, I looked forward to starting fresh while keeping my good friends close. I had this safety net at home—being cast out to Skidmore felt doable because of that.

Being stealth was still the plan. I'd talk about myself as a little boy, change sports (softball became baseball), or possibly omit some things I would otherwise share. All of this to keep things simple and not have to go through the coming out process I'd been going through for years. I'd still be online, of course, so I'd still have my community there. School would be . . . separate.

All these ideas filled my mind. The future was so close . . . but something was holding me back. The night I graduated from high school, as I drove to Veronika's house, I thought about us. She would be going to school in Boston and I'd be going four hours away. I picked her up and as we headed to a friend's chorus concert, the conversation drooped.

"Do you believe in long distance relationships?" I asked.

"No," she said quietly.

"Neither do I . . ."

I held her hand—she wasn't shaking. She was calm. I was calm.

Two months later, we decided to stay together for college.

At the time, I turned eighteen and had recently gotten my first legitimate tattoo. It was in script across my forearms, with Earth in the middle of the first O.

It was a quote from Michelangelo, something he supposedly scrawled on the edge of one of his last pieces: *Ancora Imparo.*

"I am still learning."

Stealth

THE DAY BEFORE I LEFT for Skidmore, I sat on my bed, carefully peeling off the notes, stickers, and creations that I had gathered on my walls over the years. A little drawing of a puffer fish that my friend Raven made in tenth grade. A series of three elephants Veronika had given me. A faded photograph I had printed out from one of Amy's many online albums. The hospital band from my Altoids tin incident. A Charizard Pokémon card (not my holographic one though, I'd never stick that to my wall with clear tape!)

Gathering these memories in my arms, putting them into boxes, stacking the boxes, then deciding which I would be bringing—I was ready to curate a carefully selected part of my history to come with me to Skidmore. Packing my clothes was simple; I had a million shirts, three hoodies, two flannels, two binders, and the exact same cut of pants in a few different colors. All things I felt radically comfortable and myself in. That was most important.

The million shirts made sense; every one fit differently. Some clung to my binder in weird ways. Others were too thin—I could see my binder's lines through them and then I'd have to wear an undershirt to cover it up. Some of them were too big—I had heard about the freshman fifteen and wanted to be prepared.

Mom and I drove the three and a half hours out. While I was excited, I had a pit in my stomach I knew was caused by my own transitional timeline. There was one issue I needed to tend to right away: my legal name.

The court date for my name change was a week after college classes started. It was not my plan for that to be the case. I had wanted to get it changed before I even graduated from high school, but alas. The

Massachusetts court office had been a pain when we were filing for it. We sent it out in January and got it back two months later with a note: "This must be filled out in black ink, not blue ink." Sent that back in black ink, got it back two months later in May: "The middle name does not match birth certificate. Please correct and resend."

When Mom got that letter, we both felt it was ridiculous. On my birth certificate, the initial "E" was listed, rather than my full middle name, Elizabeth, which we had written on the petition. So we sent it back, finally complete in May, and they gave us a court date four months out. Conveniently right after I started at college. *Are you kidding me?*

Even if I had not intended on living stealth in college, it would have still been emotionally difficult for me to deal with having an email address and ID card that said my name was Katherine. I preferred no one to know my birth name, even if they knew I was trans; so many folks had called me Katherine instead of Sky, using it as a tool to hurt me.

While I had reached out to the registrar's office, I hadn't gotten the answer I wanted. They stated there was not much they could do until I had my legal documents in check.

I felt overwhelmed thinking my birth name was about to come back up on a bunch of papers, and I wanted Mom there as I dealt with it.

As we checked in on campus, I muttered, "Oh, this might be under Katherine Kergil."

I got a few puzzled looks, but nothing too extreme. The folks dealing with the paperwork and ushering us onto the next stop were friendly. My hair curling over my ears and my Social Distortion shirt on, they snapped a photo of me. Instantly my ID card was printed. I ended up using a push pin in my dorm room that night to scratch "Katherine" off of it so that it just read "Kergil." Much better.

Mom helped me unload my belongings into the dorm room that I shared with my roommate, Eva. She had already moved in earlier than other students for a special program she was in. Her side of the room was white, clean, adorable, and organized—*pretty impressive for an artist*, I thought. I wanted to have a nice clean space too; however, within weeks, my clothes piled up on the floor and I had begun collecting dried tea bags for a future art project that never materialized, leaving them scattered on our giant windowsill for months. Yep.

Eva and I hit it off right away. I felt happy with the choice we had made to room together. She chatted with my mom and things felt super natural. I checked out the gender neutral bathrooms and they were perfect. Two private shower stalls, two private toilet stalls, four sinks. When I met the Resident Assistant, Natalie, she also told me about the single stall handicap bathroom on the floor, which had a shower in it as well.

"Obviously, most people don't need or want to use it up here on the third floor, but if you ever wanted to, it's all yours." She invited me to take a look at it.

Natalie was exceptionally astute. While I knew the college hadn't sent out some email saying, "transgender student, third floor, W hall," they had likely let the RA know about the gender neutral situation. Residence Life had informed me that I was the first student to select gender neutral housing. They had planned to house me in a single, right around the corner of the bathrooms, which I could still use. I argued that I wanted to have a roommate, to have a *real* college experience, whatever that was. Even though having a single (especially being long distance with Veronika) would have been sweet, I wanted the standard double that I'd seen in movies, that all my friends would be in.

Res Life had told me that no one else had selected gender neutral housing. If I wanted to live in a double, they explained, I'd have to find someone who was comfortable with living with me. I felt so isolated and alone. However, that's how I had found Eva. She was active online during the summer, reaching out on social media to future classmates ahead of time. She identified as part of the queer community and had sent flurries of friendly messages to other incoming students. I loved her gusto.

I came out to Eva over Facebook Messenger. She seemed comfortable with that, not overly curious, and she respected that I wanted to be as discreet about my past as possible.

"That's cool!" she responded, "I'd love to room with you! Let's do it!"

That's how we ended up together. Skidmore had not been very clear about the rule; they made it seem like my only option was to be housed with someone with the same sex on their birth certificate as mine. Thankfully, I felt more comfortable rooming with a female, even though we were a boy and a girl sharing a room. Definitely strange from the outside if one were uninformed about the situation.

As we began both of our pre-orientation programs, I was not surprised at the raised eyebrows regarding our living situation.

"Wait, so you're living with a girl? What? How did that happen?" Brianna, a girl with short black hair that I was chatting with, asked.

"Haha, there's this thing called gender neutral housing . . ." I outlined how it worked.

"Ooooh, got it," she said.

Our conversation was centered around the fact that we had grown up in neighboring towns. At one point, the topic of sports we had played came up.

"I played volleyball!" she said. She seemed passionate about it.

"Awesome! I did too, actually!"

"Huh?" She tilted her head as she looked at me. "But isn't it a women's team? Or did you guys have a separate men's team?"

My face turned pink. I had almost outed myself.

Thankfully, I didn't have to lie when I answered, "Our team was coed, and there were like three guys who wanted to play so they couldn't discriminate!"

Then she seemed to have a realization when she shouted, "Oh my goodness! I remember you now! So funny, we played one another in high school, wow!"

My heart started pounding out of anxiety and confusion.

It's the first day and I'm already going to have to come out to someone about my past? I tried to think of what to say.

"What's so funny is I remember a few girls on our team saying that it was unfair you were on it, but hey, it was coed and our school didn't have any boys who were interested." She laughed. "We beat you, anyway."

I smiled, knowing full well that she was confusing me with the boy who had been on the varsity team. I'd rather have her mistaken that I was *that* guy than to make the connection with my current self and my pre-transition self.

That was when I began to feel the divide. The before and the after. I used to be a masculine, androgynous girl on the volleyball team, two months before realizing I was transgender. Now, I was Skylar, a boy who had always been a boy.

I had new words to learn.

The next week, classes started. I emailed my advisor, letting her know I went by Skylar instead of Katherine. I even indicated my court date for my legal name change.

She wrote back, stating that it was not an issue at all. She even let me know that I need not email my other professors as my preferred name would show up on the roster. I felt reassured that my concerns had been addressed and everything would run smoothly.

My first class was Sociology 101. I was wearing my favorite pair of brown jeans that had an owl patch on the back pocket. I sat in the second row, surrounded by slouching, sleepy first years. I turned to a girl next to me; she had dark brown skin and her hair tied up in what looked like a snake coiling around the top of her head. I'd never seen a hairstyle like hers and it looked awesome. I awkwardly put some words together to let her know I thought so.

"Thanks so much! My mom taught me this and I hated it all through high school but now that I'm here I wanted to give it another try. That means a lot to me." She smiled. "What's your name? I'm Sheena."

"Sky." I reached out to shake her hand, although that seemed oddly formal considering I usually hugged new friends.

"That's a cool name," she said and went back to whatever she was doing.

When the professor sat, casually, on the table in the front of the room, I felt a surge of excitement for college.

As he began calling out names, I heard "Katherine Kergil."

I froze in my seat. I had to choose between being potentially marked absent, and thus kicked out of the class, or potentially outing myself.

Impulsively, my hand shot up, and I spoke in a very small, timid voice, "Yes, here, well . . . it's Sky."

Maybe no one heard that and no one will know, I prayed.

I felt some eyes on me. I don't know how many people were paying attention. My face was a deep shade of red; I felt ashamed, embarrassed, outed. I felt tricked. I felt like my advisor had been clueless. I felt hurt.

At the end of class, the professor inquired, "How many of you are in long distance relationships?"

I and a few other students raised our hands.

He smirked. "We'll check in again at the end of the year. Statistically speaking, out of sight, out of mind prove true for long distance couples. Good luck."

As if being deadnamed[10] was not enough in one forty-minute period, I was also told that my long-distance relationship, the *one* thing I felt comforted by at the moment, would be coming to an end.

I felt so uncomfortable as I walked back to my dorm and called Veronika once I was away from other students.

"I want to leave college. I can't do this," I whined.

"It'll be okay, I'll be there next week to pick you up for the court date. Give it some time," she reassured me.

That evening, I sent out quick emails to my other professors. All of them respected my name and I wasn't outed in any more classes. I was also able to talk to the IT department and get my email address switched. Unlike the registrar, they didn't need proof of my name change to do that for me. I was incredibly thankful.

The same day I got my email switched, this one guy in my pre-orientation came up to me. Mark was super tall and masculine. He seemed like the guy who would either run student council or be champion of beer pong. He wasn't intimidating but he reminded me how small I was.

"Why is your name listed as Katherine? Is that you?" he demanded.

I took a deep breath as I looked at what he was pointing at. On the roster, my name and email were listed. Not knowing what to say, I came up with the silliest lie:

"Oh, yeah! My parents accidentally signed me up as my twin sister, haha. Just a clerical error, they've fixed it now," I tried to speak as confidently as possible while totally going off the cuff.

"Huh, that's so silly! Well, glad you got it fixed." He chuckled, although he did look confused.

I shrugged and moved along. My head was spinning, I was nauseated, my head ached, and it had barely been a week. How could I do this?

The next few days were full. My senior mentor, Alex, was in this charity a capella group. Alex really, *really* wanted to make sure people were going to audition for it, so I and a few others went.

Before getting into the room, we had to fill out this form. My newest friend Diana was bouncing around, excited and nervous at the same time. Then, this girl with curly blonde hair and gigantic glasses came

---

10 Deadname is one phrase some use to describe their name given at birth.

up to me and asked to borrow a pen. She giggled as she approached me and struck up conversation.

Her name was Anna. I felt drawn to her energy; soon, we were friends. It was amazing how quickly people connected during that first week. A lot of folks stuck in the same groups, it seemed. Anna and I didn't end up in the same circle, but our paths crossed again at auditions for this drumming club. Neither of us had gotten into the a capella group (I hadn't been able to hold a note) and the Taiko drumming club was all-inclusive.

As I let the new experiences pile up, time flew by. I was glad. I still felt uncomfortable on campus. Raw, exposed. I felt like I was hiding when I wanted to be expanding . . . and it was eating me up inside.

Sometimes they say, "Time flies when you're having fun."

I say, "Time flies when you're about to become."

Skylar Tucker Kergil:
Legalized

WHEN MOM AND VERONIKA ARRIVED to bring me back to Mass, I was relieved. I would finally be able to lay Katherine to rest. When it came to the court proceedings, I wasn't sure what to expect; I knew I wanted to make a good impression, if any at all.

I wore the only nice, collared shirt I had. It was black with a few gray stripes. Skidmore had suggested packing one fancy outfit, but I didn't have one aside from full-on tuxedo world. This shirt and a pair of unripped jeans were good enough for me.

Sitting in a courtroom full of other folks, I was reeling. This was finally happening. I counted the freckles on the back of my hand, anxiously waiting.

The judge called me up. "What is the reason for the name change?"

I didn't know she would ask me for a reason, but I quickly responded, "Skylar fits me better."

She looked up at me from the judge's stand, her face apathetic, "Okay. Granted. Next."

On September 14, 2009, I legally became Skylar Tucker Kergil.

Back at school, I swiftly changed my registration and ID cards to eliminate any confusion. Finally, everything matched. I had waited to switch the gender on my license, as I didn't want to pay for a new license twice. With the letter of suggestion from my therapist (which was all

Massachusetts required) as well as my legal name change, I got it taken care of over Thanksgiving break.

One afternoon, Mark came up to me after our seminar.

No joke, he vocalized one of my biggest fears, a simple question: "Are you transgender?"

I froze but then had a knee-jerk response.

"Uh. No? Why do you ask?"

Then he inquired if Eva was, and I also said no. I gathered he was trying to make sense of the rooming situation. It had caught me so far off guard.

Thankfully, that was the only time that ever happened. It felt so weird—denying who I was. Completely lying, I suppose.

I felt guilty.

I had flat-out denied I was transgender.

I began thinking critically about my plans for being stealth. What if people found out and then Mark knew I lied?

I wondered if Eva had heard the same questions, too, then. As the semester went on, she ended up moving out before winter break. She had had a difficult transition to college and, from what I gathered, needed a break to be with her family. I was lucky to be able to move my cisgender male friend Paul into my dorm with me. He was one of the few folks I had told I was trans and he had been super accepting. I was stoked to have a male roommate. It felt more normal, though I did miss Eva.

I continued recording my YouTube videos in my dorm. A lot of covers of songs and updates on changes—my acne was the biggest addition. I had hoped for a beard, but hey. My voice was only slightly dropping and was no longer as exciting or noticeable as it had been at the beginning. I was having a great time mentoring youth as well as documenting my own progression. I felt safe online as skylarkeleven.

I got a comment that fall that made me question whether or not I wanted to continue making videos. It all seemed anonymous; then, this comment had shown me that my online presence and reality were, in fact, mixing.

"It is so nice seeing you walk around on campus, even though you don't know who I am, I feel better knowing you are here," someone wrote. I couldn't tell who it was from the info provided.

It was so sweet. It warmed my heart. At the same time, I felt there was a giant hole in my stealth bubble. Someone knew. What if they had overheard me saying to Mark that I was not transgender? Would I appear ashamed? Would they be disappointed? Am I disappointed at myself for choosing to be stealth?

Winter break swiftly approached. I tried my best in classes, but my mind was elsewhere. I was focused on my decision to be stealth.

Quickly, the semester ended. Sitting in the dining hall at the end of the semester, Diana and Anna were having a conversation about their break plans.

"I'm probably going skiing," Diana said. She gushed about a winter lodge her family had.

"Oh that's nice! I've never done it." Anna smiled, looking over at the fire.

"What are you up to, Sky?" Diana asked. "Do you ski?"

"Haha, well, the last time I snowboarded, I almost shattered my shin, so"—I laughed—"I think this winter break I'll lay low."

All I could think about was top surgery and the relief I expected from it. Right before heading off to college, Mom had asked if I wanted to schedule it. I had my pre-op appointment in July with Dr. Melissa Johnson in Springfield, Massachusetts before heading off to Skidmore and by the time I had gotten to Skidmore, they had a date available during my winter break.

I remember being obsessed with it, but day to day, I was so busy it snuck up quicker than I would have imagined.

Top Surgery

O N DECEMBER 29, 2009, I woke up ready to be cut open.

Springfield was ninety minutes away from Acton. They had scheduled me as the first surgery of the day and I was so thankful for this. It meant there was no chance of being delayed, since no one would be before me! Plus, it meant I'd get to wake up and have a large chunk of the day left with my loved ones in my hospital room.

The nurse had me get into this hospital gown, indicating I should be fully nude underneath. Mom and Veronika left the room and as I peeled my binder off of my skin, I realized it would be the last time I had to do that. I had pulled it on that morning for the last time.

I felt pure joy. Not scared, not anxious. Entirely, completely joyous.

I looked down at my chest underneath the gown. It looked bad. From the years of binding, I had flattened my chest down; what remained of my breasts sagged downward. My nipples seemed too big to me. And, after almost a year on T, I had some chest hair covering them and in between them.

I felt entirely detached from my chest. It had been a nuisance, and *only* a nuisance, for a long time. While it had been my main source of dysphoria outside of my voice, I had gotten used to maneuvering the world with my tricks and routines to hide it. It no longer brought me intense dysphoria, but that was because I literally never, ever looked at it. Ever. Until that moment; I said goodbye. With everyone back in the room, we goofed around, filmed some, and waited for about a half hour before the nurse told me I was ready to go.

Although I had had my wisdom teeth removed, I still wasn't expecting how anesthesia felt. As I was having a conversation with a nurse, the world disappeared and slipped away from me.

I woke up feeling like a few seconds had passed, but I was surrounded by tons of noise and pressure and people moving around me in commotion. I looked down at my body, but I didn't have my glasses on, so everything was a big blur. I was covered up with bandages and the noise and commotion came from a few surgeon assistants who were piling bags of ice on top of my ribs.

"I dreamt I was a snowman," I whispered, my throat sore.

"Makes sense! You were covered in ice!" Veronika laughed, kissing my forehead and taking pictures. I had wanted her to—I couldn't wait to show my followers on YouTube and Tumblr what this whole process was like.

"Surgery already happened?" I wondered aloud.

"Yep! It was about three hours, actually," Mom said, smiling at me and squeezing my hand.

"Weird. That's so weird . . ." I drifted back into a painkiller-induced sleep.

The rest of the afternoon, nurses came in and out of my hospital room and I drifted in and out. Mom and Veronika entertained themselves and me whenever I was awake. I had been given this thing to breathe into to make sure I was using my lungs fully. It was a fun challenge, the little toy.

Dr. Johnson came in at one point, as well, which was exciting as I hadn't seen her since the summer.

"You did great, Skylar! How are you feeling?" She grinned at me.

She went on to detail some of the procedure and the post-op care. I was to come back in a week to get the drains removed. They were these tubes inserted near my armpits which ran under the skin along the incisions and drained excess blood and other fluids. The tubes connected to these plastic bulbs I called "blood grenades," which had to be emptied multiple times a day. The doctor showed my mom and me how to push the blood clots through them and explained why that was necessary. It was pretty nasty and painful, but I was still too stoked to care.

"You know, when I had you in there, I was thinking we needed to shave down some of your chest bone! You're a super bony guy," she joked. "And there was also this mole on your hip, looked like it was pretty big—I almost nipped that in the bud while we had you under, but we left it."

My eyes widened, probably looking disbelieving at the idea of my bones being too bony and my mole being too moley!

"That's my birthmark!" I laughed along with her.

She made me feel comfortable, as did the rest of the nurse staff. As night was coming close, no one had taken the second bed in my hospital room. The nurse kindly let Veronika sleep there and Mom headed off to the hotel. Hospitals are weird overnight; every sound had me imagining a spectacle, like I'd seen in *House*, outside of my room.

The following morning, I remember seeing my chest most clearly. A nurse needed to clean it off and I wasn't as out of it as I had been the previous day. Looking down, I saw these huge yellow puffs keeping my nipples extended out from my chest. They were the gauze to keep them from falling off. I had two humongous incisions under them, separated by an inch of intact body in the middle.

It was weird, it wasn't beautiful.

Yet I felt beautiful.

I felt whole, even while I was oozing out of various parts of my chest. I felt complete, even though I wouldn't be able to lift much of anything for a month nor raise my arms much while I was healing. I had to work clots out through the drain tubes and then empty my blood grenades into the sink. Mom hated it.

It was cold and snowy. I didn't stay up until midnight for New Year's Eve. I wrapped a giant brown flannel around me and hung out around the house, smelling like a post-op trans guy who hadn't showered in a week. I'd say that summed it up. Veronika helped take care of me while we played board games with my mom. At night, Veronika would sleep on the floor next to my bed since I'd have to be lying propped up on my back. We held hands even from afar. Time flew by quite quickly.

Painkillers did wonders, although it was a trippy experience. I also didn't pay any attention to the recommendation of taking a laxative every day. I always pooped so much, I didn't think it would be an issue. Well, after four days of not pooping, I was crying in the bathroom as I pretty much gave birth to a football-sized turd and forced my mom to rush out to CVS to get me a laxative.

Listen, anyone who is recommended to take a laxative: take the laxative. Just take it. Don't delay. Don't ask questions. Now you know.

When I arrived back at Dr. Johnson's office to have the drains removed, I was anxious. The drains had been painful; it was exhausting having to empty them and deal with blood (something I don't do too well with). Having the tubes pulled out from under my skin was the weirdest feeling I had ever experienced. It was cool, to watch something move underneath me and then appear outside of me, but it was also rather bizarre.

In the end, the day I had top surgery felt like the best day of my life. As I healed over the next few weeks, sans blood grenades, I could appreciate my healing body. I eased off the painkillers and was able to shower. Soon after, I felt ready to apply some scar healing treatment to them. They were dark at first; deep cuts into my skin that looked jagged. I wanted them to go away immediately, but I knew it would take some time.

Documenting my body healing on my YouTube channel was amazing. I received so much advice and support from the community about my process. I got all kinds of recommendations: lightly massage the skin around my incisions once they healed, avoid working out for several months if possible, use bandages to keep my nipples moisturized, and some people swore by drinking large amounts of matcha tea to promote quicker healing.

Being able to share my experience felt important. Especially because I could only share it with my home friends and some family—exporting my joy to the Internet was a helpful release once I got back to school, where my friends had no idea about what I had been through.

During my post-op recovery, someone commented on one of my videos, offering silicone strips to even out my scars. We talked more and more, over email, about all sorts of trans things. Usually, when folks contacted me, they would have questions and I would become a mentor to them. He was a mentor to me in a time I didn't know I needed one. Over the years, he became one of my close friends. Eventually, he visited me at Skidmore, and we instantly felt like we had known each other forever. He felt like a much older brother and still does.

That's the funny thing about community.

Sometimes, you happen to meet the right people at the right time.

Coming Out Is a Lifelong Process

WHEN I RETURNED TO SKIDMORE after winter break, I was tender but joyous. I still had some Band-Aids over my nipples as well as areas on the incision that were still closing up. I wasn't solid by any means, but I felt solid (kind of like a tender sack of partially boiled potatoes).

Technically, I shouldn't have been lifting my backpack for the first week of classes, but because only my roommate and two of my friends knew of my surgery, I didn't feel comfortable asking folks for assistance. Mom helped me get everything up to my dorm, and after that, I was pretty much on my own for recovery care. Lugging my backpack around ended up stretching the scars on my right side. I was bummed at first because I wanted my scars to go away. I wanted them to disappear entirely, to blend in with the rest of my skin. The idea of stretching them horrified me, but I had to reach for things and lift my pack.

As time went on, even after blowing lots of the little money I had on scar healing treatments, I began to love my scars and not want them to disappear. I'm happy with where they are at now, I am happy they're there, and I am happy I didn't try harder to make them disappear during my first few years of seeing them as a downside. Part of that came from unpacking the shame I was carrying about them. I felt ashamed of them because they signaled to my past, to an event, to being born female.

Scars this big often come from huge traumas. They tell stories. Later, as I began to be able to tell my story, to tell people I was transgender, I began to love my scars. But I wasn't ready yet.

Instead, I carried my own backpack around campus, sore but energetic. The first night back, I sat down at dinner with my amazing friends. One of my closest ones from pre-orientation, Sally, asked everyone how their break was.

"Awesome! I went skiing and saw this movie . . ." one responded.

"It was okay, boring, I hate the snow," said another.

"Meh. Family," chimed in a third.

"Mine was AMAZING! Seriously, the BEST MONTH EVER!" I exclaimed.

"Wow, what did you do?" Sally asked.

I realized then that I couldn't tell them what had been so amazing without telling them I was transgender. I couldn't tell them about the best day of my life without telling them I was transgender. I couldn't share the details of my break without divulging my transgender status. I'd have to . . . lie?

"Oh, haha, nothing. Played a bunch of Bananagrams and saw my mom, Veronika, friends, the usual." I smiled, calming down.

"But you say it was the best month ever?" She was a curious one.

"Yeah, sleeping and cuddling my cats basically sum up a happy month for me anyway, hehe." I concluded the conversation, thinking deeply about the ramifications of this choice for myself and for these friendships.

I wasn't able to tell my new, close friends about one of the best times of my life. I wasn't able to tell them about the joy, about my healing, about the help I might need. I wasn't able to open up and connect with them in the same ways they had been opening up to me. These were going to be friends I'd someday maybe have over to my childhood home. Maybe there would be middle school pictures of me up. Maybe they'd find that old, crummy yearbook. Would I keep living my life worrying about the truth coming out? What kind of life would that be for me?

It was in that moment I decided I no longer wanted to be stealth.

Scars

OVER THE NEXT FEW MONTHS, my chest began to heal and sensation came back. I began to feel stronger and after two months, I was back at the gym. It felt amazing to be able to work out without a binder on. Sweat felt different on my skin; I felt cleaner. I felt complete, even though I was so weak after having laid low for a few months. I lost fifteen pounds total but I was still healthy.

I admired my chest each morning and night. It felt surreal; as muscle began to grow in my chest, I felt less bony and more solid. My goal was to be fit and comfortable being shirtless by the spring, when outdoor events could be worthy of tank tops, which I hadn't worn previously due to my binder being visible. I was also stoked about going swimming in the river—it may have been shallow at the time, but I was too excited to not look forward to being shirtless once the northern New York winter subsided.

One night in March, two months post op, I was hanging out with Anna in her dorm room and we were playing a game called "Tell Me a Secret or Ask Me a Question" and I chose to tell her a secret.

"I have two giant scars across my chest," I said.

"Hmmmm . . . intriguing." Part of the game was you couldn't ask more about it.

A few nights later, we played the same game. She chose to ask a question: "Where are the scars from?"

"I had top surgery in December, a double mastectomy. I identify as a man but I was born female." I smiled, feeling confident.

Her eyes got wide, but she said, "Cool! And thanks for trusting me!"

As I began opening up to more and more of my friends, the responses were entirely positive. There were no moments of people doubting me because they could see me. Instead of having to prove myself and my identity, I had control over sharing where I had been. They all saw me as the man I was. The progress I'd made in my transition lay to rest any old, abusive outcomes, like a response of "but you look like a girl," or "you are so much prettier as Katherine." That was no longer possible, since they hadn't known that part of me.

Sophomore Slump

SOPHOMORE YEAR ROLLED AROUND; MOM wasn't in the best of health. She needed to get a stem cell collection done. I wish I could have been there to support her, but I had to head back to school.

Going back to Skidmore put a strain again on Veronika and me. We broke up for a brief period upon my return. I ended up writing a song to try to get her back and drove in the middle of the night to play it for her. We lasted a couple more months after that; in the end, the distance was too much, and we were growing into different people. When we split, it was the most final breakup I had ever had. We didn't see one another or even talk after that.

Veronika had been in a few of my YouTube videos, so I felt I needed to explain to my subscribers why she wasn't around anymore. A lot of couples had been inspired by our videos, which were such a powerful project for me and her to work on. Still, I didn't want anyone to think our breakup had to do with my being trans. This was the first time that it had been entirely for other reasons.

Unfortunately, the Internet was not a super safe place for me at the time. Friends and fans whom I had drawn support from were reacting in less than supportive ways. When I began dating someone new, way later on, comments asked where Veronika was and why I had "downgraded" in looks of my partner. It was disheartening and something I had never before heard from the Internet.

The majority of my followers were fantastic. Still, there was something about how among a hundred kind comments, the one negative one would eat at me for hours. I focused my energy into working on that issue and continued to record my chest healing and the changes on testosterone.

I had my own dorm room sophomore year, but as winter came around, I could feel an ache in my stomach. Something was wrong. My moods were shakier. I confided in my close friends at home and at school that something was up.

Late one night, Hank and I went for a walk around campus. He had been working out lots lately, getting more muscular than I'd ever be. He also had the best smile although he didn't trust many people, but he seemed to trust me. It was two or three in the morning before we headed back to our dorm rooms. Not feeling myself, I bummed a cigarette and told Hank that I felt like I was going to die.

"I've felt that way, but dude, this is weird from you." He frowned, looking at the ground.

"I've always felt I wasn't going to belong in this world, but not like this," I said, grasping for words I couldn't find.

"Dunno man. I don't fear death and so the feeling passes . . . or becomes normal, I guess?"

"I don't want to die." I felt more sure saying it out loud. "For so long, I thought I'd have to kill myself in order to be reborn as a boy. But then I looked around and I wanted to keep my family and my friends and my personality and my favorite color and my ability to bike and all that stuff. I didn't want to be reincarnated because of that, but I didn't fear death because of the opportunity it may have provided . . . I don't know. Now I've had surgery. I'm over two years on T. I am myself and I finally feel content with where I'm at . . . but my body and mind feel like a rollercoaster now." I picked up a stick and snapped it in half.

"Ah, that's how I always feel. The pull toward death. Maybe it's the hormones, dude? I don't know, I hate doctors, but probably worth checking in."

Some Days It Feels Like

Fall 2012

I killed my twin sister,
but I still feel her every day
through my fingerprints
and the caverns of
the life lines in my palms.

Every now and then, I see her
in that moment between
eyes closed and open
in front of my reflection on
dark car windows or scratched mirrors.

Then softly, I hear her voice
shaking between the scars she left—
two small and two big,
across my chest.

How I will never forget my mother's tears,
my brother's fists,
and my father's closed ears.

As if I killed their only daughter, our only sister—
I shake through the consequences,
the infinite "what if?"s
until I feel her smile

spread across my lips
and know.

While the possibilities of what could have been
never cease to break me open again,
at my very worst, at the very least

I am an honest son,
a loving brother,
a better man.

Kissing Is Just Like Falling Right on Someone's Face

DURING MY SPRING BREAK, I had my hormone levels checked. Dr. Spack called me to let me know something was up. My estrogen was triple what it had been last time. He recommended upping my testosterone dose, slightly, to help suppress it. I always thought science was exact. If X happens, treat with Y. Turns out, the medical field is very much about problem solving. Bodies are a funny little variable.

Upping my dose helped temporarily, but my levels then revealed my testosterone was too high. He put me on a type of birth control that didn't have estrogen in it, so as not to worsen the problem. I still didn't feel well.

As things progressed, I began drinking more at parties, something I hadn't been into for a while because I didn't like the way it felt. I suppose, like others, I wanted to brighten my mood, party, and dull the pain. At one of our huge end-of-semester dances, I drank too much. Rum and cokes tasted good, but I hadn't noted how much rum was really in there.

Behind the building, I was chatting with Anna with my hands on her shoulders. I don't know what we were talking about, but midsentence, I paused and kissed her.

". . . and then I saw this guy with a purple velvet hat . . ." I continued my sentence.

She interrupted me with, "Um, Sky, you just kissed me."

Bewildered, I looked at her and swore, "No I didn't! I fell on your face!"

I denied kissing her for that whole night and then it took me weeks to own up to my actions. I felt ashamed, or shy, or awful about the whole shindig. I had liked her for a long time . . . a lifetime, it felt like. To have that be my drunken douchebag first kiss? I shuddered.

Still, I hadn't thought such a vibrant, wonderful person could like someone like me. Even when the first song on a mix CD she gave me was "Say Hey (I Love You)"—I was too clueless.

When she told me how she felt about me, I sensitively approached the transgender thing.

Both laughing and serious, she admitted she had gone home over the weekend after I had told her about my gender identity and had had a crisis. In the end, she thought for a while and established I was a boy. It was that simple. She saw me as a boy and therefore it wasn't some type of sexual orientation questioning fiasco.

I breathed a sigh of relief. She saw me for me.

Period

AT THE END OF SOPHOMORE year, Paul and I started to discuss the idea of going to the Newport Folk Festival, considered to be a legendary showcase of amazing folk artists. We were super into folk—he liked the Decemberists more than anyone I knew and I had an affinity toward lyrically beautiful bands like the Cave Singers. But let's be honest—my inner queer kid immediately saw that Tegan and Sara would be there; after the show in 2008 that didn't quite go my way, I was feeling ready to trump that experience by embracing those festival porta-potties and not letting anybody police my gender! NO WAY THIS TIME!

In June, Paul and I moved into a seven-bedroom apartment on campus for our summer classes. I was super extra excited because Anna was also living with us and it felt like a dream come true. Hanging out with her was fantastic and living together was incredible. Our relationship progressed quickly, but every day felt like weeks as I savored the moments.

Our friends clearly knew what we were up to. Things were going well; we finally had the freedom to be open and fall in love. I was hesitant, as I had (and still have) issues trusting intimate partners. She was working on a translation project for the summer and saving up money while working on campus—she was heading off on an entire year abroad at the end of summer.

Knowing our days together were limited, living together seemed to speed our relationship up, but there wasn't a destination. We didn't talk about what would happen at the end of the summer. Neither of us were interested in long distance dating; we had been clear about that for years in discussions as friends.

Before moving in together, I thought about sex. She would be the first straight cisgender girl I'd been involved with. With no desire for bottom surgery,[11] I knew I didn't have the parts that she may have expected from previous hookups with cisgender men. Honestly, most of my interactions with folks could stop at making out and I'd be satisfied enough. I'm somewhere on the asexual spectrum, but haven't spent too much time pinning down a label for it. I'm attracted to folks when I'm attracted to them.

I had never had a desire to own a prosthetic device for sex up until that point. All-natural bodies interacting was my go-to . . . but I got nervous. I didn't know what to do. In the few weeks between the semester ending and moving back into summer campus housing, I posed the question to a bunch of my girl friends at home during an impromptu band practice. To my surprise, they were all excited, especially my friend Tina, who was fascinated by all the possibilities. We decided to use Amy's computer to look online.

"OOOOOOOH! What about that one?" Tina giggled as we pulled up a website that featured more color options than the last website had. She was pointing at an eight-inch neon green prosthetic cock. I laughed along.

There were some that could do some magical things, like a 3-in-1 type. It could be used to pack, pee, or play. Pack was to create a bulge in pants. Pee refers to the ability for one to urinate through it standing up. Play usually means penetration or sex of some sort. We all mused about this type of prosthetic, and decided that the idea of having one I both peed in and used for sex wasn't the best option. Obviously, cisgender men use the same part for all of those things, but bodies are more self-cleaning than silicone.

I had a very limited budget. I didn't want to spend more than $75 but it became very clear that I would end up with a neon pink thing for that price. I knew that wouldn't do the job. I wanted something realistic, natural looking, that I could pretend was actually a part of me.

---

11 There are many types of bottom (genital reconstruction) surgeries for transgender masculine folks, including metoidioplasty and phalloplasty, options to relieve bottom dysphoria and create a functioning phallus. Bottom surgery can also refer to a hysterectomy.

After looking at a few other queer sex toy sites, we found a list of popular hard prosthetics for transmen. The Doc Johnson was recommended. It was $75 plus a cheapish harness that would run about $25–40. In the image, it looked okay. I don't know what I was looking at, but it was what it was. A giant dong on the small computer screen. We were huddled around the image and scrolled down to the details.

It had several tones and I chose a realistic looking tone for a pasty white person, one with faint pink veins. Didn't look too big or too small, maybe six or seven inches. I had never had any interaction with a cisgender penis, so I had no idea if that was considered normal or not. Tina assured me that seemed about right and well enough. I felt confident ordering it. We decided to have it shipped to me once I got back to school.

They were excited for me as we were perusing, offering useful pointers and opinions. I've been truly blessed to have such incredibly welcoming, curious, and kind friends. I felt awkward discussing it, but sitting on Amy's bed as we all looked at this new world felt comforting.

I brought up how I didn't know whether or not to have it on before we started messing around, or how the transition would go to getting into a harness, or how to even . . . know what to do with this new prosthetic. My friends counseled me through it, helping me realize that my dream of being able to "whip it out" in the moment would be hard to fulfill. It would be awkward. It would take some time to adjust. There would be a pause—but that pause could be natural, like when a cis man puts a condom on.

When it arrived at school, I was not prepared. I got the box from the mailroom and knew immediately. Giggling and awkward, I asked Hank if he would come into my room real quick. My room was right next to Anna's—thankfully, she was at work when this all went down. Poor Hank had no idea what I was about to show him.

As I opened the box, I was like "HANK, WHAT DO I DOOOOO?"

And when he saw what was in the box, he squealed and waved his hands around like "AHHH I DON'T KNOW AHHHHH I DON'T KNOW!"

First, it looked huge. Gigantic, in fact. It was a behemoth. Second, this is not what I imagined penises looked like, even prosthetic ones. It looked ridiculously wide, weirdly long, and weighed a ton. Neither Hank nor I had ever experienced a prosthetic penis up close so we had no idea what we were looking at. I had to share it with him. I knew it was wonky. I knew it was private and weird. I couldn't contain my laughter, my awkwardness, my silliness about this very serious purchase.

"Literally. What. Do. I. Do."

There are no handbooks for what to do after receiving your first penis, okay?

As it turned out, I hardly used it. It was too big, it was foreign to me (and remained so even after months of owning it), and the harness wasn't very secure. Later down the line, I spent some more hard-earned money on a nicer one. That one proved to give better experiences, but I still rarely used it.

Sometimes, using it actually made me feel *more* dysphoric. Having sex, making love, whatever I called it at the time, it felt like this intruder had been introduced and became another player in the game. I sometimes felt worse when I had it on, because it replaced a part of me that was functional and felt good and made me overthink the idea of "needing" it as a way of providing pleasure to a partner. Pleasure comes in many ways. And then, when I would take it off, I would feel like I had a "lack" of a penis, rather than feeling content with my own body's capabilities.

I had similar feelings about packing. Others around me talked about how doing so helped relieve their dysphoria. How could I explain that it actually caused mine to be worse? It made me feel fake. I felt like a whole, "real man" without one. Packing made me feel like I was pretending to be something I wasn't. Like I was lying with my appearance. I felt extremely uncomfortable and wondered how others could feel so fulfilled by packing.

By this point, there were many other trans-identified YouTubers out there. I had watched some videos about packing and everyone raved that it was fantastic. I felt weird that it didn't help my dysphoria but made it worse. Someone even told me that I wasn't a "real transgender person" because I didn't feel such crippling dysphoria about my genitalia that I felt I had no other choice *but* to pack. It wasn't even that—I didn't feel connected to my genitalia, but having something foreign down there to worry about made me hyper focused on my lack of connection to my genitalia.

A casual reminder: we all experience things differently, and that's kind of beautiful.

Aside from obtaining my prosthetic penis, I had signed up for a class in human genetics with a professor I had heard was phenomenal, and it would also fulfill my science requirement. I chose to take it as a pass/fail course so that I could potentially slack off if I wanted to (hey, it was summer after all).

Some of us living in the house were taking classes, some were doing research, and some had jobs on campus. Our first weekend there, Anna and Paul were working at this alumni reunion. They were compensated amazingly but worked long, long, looooong days. There were fireworks, bands, free meals, and older alumni who needed to be driven around in golf carts. I had a blast sneaking into some of the events to say hey to them.

We started a tradition called "Magic Mondays." Basically, we would all get drunk or hyper, sometimes smoke some pot on our back porch, and dance around all together on Monday nights. It got us through the Monday blues and somehow magically became a weekly event that I will always remember as a legendary tradition in college.

And with Anna—it was wild to go from a very unhealthy long distance relationship to an extremely healthy one where we had mutual respect for one another. We would go for long walks, hold hands while we slept, and eventually started hooking up.

Many of our friends were super excited for us. A lot of them had been waiting for us to finally acknowledge our mutual love; they had sensed it in the years prior. I felt so free and so happy. I truly, finally felt *healthy* in all aspects of my life—relationships, school, goals; past, present, future!

But as July rolled around, I entered a period of sleeplessness like never before. My sleep had been rocky throughout my life, but for whatever reason, even with my early morning class, I couldn't get to sleep any time before two in the morning and even then, wouldn't have slept much or well at all. Lying awake next to Anna, who could fall asleep pretty much anywhere at any time she chose, I started to feel like I was going crazy. Thoughts swirling around. Head pounding, room spinning.

At various points since beginning testosterone, I've wondered how much my hormone levels are impacting my sleep. Placebo effect can be strong—I often find myself saying I feel exhausted because it's Tuesday, then I'll do my shot on Wednesday and eat twice as much, and then on Thursday I'm all like *wow I have sooooo much energy!* In the end, it likely is a fluctuation of hormones and routines that impact my sleep.

Regardless, my summer routine was way off kilter; on the nights where I couldn't sleep, Hank and I would go for long walks or bike rides. I had brought my childhood bike to college, the one with the blue pegs, even though it was much too small for me by that point. As the Folk Festival got closer, my late-night bike rides with Hank evolved into full-blown all-nighters of venting and frustration. I couldn't sleep. Couldn't rest. I was stoked to be with Anna, cuddling in her bed many nights, but I often became angry and more upset than I had been in a long time. I still tried to be my happy hyper self, and I'm pretty sure I succeeded in hiding the fact that I felt I was going crazy from others aside from the few close friends that I would break down to.

In retrospect, these moods and moments were a definite result of a hormone imbalance. I didn't know it until one of the best (and worst) weekends of my life.

My summer course in genetics wrapped up and I had to move back to Acton for the rest of the summer. I dragged my feet as I packed my room into my little yellow car. Since starting college, I'd never had such a fun time on campus, even with my sleep woes. Driving up the Hudson River and swinging off dangerous but thrilling rope swings. Losing my earrings from the impact of falling forty feet into the river. Stealing a "Speed Hump" sign. I kissed Anna goodbye and wished I could rewind six weeks to do it all over again.

Anna and I decided we would write each other letters and I planned to go up to her place in Vermont at the end of summer. We also had Newport Folk Festival in July to look forward to.

We were thrilled beyond belief when the weekend of the Festival rolled around. Our plan was to crash at my house in Acton, as the drive to Rhode Island was a couple hours down and back. Paul had recently gotten a leased car that was much nicer than mine, so on Saturday morning, we opted to take his and drove down. There's a stereotype that drivers from New York State are insane, angry, aggressive; Paul wasn't insane or angry, but he was fast. Hey, at least we got there quicker than we would have in my car.

Waiting in line, I noticed so many colors around us. People with rainbow bandanas, sparkles, beads, and light sticks, like those glowy ones from the nineties. We had brought plenty of snacks and water, knowing what was ahead; a bunch of dust, a lot of sun, and a rollicking good time.

They had to check our bags once we finally got to the gates. The woman checking out my backpack seemed super stern—wearing the type of scowl you get after hours of confiscating various water bottles full of alcohol. I did what I felt was necessary—I tried to crack a joke.

As she looked through the front flap of my backpack, I saw her reading my bright pink THIS IS WHAT A FEMINIST LOOKS LIKE pin.

Laughing, I pointed to it and said, "Yeah, that's what a feminist looks like—an old, worn backpack!"

Her face went from stern to hatred. Sometimes, I don't *think* before I speak. I apologized, realizing she wasn't in the mood for a joke and that wasn't a very good one anyway.

We had a whole list of bands we definitely wanted to see (The Decemberists for Paul and Anna, Tegan and Sara by my request) and others that we wanted to explore or potentially see. The various stages wound around gateways and food and blankets.

Sometime in the afternoon, we caught Tegan and Sara at a smaller stage. It was half covered, providing some shade for the lucky few squeezed under. We were able to wiggle our way into an edge and were about twenty feet from the stage. Seeing them up close felt intimate. Like we were hanging out with them.

Reliving my young queer memories, holding hands with a beautiful blonde-haired babe, I felt a sense of belonging. I've orbited around the feeling of fitting in, of belonging, of being present, of trusting I am in the right time and the right place. When it comes to me, I can feel it so strongly. And bobbing along to an acoustic guitar riff, I felt it.

When their set ended, we wanted to stick around to sit, relax, recharge. We meandered over to a sunny spot, and as we did, someone started walking up toward us. I saw her in the corner of my eye—she had short hair and an androgynous vibe. Many people at T&S did, though, not going to lie about that.

She stopped a few feet from me, fumbling with her hands, before I heard the faintest voice.

"Hey, um, are you . . . Skylar Kergil?" she asked.

All at once, I felt excited, anxious, terrified, and completely calm. Excited because I had never had a stranger recognize me. Anxious because I didn't know to what extent Anna was aware of my online life. Terrified because what if this person was actually going to harm me or ask something of me that I couldn't give? And entirely calm because, well, I had my people right there. Best friend and best friend/girlfriend. Nothing could have gone wrong, but a whole lot went right.

As she explained that she had been watching my YouTube videos for years, I couldn't stop beaming. It was my first time being recognized in public! She wanted a picture together so I put my arm around her shoulders and Anna snapped it for us. After this fan walked away, Anna turned to me with her eyes super wide and mouth all the way open.

"WHAAAAAT!" Anna exclaimed.

I shrugged, smiling, still reeling in the aftermath. Paul had been right nearby, so we were quick to run over and tell him about the interaction.

"What? That's so cool! I mean, well, it is Tegan and Sara at least—it would happen here of all places," he said.

I made sure to let Anna know that was the *first and only* time that that had ever happened to me.

"Suuuuuuuuuuuuuure," she replied.

"No! Actually!"

"Seriously? That's so cool."

Getting home late that night, we were all exhausted. Lather, rinse, repeat.

While Saturday had proven to be a sunshiny day of happiness and joy, Sunday would turn my world upside down.

Because Paul was heading back to NY after the festival was over, we took separate cars on the second day. Anna came in my car, and Paul was already miles ahead of us within an hour (Theo could go about 60–65 mph, tops). Neither of us had smartphones or a GPS device, so we had a printout of the directions and Anna accidentally had me get off at the wrong exit.

Not a big deal, a minor setback.

As I got back onto the highway, I had to accelerate pretty fast because it was a short on ramp going up a hill. Something felt off. Looking at the gauges on the dashboard, everything started moving toward the right. The speed, the rpm, and the temperature.

Behind me, I saw a white cloud.

"We . . . are pulling over." I gripped the steering wheel tighter.

"What's wrong?" Anna had no idea about the cloud behind us.

"Just stay in here," I commanded, probably in an unfairly terse tone.

Whenever anything went wrong with Theo, I didn't want anyone's advice unless they were a mechanic. Having a car that was constantly in and out of working condition did not make me feel a sense of pride, but I did feel proud knowing pretty much all of the ways it could break down and what each looked like.

Something was up with the radiator; it seemed to be dumping water out—white smoke was most likely vapor, which is much better than fire. I popped open the hood to a face full of steam. Anna stayed in the passenger seat, wide-eyed but calm. I came up beside her, opened her door, and informed her it didn't look good.

"What's wrong? Is it fixable? Where do we go?"

"Honestly, no idea. But I need to get it to a gas station right now because it's out of coolant."

It was a Sunday morning in the middle of nowhere. I closed the hood, hopped back in, and was able to get Theo down an exit ramp and put him in neutral as we coasted down into town. The hill was about to run out, and it looked like everyone was in church or simply did not exist.

There weren't any human beings anywhere and there was no cell phone service.

As the hill ended, I went around a curve, crossing my fingers, and found myself at the top of another road heading downhill. I pulled over to the side of the road in between two houses, not knowing what to do.

"I'm going to go knock on this door and ask where the gas station is or maybe there's a mechanic around," I told Anna as I headed toward a stranger's front door.

A woman appeared, cautiously speaking to me from a distance. I suppose I did look a little rugged—tye dye, tattoos, baggy ripped jean shorts. The person who would stop at a random house in the middle of nowhere to use their bathroom and leave it smelling like patchouli and mud.

"There's something wrong with my car and I coasted it to here, I'm so sorry to bother you . . ." As I went on, she seemed to have a great idea.

"Oh! My neighbor is a car dealer! Go on over there." She gestured to the house next door.

Confounded, I walked next door. Car dealer and mechanic are not the same thing, but worth a shot.

The man who answered the door seemed nice enough and told me to bring the car around to his back driveway. I did my best fake grin as I hurried back to Theo and told Anna to buckle up because we were going to try to move this dehydrated yellow banana slug back uphill.

When I pressed on the gas, it felt like air coming out, just gears spinning and no gas. It would have been hilarious if we weren't about to miss the first few bands at the festival.

The car dealer took a look at what was going on and said, "Hmmm, you're out of transmission fluid. Let's put some water in there."

I had no idea what he was doing, but watched as he stuck a hose under my hood and pumped the whole thing full of water.

Theo spat and sputtered water out as Anna and I headed down into town where he instructed there was a gas stop that almost always had a mechanic. Except that day, of course, no one was there.

We finally got cell service as we pulled in and stopped Theo by one of the pumps. The gas station looked abandoned. The whole place looked like a ghost town.

I called my mom while Anna called Paul. He had managed to get about forty minutes ahead of us and was pretty close to Newport but turned back to come to us. My mom looked up where we were at that moment (we were about ninety-six miles from home so our AAA membership would cover towing).

While we awaited the tow, Paul arrived and joined the saga. Making light of the situation, we took some selfies in front of the graveyard that he noticed was right across the street. Ghost town, cemetery, dead car . . . we were ready for a movie deal.

Eventually, we got down to Newport, having missed a couple of bands. That afternoon, we happened upon a folk band we hadn't heard yet called The Head and The Heart. Alongside River City Extension, they became one of our best finds of the event. Standing under the small tent, crowded into this intimate folk show, I couldn't help but imagine a future where I'd be up on stage with Anna playing songs about our stories.

As the evening progressed, I started to feel this crampy feeling in my stomach. I figured it was maybe because I was nervous—I felt a little awkward having my mom drive down that night to pick us up since Theo was dead. And we had been eating festival food so who knew what was up. I stopped by the porta-potty on our way out but I seemed to be fine and figured I could make the two-hour drive back without any problems.

We hugged Paul goodbye and he took off into the night for his much longer drive home. When Mom and her friend picked us up, I wasn't feeling very good at all. My mood had plummeted, but I figured,

Okay. It's the end of a long, amazing, exhausting, emotional weekend. Of course I feel out of whack. Having Anna next to me in the backseat to hold my hand helped.

We stopped about a half hour into the drive at a cute roadside ice cream stand to get some grub.

Still feeling weird, I left my mom and Anna outside at the ice cream window and went to the men's room (which, thankfully, had a stall).

Popping a squat on the toilet, I felt an unfamiliar sensation as I pulled my boxers down. Something wet. Something sticky.

I look down to see blood. Blood everywhere. My head started to spin. I've never liked blood. I knew this blood must have come from somewhere. My body.

HOW? WHAT? NO! I mentally screamed.

The walls of the bathroom felt like they were closing in. I sat down on the toilet with my head in my hands and started to bawl. I grabbed as much toilet paper as I could and tried to clean up some of the mess. A little bit of blood had soaked through to my shorts. I managed to tidy myself up a little bit, my eyes bloodshot and still teary as I snuck out of the stall to the faucet to wet some paper towels and ran back in.

I texted my mom that I needed to talk to her, privately. She didn't register the crisis via text, but I got her to meet me on the other side of the parking lot while Anna was at the ice cream stand so she couldn't see me. I proceeded to cry into my mom's arms.

I felt I was drowning as I blubbered, "I think I got my period."

"Oh sweetie, it's okay." Mom thought for a moment, looking confused. Then she held me tight, no doubt realizing the ramifications.

As I started reeling off a list of ideas, what could have caused this, what was wrong with me, am I going to die . . . my usual panic response, Mom calmed me down.

"Everything will be okay, we will figure it out," she said.

Mom was in menopause, and I was set on not telling Anna what had happened, so I wasn't going to ask her for any supplies. I basically stuffed my boxers with toilet paper and prayed the whole ride home that I wasn't dying. I couldn't stop thinking about the unknown horror going on with my body. Over two and a half years into my testosterone treatments and now this? I knew enough to know it wasn't normal—I hadn't had a period since the day I took my first shot. It had been suppressed so easily; how could it come back so suddenly and so violently?

Not only that, but I was nearing my last month with Anna before she headed off for the year. Being transgender by itself was enough to make me conscious of the many changes that Anna had to adjust to while dating me. She had never dated a boy that didn't have cismale genitalia . . . and now she was dating a transgender boy who had his period? I felt so scared, so gross, and so unlovable.

It felt like a cruel trick.

Just as the pieces of my life began falling in place, my body decided to fall apart. I didn't even want to confess my plight to Dr. Spack, but I knew I would have to.

After I dropped Anna back at school the following day, I cried my whole drive home. Somewhere within me, I felt like I had regressed back to high school. The love for my body dissipated rapidly. My dysphoria went through the roof. Even though I'd been lifting some weights and finally showing some muscle under my skin, something I'd been proud of mere weeks before, I couldn't face myself in the mirror.

I couldn't believe what my body was choosing.

A Primary Care
Physician, an
Ultrasound Technician,
and a Surgical Assistant

FOR A WHILE, I WAS not fond of doctors other than Dr. Spack. This originated from a series of unfortunate events at various doctor's offices I had been to while in the process of transitioning. Because of these mishaps and misfortunes when I was younger, I still feel anxiety any time I must introduce my body to a new doctor, fearing rejection.

At the end of junior year of high school, I felt a stabbing pain in my abdomen. One evening, I whined about it to Mom to such an extent that she suggested I go to the doctor if it was that bad. I decided it was that bad and scheduled a time at my primary care doctor's office. It was going to be in three weeks. Fine.

Walking home from school one afternoon, I keeled over in pain from the stabbing feeling. That time, it felt like someone twisting a knife right into my intestine. I started keeping a food journal, as Mom suggested—maybe little clumps of seeds were getting caught somewhere. Maybe she had read that online.

"Screw you, seed clump," I moaned out loud as Amy looked at me like I was crazy.

"Couldn't it be like, your ovary?" she asked.

Even though I was identifying as a boy, I was still getting periods, and expected them every month until I started testosterone. A boy with periods. But I had never gotten cramps before and my periods sometimes missed a month or were only a few days long due to how much I exercised and played sports. I was quite lucky, overall, on that front.

"Oh, yeah, it is in that spot!" I pondered. "Maybe it's the feeling of the egg being released or something?"

"Dude, you are so sensitive."

"I am so sensitive, I know." I laughed, knowing she was playing. "I can feel my intestines contract when a poop is coming."

"You're disgusting and I don't know why anyone likes you," she joked.

"People like me because I can predict when a poop is coming."

I twiddled my thumbs as I waited for my primary care doctor to fetch me from the waiting room. Wearing my sewn-together Social Distortion shirt, my black undershirt over my black binder, and black skinny jeans, I did not fit the scene of an upper-middle-class doctor's office. When I finally got into the exam room, it hit me that I had not been there since the previous summer when I had a physical. That was before I had begun socially transitioning and binding my chest and going by Skye.

Mom had work and couldn't come with me, and I did not particularly want to tell Dr. Christie about my gender transition plans. It didn't seem important since I still felt eons away from starting hormones. She wouldn't know the difference between me last time and me this time. I resigned to responding to "Katherine" and she/her pronouns, to get it all over with quicker.

After I explained what was going on, the doctor asked me to remove my shirt and bra so she could better examine my abdomen and upper body.

I looked at her with eyes wide and mumbled, "Ummm . . . I don't wear a bra, I actually wear a chest binder, but it only goes down to right below my chest and the painful spot isn't covered . . ."

"What?" she asked.

"I don't feel comfortable taking it off?" I felt extremely uncomfortable either way at that point.

"You are binding your chest why?" She had an accusatory tone.

"Uhhhh, I identify as transgender—as a boy—and binding my chest is making me feel more comfortable for the time being, I eventually would like to have a mastectomy, but obviously, I'm sixteen so—"

"Okay," she replied, cutting me off. "Just lay on the table."

Her face looked disgusted, like I was some less-than-human creature totally grossing up her office. I wanted to cry. Not only was I in pain, my abdomen in a constant battle against some sharp object, but I was now feeling emotionally unsafe. In a doctor's office. In a place where I should feel safe. In a place where I should be able to be honest in order to receive the best care possible.

"Well, there isn't anything wrong from what I can tell," she said dismissively.

"But, I mean, it can't be normal?"

"I'll order you an ultrasound, you can go schedule it on your way out." She left the room quickly.

I pulled my shirt back over my head. I never wanted to see her again.

Luckily for me, she never happened to be available whenever I went back to that office. Essentially, my primary care doctor began avoiding me. She never confronted me and none of the office staff mentioned anything, but for the six or seven other times I had to stop by there throughout high school and the beginning of college, she was always "unavailable." Instead, I would see a nurse practitioner who seemed to have no issue with my gender identity. Prior to uttering the word "transgender" during that exam, I'd only ever seen Dr. Christie. She had never cancelled my appointments. I assumed the one thing that changed—my gender presentation—was the catalyst.

On my way out, I picked up the ultrasound instructions. It would be the next day, at three in the afternoon, at a nearby hospital in the radiology department. Mom was going to be at work, so she asked our neighbor Sandy to take me.

Sandy was fluent with hospitals, having been an administrator at one locally. I felt comfortable as we drove down and she went over what an ultrasound was like.

"I figured people only get ultrasounds if they're pregnant, haha, which I'm not, haha." I stumbled over my words, trying to be casual.

"Oh, people get them all the time for other things! Intestinal things, things like that. Even men will get them done, especially for organs and stuff. There's lots more in there than ovaries and a uterus, that's for sure!"

I checked in at a desk in reception. The receptionist looked at me funny, like something was wrong. Sandy asked if there was a problem.

The receptionist reattached her lower jaw to their upper jaw before faking a, "No, no, an error in the system here."

"What error?" she asked.

"Are you Katherine's guardian?" the receptionist asked.

"For this appointment, yes," she replied.

"And this is Katherine?"

"Yes. What's wrong?" she demanded.

"Nothing, I am just confirming our medical record information," the receptionist replied, getting antsy.

She handed me a sheet with a sticker in the corner that stated "Katherine Kergil, 05/19/1991, F." Sure, the F may have been the cause of confusion. Whatever. I wanted this all over with.

I entered the ultrasound room with a nurse while Sandy stayed in the lobby. Technically, I was permitted to invite her in, but I didn't want more people involved than had to be. It didn't cross my mind that I'd need an advocate.

There was a woman with caramel skin and big brown eyes navigating the ultrasound machine. She reminded me of a girl I went to high school with. When I looked to my side, the nurse had dropped off my record and split without me noticing. I turned back to the technician not knowing what to say. This woman was smiling and showing her assistant something when I walked in, but when she turned to look at me, her face looked angry.

"Excuse me? Can I help you?" she asked in a nasty tone.

"Ummmm . . . they sent me here for the ultrasound?" I begged in my mind for her to be accepting.

She looked surprised. "What for?"

". . . I don't know? I have an appointment due to unexplained pain."

She scoffed at me. I wish I was kidding.

"Where is the pain?"

"My abdomen?" I kept sounding unsure of myself because I had never been treated like this in doctor's offices. Plus, my record was right there. I'm sure it explained everything. Instead, she was quizzing me and asked me a few more questions about my "intentions" for being there. A few times, she referred to me as "child" and in the third person to the assistant she had, who seemed uncomfortable during these interactions as well.

She told me I would need to lie on the table and roll up my shirt to expose my abdomen. The way she demonstrated it made it very clear that I could still keep my binder on. I felt a small sense of relief knowing I'd at least have that comfort.

While I was laying on the table, the technician, holding this ultrasound device with this jelly liquid over my stomach, looked up at me in a very concerned way.

"Are you sure you are a girl?" she said. "You look like a boy."

"What?"

"Boys don't usually get this ultrasound, that's why I'm asking—you are sure you are a girl because you do not look like a girl."

I was silent, mulling it all over as she asked me again. I'd made such huge progress that year, being recognized socially as a boy. Coming out as transgender and having my friends become my allies. Almost everyone in my life was using Skye and he/him pronouns for me, or they were at least working on it and more than half shifted in that direction. I identified as a boy. I was a boy.

And I had come so far in the eight months since I had finally found those words.

She was in a position of power; I was lying exposed on a table in a dark, cold room with someone making me feel extremely uncomfortable. I looked at her and felt I had to respond with, "Yes, I am a girl."

To which she repeated a third time: "Are you SURE that you are a girl?"

I gave up.

She continued to make comments questioning my gender identity and my body. When I got out of there, I didn't want to tell Sandy what had happened. But I'm a talker. And I had to. I couldn't keep it in. I felt wronged.

Sandy was floored. Thankfully, we were already almost home. She told me she would have run right in there and gotten that technician written up for what she had done to me. I told her I would tell my mom and go from there.

Mom was also floored. What had happened was not fair to me. I didn't want to file any complaints or cause any trouble or talk to anyone official about it. I never wanted to see that woman again. And I never did.

Fast forward a year. I was six months on testosterone. I was happier, healthier, and more confident than I had ever been in high school. I had just graduated high school, in fact. Things were exciting, things were looking good.

Before college was to start, Mom thought it would be a good idea for me to get my wisdom teeth out. Amy's parents had had the same thought. However, during the week that I had mine scheduled, Mom had an unexpected business trip come up.

Knowing full well that I wouldn't be able to drive after anesthesia and that I would need some solid medication distribution care for the first few days, Mom solicited the help of Amy's mom. Amy was getting hers out on Monday, and I was getting mine out on Tuesday, so we could commiserate in pain together. We were stoked—we would get to basically have a week-long sleepover while my mom was out of town! Sure, we would be incapacitated and immobile. But it was still going to be awesome lying on her comfy couches, binge watching *Law & Order: SVU.*

Amy's mom drove me to my appointment while Amy stayed home, still resting from her surgery. After six months on testosterone, I was very rarely misgendered, something I was thankful for. However, when I arrived at the oral surgeon's office, they plopped my wrist band on me: Katherine Kergil, 05/19/1991, F.

I figured no one would look at it. I was wrong.

The surgeon came in to set me up and talk to me for a moment. He introduced me to the surgical assistant. I was surprised—she seemed young, maybe mid-twenties, and had tattoos all over her arms; birds of various colors, nothing too risqué.

When the surgeon left the room, she explained to me how anesthesia worked.

"Have you ever been put under?" she inquired.

"No! But I'm excited! It seems fun!"

"Yeah, I think so too! What's that there, though?" she asked, pointing to my tiny bird tattoo on my finger.

"It's a bird, since I go by the name Skylar and my last name is K, I feel a connection with skylarks."

"Oh cool! And why does it say F on your bracelet?"

"Uhhhhh. Well. I'm a transgender man, but I was born female. I've been on hormones for six months and I'm feeling great."

Unlike during my ultrasound, I had the confidence and ability to say those words and own my identity. I didn't like to come out unnecessarily to people, but now, when asked, I was able to provide more accurate information. Gaining that language was crucial.

Unfortunately, I did not have the words to respond to what came next.

"That's so cool! I've honestly never met a tranny before! I never would have thought anything other than you being a young, attractive boy! Like, who would have known! Right?"

I looked at her, patiently, not knowing what exactly to say or do.

She began talking more about how she would not have known I was transgender. While some may read that as a compliment, she was realistically saying "I can tell when someone is transgender because they look a certain way." That can't be true. My brother had expressed this sentiment many times—like he had "trans radar." It was very frustrating.

Things moved toward the actual anesthesia process. I was hooked up to an IV and still surprised to be alone in the room with her. I figured the surgeon should be back in.

"So I'll have you count down from twenty," she said, before quickly adding, "Oh and like, do you have a penis or a vagina?"

I wished I was hallucinating. Was I? I looked around the room. I could still see everything clearly. I could still think clearly. But fluid was coming down the IV. Time was running out.

I tried to think—what should I say? What do I do?

Right as I felt myself slipping out of consciousness, I muttered, "It's more complicated than that . . ." and she seemed to take that as the answer, or I don't know what happened. I woke up and she was no longer there. I never had to see her again.

But I left with this feeling of being violated. I was violated. I had been asked an extremely inappropriate and offensive question by someone who was administering anesthesia to me. Not even my best friends would have the guts to ask that.

That was my first ever surgery. That was my first ever experience with an anesthesiologist. I didn't want to burden Amy's mom with the information, so once I could talk, I told Amy. She was so angry on my behalf. We ranted and raved for a long time before switch to conversations about our love for Mariska Hargitay and drifting off into a post-wisdom-teeth-extraction slumber. I was, and still am, so incredibly lucky to have a friend who cares about my safety and well-being like Amy has.

Bellybutton

WHEN I FIRST WENT TO a gynecologist, I was a twenty-year-old man. I went to Brigham and Women's Hospital and tried to ignore the name. I understood why I was uncomfortable—the "Women" bit. I had been shedding that label.

The doctor was a man in his fifties but he greeted me with respect. When he asked me what was going on, I starting rattling off my symptoms. When I was done, there was a moment of silence.

"Yes, Sky always talks this fast," my mom chuckled.

The doctor laughed as well. He recommended we do an exam; it was then that a huge wave of dysphoria hit me. I tried to breathe, but barely could. Walking down the hall, I felt faint.

In the room, with my mom there, I had to strip down to a gown and spread my legs. I felt so uncomfortable; nausea began to build up in my stomach. I hoped I wasn't going to puke; I wanted it all over with. There was a nurse in the room as well, and while I thought that may make me more nervous, she was actually the most reassuring.

"It'll be over in a moment," she kept saying, as she smiled. She used the right pronouns and name for me. "Think about something you're looking forward to, like when you get back to school."

It helped time go by faster.

After it was over, he put in an order for an ultrasound, after which we would meet back up to discuss the results and options. I had told him about the mysterious pain I had had since I was younger, seemingly in my right ovary, and he added that this might reveal the cause of that, too. I felt hopeful.

The ultrasound was the following day and was easy. They respected me, unlike in my previous ultrasound. When I checked in, the receptionist looked up at me with a compassionate expression.

"Also, sweetie. You can refuse to have the internal ultrasound. The doctor ordered both, but in almost all cases, the patient has a choice because the outer one gets the best image anyway." She smiled.

"Thanks so much! Yeah, I only want the outer one," I felt relieved that I had a choice and that she had been so kind as to tell me ahead of time.

The results of the ultrasound showed that my right ovary might have cysts and/or might be twisted. I had an appointment with Dr. Spack right after and we went over what was going on.

"Well, your estrogen came back at an extremely high level again. The birth control doesn't seem to be helping at all," he said. "Your testosterone is also way too high. It seems like your body knows the testosterone is foreign and is trying to compensate for that and force it out, but it isn't going that way. How have you been feeling on the birth control?" he asked.

I took a moment to think. He had put me on this birth control right after I'd called in about the period. It had been a month or so, though. While my impulse was to say "fine," I paused and thought about recent events.

"You know, I've been feeling depressed. Like, something awesome happened a few weeks ago, I began this relationship with this amazing girl, but I don't feel the way I know I should. I used to feel so inspired. And I've also felt maybe suicidal. Not with a plan to kill myself, or anything, but this thought keeps coming into my head when I can't sleep at night. My insomnia has been so bad. I've felt out of control and I don't know if that is the birth control or something else. I feel crazy."

"Alright, let's stop the pill for now. I think that should help. Those side effects are very strong and it's better to be careful. I think the best bet is a hysterectomy. I'll put it in for your insurance to approve, over with the doctor at B&W hospital." He smiled.

I let out a sigh of relief. This could all be over soon. I started to process what a hysterectomy meant—no longer being able to carry my own children. No longer being able to have my own biological children, in actuality. Science may progress (cool!) but as of right now, it would be impossible for me to reproduce. I didn't want to harvest my eggs after so long on testosterone; it just seemed impossible and unlikely they would be viable—plus, the process can be quite taxing on the body and so anyone who goes through it (shout out to awesome friends of mine!) is incredibly strong.

When I began on testosterone, I had accepted the possibility that I would no longer be able to reproduce. Technically, my ovaries were still working and my eggs still okay at the time of my gynecologist appointment. At least, that's what they said. I knew that I never wanted to carry children; while the reality was difficult, sometimes seemingly unbearable to cope with, I had made a choice and I reconciled my difficulties in letting go of my reproductive organs by accepting my past self, present self, and future self.

The date of my hysterectomy was going to be in July, but then I got a letter back from my insurance. The letter stated:

> . . . *our recommendation is that the patient, an overall healthy twenty-year-old female, stop testosterone treatment and start on an estrogen birth control. Our doctors have reviewed the case and until this is followed and results are reported back, we will not endorse the total hysterectomy.*

Will I Die?

THERE HAVE BEEN A FEW moments in my life when I did not know if I would be able to go on.

Receiving the letter from my health insurance company denying my hysterectomy, which was so insensitive to my crisis, almost pushed me over the edge. I was home, thankfully, and was able to retreat to my childhood bedroom and weep. Ever since I had begun feeling wonky with hormones and getting my period, I'd been able to cry for hours. It was a helpful release during this time, but I felt like I was drowning in tears.

A shitty situation was made even worse.

Over the next several months, I experienced a never-ending crampy-bloaty-painful-droopy-goopy-poopy period. I felt like I was physically dying while also mentally trying to stay strong.

I recalled a time in middle school, sleeping over at one of my friend's houses. Her older sister's boyfriend, Josh, had been entertaining us with his thoughts and ramblings.

"What I always say about periods is: anything that can bleed for a week and not die? That's spooky!" He laughed as we all laughed along with him. Back then, periods weren't something that felt applicable to me. Now? I thought of the joke in a whole different way.

During those months, I fought with my insurance company to get my hysterectomy covered. Letters from two therapists and two doctors still didn't sway them; until I stopped testosterone for six months and began on estrogen treatment, they wouldn't consider it. In the end, I fundraised over half the amount I needed and sought a cheaper doctor to perform the surgery.

Starting a fundraiser for transition costs was a difficult decision for me. Reaching out to my followers and asking for money felt unusual and new. To my disbelief, a large number of compassionate, incredible people pulled through. Right when I felt like it wouldn't be possible, strangers donated to help me have a surgery that was necessary. I cried when I received every donation, and especially when a kind stranger donated $1,111.11 to me, knowing that eleven is my favorite number. It melts me inside, turning me to a mac and cheese puddle of love and gratitude.

After I'd raised enough money and my mom had fought with the insurance over and over to have at least part of the procedure covered, I had my hysterectomy in January of 2012. My surgeon was so kind and respectful of my gender identity. He seemed sympathetic to what I was going through and used vague terms. I appreciated that he wasn't too descriptive with the process. He told me they'd basically go inside in three different places, cut up the organ and everything, and slurp it out through my bellybutton.

As I celebrated the two-year mark after my top surgery, Amy and Winnie were beside me while I recovered from the hysterectomy.

Anna was abroad, and though we had some phone talks, I leaned primarily on my family and home friends. They were incredibly supportive.

Over the following weeks, I recovered quite fast as the incisions were small and the pain minimal in comparison to top surgery. They had filled me up with gas to do it laparoscopically and the gas still puffing me up under my skin was the most painful part. My shoulders and back and neck swelled up and hurt like crazy.

No, the gas couldn't be farted out. It was destined to leak out slowly through my skin pores.

While I hadn't expected it to, the hysterectomy lessened my dysphoria. I began to care less about any future bottom surgeries that are available to transmen. I began to feel more comfortable with what was going on down there now that I no longer had this organ to worry about. I had no idea I would feel more free after the hysto, but I did.

When I got back to school, I was able to open up about what I had been through. My experiences began to seep into my art and poetry. I started to realize how I felt—without the hormonal difficulties and fluctuations. I began to feel like myself again even though a large part of me had been taken out.

I had to answer a lot of hard questions about how I felt.

I felt grateful and amazed that I had overcome the constant pain, the suicidal thoughts, and all else that was stirred up in this major moment.

Yes. There are a few moments in my life when I didn't think I would make it. But when I reach toward my guitar, toward my pen and paper, toward my YouTube channel, toward my empty canvas and paint, I know I can. When I reach out to my closest friends, to strangers on Tumblr, to my mom via text, I know it will be okay. There are some moments in my life when I didn't think I would make it, but I did. And I do. And I will.

Daughters

November 2012

I.

Across from me,
an acquaintance mentions
she just learned
'women are attracted to men
because they know men can give them babies,'
as she winks at me
awkwardly.

II.

Last January,
I put my life in the hands
of a doctor with a warm smile,
who demonstrated how
my very own womb could be
sucked up and out of
my own little
bellybutton.

III.

My daughter would have had
a dimpled nose

and curly brown locks of hair
coupled by cancerous genes
and mild manic episodes—
in any and every case,
she would be
magnificent.

Day of Silence

THE DAY OF SILENCE IS a youth-led event where students from middle school through college can take a vow of silence as a way of highlighting the LGBTQ+ voices silenced by anti-LGBTQ+ violence, harassment, and abuse. In high school, our GSA organized it every year and it felt so hard for me to keep my mouth shut, but I would.

People would pick on us and say it was silly, but it helped us unite our voices in the school. Especially because in high school, teachers would often make kids speak every class. That's at least five or six times a day. Even without raising a hand—the teacher always seemed to know who hadn't spoken in a while.

It was easy to notice a lack of voices in that crowd. When college rolled around, I didn't know what the impact would be. Instead of participating in the Day of Silence, I found that a lot of the youth needed support for the events surrounding it. Our GSA helped with some small events to raise awareness for it.

In the fall of my senior year of college, I received an email from a local trans guy named Kaleb. He asked if I'd be willing to come to his school to play some music, citing that it was hard to do trans education for the staff when he was the only currently "out" trans man.

"They're tired of hearing my voice," he laughed, explaining he also was a fan of my YouTube channel and was happy to find I lived nearby.

I was stoked! I went on a weeknight and had a fantastic time with a group of students, sharing my story, playing some music, and having a Q&A as well as private conversations with students. I had hoped it went well—and I think it did.

In the spring, Kaleb contacted me again for a local pride event. He asked if I'd be the keynote speaker at the Egg in Albany, a huge performing arts center shaped just like an egg, to celebrate the Day of Silence.

"Wait, you want me to *speak* on the . . . Day of *Silence?*"

Anna and a close photographer friend of ours, Julia, came with me. I was nervous—I held the speech I had written in my shaking hands.

There were hundreds of high school students there. I sat out with them to watch performances and hear other speeches before it was my turn. Being around the youth right before it, I had changed the tone for my speech. I knew that, like when I open my computer and speak candidly to YouTube, I work best off the cuff.

I started off by saying that I was nervous. That my voice and hands would be shaking. That I might make some mistakes. That I didn't expect to be standing there because when I was in high school, I didn't anticipate being alive at twenty-two. It seemed unreachable.

Then, too nervous to go further, I read off the paper in front of me, occasionally looking up to meet the eyes of a teenager and then winging whatever was coming next. I shared about how it felt to grow up transgender, to feel alone, to face discrimination and harassment. I asked the audience what they want to see in this world and to become it. At the end of my fifteen minutes, people applauded. As I walked off, I received hugs from a group of students who had questions upon questions.

Answering their questions and hearing their stories was my favorite part. Ever since, I have always made space to hear stories before or after I have a gig. And I always, always, always ask people to ask questions.

I will never forget how I felt after speaking that day. Every day is a blessing. Seeing the youth, being a part of their Day of Silence, and hearing the struggles that they continued to face broke my heart while simultaneously giving me purpose. I ached for them. I ache for the young queer people in this world.

After my experience at the Egg, I began to be invited to more and more schools to share my story, play some music, host a workshop, bring my thesis project, or a combination of all things. I am thankful for these opportunities and the amazing people I continue to meet on those trips.

I continue to speak often, sometimes declining if I am too nervous, but always trying to push myself to be out there. I will never forget the parents who have told me I helped them accept their child. I will never forget the kids who have told me they brought their parents to my gigs and that it helped. I will never forget those timid emails I receive after speaking, from that sweet person who was too shy to come up and chat with me after. I will always remember how each and every person has helped me refine my speeches, inspired me to write better songs, and encouraged me to share my story and stick around after to hear others'.

I mean, I wouldn't be writing all this without them. Dang.

Why I Out Myself

S OMETIMES, I WORKED ON THIS memoir while I was at my day job. Yep. Anywho.

It was a Thursday evening, a little bit before we were closing the bank, and a large man in a black shirt with baggy pants came running from across the street to do a withdrawal. While I was processing the transaction, he commented on my gauges.

"What size are those?" he asked with a tone reminiscent of people who had inquired about them in the past only to scoff at them.

"Double zeroes," I replied. "I gauged them when I was, like, fourteen."

"They look good! I like 'em. Why did you do that though?"

"Honestly, I always liked the look, wanted my ears pierced at a late-ish age, and also didn't like the look of stud earrings in guys' ears."

"Oh I agree, I agree!" He was amused; he then pointed at the little tattoo on my thumb and asked, "Is that a bird . . . or a spaceship?"

"It's actually a bird! You're one of the first people ever to get that right. People ask me if it's a pizza slice." I loosened up. "I actually gave this tattoo to myself when I was fourteen . . . wow, about eleven years ago."

"Where were your parents? Geez. Well at least you seemed to turn out okay!" He joked, but seemed to sincerely ask about the parental situation.

"To be fair, my older brother went through a lot and they pretty much let me do whatever so long as I was somewhat safe and happy. I used to dye my hair all the time and they didn't care about any of that until I started getting tattoos and pierced my nose. My dad was very happy when I shaved my head and took my nose ring out!"

"Aha, I bet he was! So then what do you do outside of work? You're a musician, artist?" he asked.

All of this is happening while I'm gathering up lots and lots of cash to give to the man. I looked down at his withdrawal slip and see that his name is Frank.

"Yeah, Frank, I suppose artist is the easiest way to describe it! I'm currently recording some of my songs and writing a memoir," I replied.

Frank leaned further forward and got wide-eyed at this comment. He had such a cheery face though, like an overall nice, gentle guy who happened to also be gigantic. With disbelief and raised eyebrows, he asked, "A memoir? Really. Who at twenty-five has enough to write a memoir about?"

I definitely laughed out loud. Sometimes I do that when I feel uncomfortable or don't know what else to say right away. Here comes the big choice again—do I say it's about a tumultuous experience in high school and college? Do I lie and make up something entirely bizarre? Do I simply *tell the truth*? And as a bank teller behind a counter, I'm easily accessible if someone wanted to, you know, reach over and punch me in the face.

"Actually, I transitioned from female to male when I was fifteen and folks have expressed interest in reading my story . . ."

He looked like I had told him he won the lottery (that is definitely not a typical reaction). He proceeded to tell me that if I hadn't told him, he would have never known. Sometimes, I see people say this as if it is a compliment, akin to "but you don't *look* transgender!" For Frank, though, I could tell in his tone that he was more bewildered to be meeting a transgender person rather than trying to say I looked super cisnormative.

This was further backed up by what he said next. "That's truly amazing. I mean really, amazing. And it is so cool that the bank is cool with you!"

I looked at my coworker who came up to my side to help me get all the funds I needed for this transaction and nudged him. "Yeah, except Rulx secretly hates me and legally can't discriminate against me."

In his thick French accent, he joked back, "You see, the bank may be okay with it but I never said *I* was okay with it *sooooo* . . ."

"I have a niece who is going through the same thing. My sister is handling it pretty well, wants her to be happy and healthy," Frank chimed in. He explained that she had said she was a boy ever since she was five and everyone had been cool with it, even now that she was fourteen and wanting to take the next steps. I knew it was likely he was using the wrong pronouns, but I decided it wasn't important for me to correct him in that moment, especially since I wasn't even aware of what pronouns his niece preferred. I chose to call them by gender-neutral pronouns when talking back to Frank, which is something I do whenever I am not aware of what someone's pronouns are. (Also, why aren't there any gender-neutral words for niece/nephew or aunt/uncle?)

I let him know that I make some videos online as resources for youth and would love to meet his niece.

"Oh, I'll bring her and the whole family in now to meet you! I think this is my favorite branch of the bank now!"

It's not every day that a customer gets this enthusiastic with us, and it's definitely not every day that I tell a customer I am transgender. It would have been just as easy to not open up—it's not my job to connect with customers on that level—yet every day I am reminded of my purpose in remaining out as a transgender man. This man genuinely seemed thrilled to have met another transgender person, possibly the first one he'd met in person other than his family member. And the potential for that excitement, that happiness, that innocent curiosity, to bloom into a safe space for this transgender child—that's it. That is all. He left happier than he came in, he left seeing an alive, adult transgender person, and he left with his perspective changed. I left happier than I was before he came in, I left alive, I left work smiling on my way home to my partner to let her know about this heartwarming interaction—and maybe, that night, one transgender kid found an ally in an uncle.

Then Love Lets
You Let Go

WHILE ANNA WAS ABROAD FOR a year, I wrote her songs to play for her when she got back. Sitting in the field behind her house in Vermont, the morning after she returned, I felt more in love than I had ever been. I knew college was coming to an end, one year left, but it was the best year. I'd finally been with my best friend in the way we wanted to be together.

We graduated the day before I turned twenty-two. Her plan was to move back to Vermont, and I was off to go live with my mom temporarily. Mom had recently moved up to Maine, and the idea of going some place where I knew no one was appealing to me. I spent some time with my mom before I found a job at a bank in Montpelier and ended up hauling my butt over to the small farmhouse room Anna had rented on the outskirts of Montpelier. This was only a couple weeks into the summer, to be honest.

I've always believed love tells you when to stay together.

Getting dressed up in a suit and working at a bank felt like a funny contrast to coming home, making YouTube videos, recording songs, gardening, and flying out once a month to a speaking or music gig. We felt at home in the town. And then, one day, I thought about the boyfriend I was. I had thought I was a good one, because I wrote love notes and songs and liked to give attention to my partner and support her, but I was still growing.

I was jealous because some guy had a crush on Anna. I didn't react well to her reacting well to his advances. She had done everything right—said she was flattered but she had me, so she let him down easy. But she was stoked because, hey, it feels great to be desired. My bruised and battered heart couldn't join her in that joy. I felt defensive and not myself.

I couldn't wrap my head around it, and as I dealt with those emotions, I came to the conclusion that I wasn't very secure with myself. I had been in back-to-back long term relationships . . . basically since I was fourteen, starting with Ashley, who had cheated on me and then broken up with me because I was trans. Then there was Rex's quote ringing in my head—that I'd never be happy.

I began to think about how this was shaping me to feel more jealous and, in return, less secure with my autonomous self. Anna had had experiences abroad that helped her grow, find herself . . . but how could I do that if I was constantly relying on the love of someone else to help me love myself?

Still in love, we had many talks about what the future would look like. I'd go to Boston while she'd stay rural. I'd move in with Amy and Winnie and Clare in Cambridge and transfer to a bank down there and try to make it in my music career. I'd be single and I'd try to find myself. She'd go to Virginia, farm, follow her dreams.

I believe that love tells you when to let go.

Re-Humanizing
the Transmasculine
Community

AFTER COMING OUT FULLY TO my college campus, storytelling and transgender advocacy became my priority. I began embarking on my senior thesis project, focusing in re-humanizing the transmasculine community. I had a desire to gather stories and hear about folks' day to day lives. I received a grant to send out disposable cameras to participants around the world.

I asked them to photograph their lives and write some notes about the pictures, if they chose. What I got back blew me away. There were people of all ages, all skin colors, all backgrounds, all sexual orientations, all abilities—showing me their lives and what they were most proud of. Some didn't even mention they were transgender, because that wasn't even in the top thirty-six things they cared to show the world. Others focused entirely on it, showing me their binders, packers—it was an individual choice.

I also photographed some local trans-identified guys. I printed and framed their images alongside handwritten notes they wrote. My thesis was hung in our on-campus art museum, and I was awarded my degree in studio art. Right after, I was heading down to a transgender conference that I hadn't been to yet and I decided to book a table and bring the photographs and project down with me.

At the Philadelphia Trans Health Conference, there were a wide variety of workshops and vendors. I spent a long time talking with a black transwoman who was going through a mental health crisis. The bathrooms were gender neutral and we were able to talk by the sinks. When I emerged, there were some people standing around.

"Are you Skylar Kergil?" One of them, with bright green hair, approached me.

"Uh, yeah! Hi! Do you like hugs?" and then I was swarmed with young transgender folks.

"Your videos helped me so much!" one shouted.

"I can't believe you're real!" another one exclaimed.

"Oh my god—I can't even breathe!" One seemed to be explaining to their friend that they might pass out.

I gave so many hugs but was caught off guard. I hadn't realized the impact my videos had had on others. I mean, reading comments, conversing over email . . . it was all something I had done without being physically around my community. Now, I was bombarded with physical love that I didn't even know existed before then.

I spent much of the trip listening to excited fans. For them to talk and me to listen was my favorite part—it's the opposite of my YouTube channel at times. At one point, I asked the cupcake vending folks next to me to keep an eye on my table as I wanted to check out what else was around. Sometimes, it was difficult to get to the bathroom when a fan wanted to chat on the way. I tried my best to give everyone as much time as possible, but sometimes I wish I could have had an invisibility cloak to quickly go pee! It ended up okay; sometimes I happened to take bathroom breaks with fans. No biggie.

After meeting some awesome artists, writers, activists, and other empowered transgender people, I met up with guys from the Internet to go to an FTM-specific workshop.

When I got back to my table, I met Zane. He wore glasses, but they couldn't obstruct his cheery eyes. He introduced himself to me. He had seen some of my videos, but we also had a friendly mutual connection.

Talking for a few moments, I liked him and felt drawn to the stardust that he is made of. He says he was all anxious and shy and awkward, but he was perfect. I had never felt myself vibe so well with another human, let alone another transgender human.

We orbited one another for the rest of the conference and exchanged phone numbers. We took a long walk around Philly, getting lost, debriefing after the conference. What drew me to Zane was that he could both talk and listen in this perfect balance. Like, he could sense emotions and he could sense maybe when I needed silence (the conference was chaotic at times) or when I needed lots of talking to distract my busy mind. We hugged so much and we hugged goodbye, but it was more of a "see you next year."

Then, in the fall, he showed up at one of my gigs in Pennsylvania. He had driven out for the night to come see me. That's when I fell in friend love with Zane.

Since then, we talk almost every day. And while the transgender conferences have gotten more and more packed, and I've become more and more well known, he is a huge help in keeping me sane.

Amy and Winnie came with me to the next year's conference. Amy is pro at dispensing my shirts and generating hype while Winnie is incredible at talking with those who may need to have a longer conversation than what I am able to give them. I've got a dream team, and I couldn't ask for more.

While I had fans rushing up to my table, wanting autographs, wanting my time and to chat, they told me how important it was for me to continue making YouTube videos even without there being any exciting physical changes left to expect. Knowing I still existed seemed to be enough for them, and I was happy to oblige and continue vlogging after my brief hiatus at the end of busy college times.

"You made me feel not alone," one fan told me as they cried into my shoulder.

I leaned on theirs, too. At my best of times and at my worst of times, I know I can count on these amazingly sweet, caring, and compassionate people to be a safe space for me to speak from my heart.

At the conference, I heard Janet Mock speak for the first time. I had read her groundbreaking memoir, *Redefining Realness*, fallen in love with her impeccable prose, and was moved by her attitude toward approaching the spotlight. One of the things she shared during this speech has stuck with me so fully, it has guided my activist work since. Janet was speaking around the time that Caitlyn Jenner had made a huge coming out via multiple news channels and releases.

"The media wants us to believe that only one story can be in the spotlight. That there is only enough light for one transgender person, for one narrative, for one of us. It is our duty to show them that there is enough light for *all* of us. We must share this light, spread this light, and bring our stories to light." She lifted her hands up in the air, demonstrating light spilling out from the confines of a spotlight and instead taking over the whole room.

Zane and I were squeezed inside of a group of new friends in the back of the room. I felt like a puddle of mush, listening to one of my idols speak. Leaning my head on Zane's shoulder, gazing up at Janet with wide eyes of admiration, I felt ready.

Ready to play a role in the community that I knew was necessary. To keep telling my own story, but only if I believed it would open the space for other stories to be shared. To push back against the media hand-picking transgender narratives that fit the media's narrative. To say no to being exploited and to say yes to listening. To say yes to being humble and to say no to the systemic oppression and erasure of the diversity that made the transgender community strong in the first place.

Janet's words bounced off my ribs until my heart felt at home. I will be radically honest. I will live and I will exist. There is more than enough light for every one of us; we just need to share it.

Inspiring Toward Wholeness

IN 2014, ONE OF MY YouTube videos went viral. It was a monologue with pictures, detailing my transition so far and the emotions that went along with it. After it was seemingly everywhere, I started getting contacted out of the blue by organizations that wanted my help, or for me to volunteer for them, or to visit to speak and share music. It was amazing.

And then, that fall, I was contacted by the Trevor Project, an organization I had adored for many years for the lifesaving help they provide to LGBTQ young people. I figured they might want me to volunteer some hours or spread the word.

They told me that they had chosen me for their Youth Innovator Award.

"We wanted to let you know that you are receiving this award for the extensive work you have done to inspire LGBTQ youth toward happiness and wholeness in their lives," the woman explained to me over the phone. "And we would love if you would come to LA in two weeks to receive it in person at our Trevor Live event!"

I felt butterflies in my stomach. Me? I had idols who helped me, like Janet Mock and Tiq Milan . . . I felt so undeserving of the honor at first, until I reflected on the time and energy I had continued to put into my activism.

Mom reassured me that it wasn't some sort of prank. I picked her as my plus one. Soon after, my boss took me to Nordstrom Rack to find a cheapish but modern suit for the occasion. Mark was the best.

Before Mom and I flew out there, I had my speech written. They had wanted to see it ahead of time and then told me there would be teleprompters. I didn't know what those were, but essentially, I wouldn't have to memorize my speech. That took a huge load off my back.

We arrived at a nice hotel and they sent a black car with tinted windows to come pick me up. It was about five hours before the performance and they wanted to do a sound check as well as tell me where to walk on stage.

On the ride over, the driver asked what I was up to. I didn't know if he would be friendly or open-minded, since he was pretty masculine and about my parents' age. I tried to be vague.

"I'm actually receiving an award tonight."

"You seem too young for that! What award?" he asked.

"Well, it's actually an award given to folks under the age of twenty-four. It's called the Trevor Project's Youth Innovator Award. It's for helping inspire LGBTQ youth—I've been documenting my entire transition from female to male since high school." I calmly tried to own the experience, even though it felt surreal.

He went completely silent for a moment.

"My daughter is going through that right now." He spoke slowly, searching for the words. "I mean, my son, I guess. Sorry, it's still so . . . new and she doesn't often talk to me about it."

"Maybe give your kid some time, and let them know you need some time, too. My dad took a while to get used to the idea, but the most important thing he did was told me he loved me no matter what."

"I haven't talked to her in a few weeks because I think she's mad at me . . . I think I will call her, I mean him, after I drop you off." He looked at me closely. "You seem alright. Maybe . . . maybe my kid will be alright, even if this is what it is."

They were setting up the red carpet when I left the cab. I met the director of the event, who hugged me and thanked me for my work. My head was spinning that this was reality. They gestured to the podium and I noticed the two glass prompters. They blended into the audience, but facing me, my speech was scrolling through in big white letters. Having not studied my short speech, I tried my best to only occasionally sneakily glance at the prompters. It wasn't going well.

The director of the event asked me what was up.

"It's . . . a lot. It's new to me, sorry." I apologized profusely as I was definitely not delivering a picture-perfect speech.

"I know you can do better than that, Skylar! I've seen your videos, you are so eloquent. Relax once you get home, take a deep breath, and I'm sure you'll rock it tonight, but you can't stare right at the prompters. That is a huge no-no!" He was friendly but also stern.

When I got back to our hotel room, I looked to Mom, feeling determined. "I am going to read this speech over and over and over and over again until it is memorized. I embarrassed the living daylight out of myself. Whoooops!"

Mom was optimistic while I was definitely stressing.

Some hours later, we were at the event. I walked down the red carpet and had an interview with Tyler Oakley that totally melted my world. His hair was bright blue. Here was a super famous, incredibly kind and funny YouTuber, chatting with me casually at the event. Everything was like stars left and right.

Many celebrities surrounded us as I sat toward the front with my mom. I'm not so good at remembering faces, but I could tell that these were important folks who had come out to support the Trevor Project and I was beginning to get excited (albeit about to piss myself) as the moment when I would receive the award got closer.

All of a sudden, it was the part we had rehearsed previously. The two guys introduced me as I ascended the stairs at the front of the stage. Everything felt like it had paused.

Tyler Oakley handed me my award, and I stood between the two teleprompters, in front of thousands of people, on a beautiful stage wearing a suit slightly too big on me.

As I began to speak, I got in the zone. I was holding this long crystal award and the weight kept my hands from shaking. I didn't even look at the teleprompters once; I was too busy gazing out at the crowd I was addressing. When I finished, I couldn't believe how smoothly it had gone—a few hours before, I had been so unprepared.

The audience stood up to clap. I saw a woman in the front row wipe a tear from her eye. When I sat back down at my table, I felt like I had accomplished something huge. I had fought my fears, fought through the stress of schoolwork for six years while continuing to make videos, and fought through my sleepless nights by answering emails to youth.

I couldn't believe I was there, that this was awarded to me, and that, for the first time in a long time, I felt a sense of pride in the work I had put in to help our community.

Moms

IN 1999, I MET TIGER. He was peeking out from a cage at an animal adoption clinic, bright orange and young. He looked mischievous. His nametag stated "Sneakers" because his paws were white.

JT found a little tortie cat named Olivia. Our parents let us adopt them and bring them home to our other two kitties, sisters Thelma and Louise. Having four cats was basically heaven.

When Tiger was young, I'd gently bite his ear. I know, it sounds weird, bear with me; I'd kiss it with a slight nibble and then tell him that this is how he'd be able to tell who his mom was.

"I'm your mom and I'll always be your mom," I would say to him as I cradled him in my arms.

Years later, my mom adopted a Bernese Mountain Dog named Toby. It was very clear that Toby was Mom's dog, so I called myself Toby's sister. He would always sit in this one spot between our living room and our kitchen. He'd be there, with his big floppy tongue dangling out, smiling and waiting for someone to pet him and cuddle him. I'd run up to him, get down on my knees so that our shoulders would be the same height, and hug him for so long.

Tiger liked Toby. He would follow Toby around and vice versa. Sometimes, they'd get into trouble together going berserk watching animals outside the front door. They wouldn't cuddle together, but they'd sometimes lie pretty close nearby.

A few years after Mom adopted Toby, she was diagnosed with cancer. The doctors didn't have very many encouraging words about her timeline . . . at first. She was on the younger spectrum of folks at diagnosis—a good sign—and was also otherwise in pretty good health. I didn't and I don't believe in god, but I began to pray to whomever or whatever was up there. I began to ask the world, out loud, for more help.

And I also talked to my pets about it, too. They didn't seem to understand, but they were always there. Mom didn't change her routines. In fact, having Toby probably helped her. Having that responsibility and need to get out of bed—Mom couldn't (and wouldn't) sit back and be depressed. She's a fighter; if not for herself, then for her family and, these days, for transgender youth.

During this difficult time, feeling like I'd be losing my mom as well as feeling like I couldn't go on living as a female when I knew I was a boy—I spent a lot of time venting to my pets. My friends were great but didn't always understand. While I was searching for the words for my feelings, it was nice to speak them out loud to Tiger and Toby.

After telling my mom about how I wanted to transition and feeling frustrated by it not happening instantly after that moment, I punched my bedroom window. Tiger was in my room at the time and saw me do it; I shattered the first panel of glass and my fist didn't make it through the second one. I felt angry and upset because I knew I'd never be able to afford transitioning on my own. Tiger looked scared—I probably did scare him. I felt so bad.

I felt embarrassed telling my mom what I had done. She was upset, of course, but she took it in stride.

Tiger slept on my bed that night, something he didn't always do.

When I began my transition, binding my chest at home and being called a different name, I didn't think about how it would affect my pets. As I got closer and closer to starting testosterone, I remembered hearing my smell might change. That my voice would change. Would my pets recognize me?!

During some of the most difficult times, feeling rejected by a partner or my brother, I would cry into Toby's fur. He would sit there, breathing, being a dog, and I would tell him about everything going wrong in my life. He picked up on my emotions way more than Tiger did back then.

I'd look him in the eyes and ask him if he recognized me still.

He'd lick my face and love me, regardless.

While I was in college, Toby passed away. As he had gotten sicker, Tiger followed him everywhere. He would lie down by his tail and stay by his side. Toby began to not be able to stand up, and that was when we knew. Big dogs don't live as long as smaller dogs, but they have a lot of love for this world. I went with Mom to the vet and held Toby's head as he drifted off to sleep.

I was over a year on testosterone and it was the first time I had truly wept since beginning it. I didn't know I could; I suppose that's what happens when you feel like you are losing your brother.

We went home and the house felt quiet. I was on break from school and didn't know how to cope with a lack of Toby.

Tiger slept in Toby's favorite spots. It was like he was waiting for Toby to come back and didn't want to miss him when he did.

I picked up Tiger. He had aged. He was thirteen years old when Toby passed away. His mouth had gone from bright orange to white. He was going gray. I poked fun at him and then bit his ear.

"I'm still your mom," I said to him, "even though I'm technically your dad now."

After college, Tiger moved in with me for the rest of his time. He had traveled to more places than a lot of people had. Born in California, lived in Massachusetts, then in Maine, then in Vermont, and finally back to Massachusetts.

More of my friends got to meet him. When he was younger, he had been a hooligan, clawing at doors and opening cabinets and keeping us up all hours of the night. As he grew up, he mellowed out and became a cuddly lap cat. Anna nicknamed him "the best cat" after we moved in together. Tiger "The Best Cat" Kergil was his full name after that.

My mom travels cross country twice a year. It helps her to avoid the snow in the winter. The past ten years of chemo have made her bones brittle—holey rather than holy. Because of this, it's safer for her to be away from ice and snow (which likes to trip us human beings).

She adopted another Bernese Mountain dog, Izzy, a few years ago. Izzy is such a princess in comparison to giant, mellow Toby, but she is fiercely loyal to my mom. And she gives my mom a wonderful reason to get out and about, even organizing Berner meetups in Maine.

In 2016, I was leaving to drive my mom back from California. As of late, Tiger had been sleeping on my bed, wrapped under my arm every night. It was a new level of cuddling that was unusual, but welcome. Except that Tiger began to have trouble jumping up on my bed . . .

I took a long, hard look at him before I left for my week-long trip. He had been eating less and less. He was still purring, but he rarely moved from a big blue pillow in the living room. I hugged him tight.

I was living with Amy and Winnie at the time and asked them to keep me updated. While I was driving through Arizona, I received a text from Winnie. Tiger wasn't doing too well. As tears welled up in my eyes, Mom and I pulled off the highway. I called the vet and scheduled him an appointment for the morning we were set to arrive back.

Once I got home, I knew it was Tiger's time to go. He seemed to know as well. Winnie came with me to the vet and Tiger lay calmly on the counter. I bit his ear softly and told him how much I loved him and how proud I was of him for being such an amazing cat to every creature that had come into his life.

I feel like I was a good mom to Tiger. There is nothing I would have done differently. Just like a mom, I am still so proud of the amazing cat he grew up to be.

And as a son now, I am so thankful for the amazing mom I have had in my life who has shown me how to stay strong and be true. A long time ago, I accepted that life was finite and I'd have to say goodbye to my mom, but she didn't. She accepted the indeterminable future and continued living. I am so proud of the amazing person my mom has become.

I asked her if she always wanted a son and a daughter, if she always wanted us to go to college and have successful careers. I mentioned that I'd delayed coming out, out of fear it would break her heart.

"I realized after my diagnosis and all you and JT went through as kids, all I want is for you to be alive and well. That's it. I couldn't be happier to know that you two are," she responded. "I wish other parents could see this, too, but the most important thing to know is: I am so proud of both of you."

When People
Aren't Kind

ULLIES ARE PEOPLE. I PREFER to remove the label "bully" and think about the actions that people take. "Bully," in and of itself, almost sounds acceptable. Like an excuse. As if there's a position with a defined title that exists in this world for people who are mean to others: bully.

I refer to people who have bullied me as people who have bullied me. This world need not be a place where any form of bullying should be acceptable, but I also bullied someone at one point. I had made fun of her weight on an online forum because she had made fun of a friend and me on the bus to school.

Her mother printed out the website and marched it over to my mom. I had to own up to the words, the violence I had created, the pain I had caused. I went over and apologized profusely and then avoided that family for a long time. I realize now that what seemed like a small comment about her weight could have spiraled into years of issues with body image, or added onto already existing issues with body image—it breaks my heart and no amount of apologizing can fix it. Since then, I've tried to say kind things or say nothing at all if I'm not sure.

I did realize that instance came after years of me being bullied for a variety of reasons. I can remember a lot of the moments, but many of them slipped into a category of "bad days" in my mind. Some of my bullies were family members. Some were close friends who soon became ex-close friends. Some were complete strangers. Some were older than me, some were younger than me, some were in places of power, some I was in charge of. All were human.

When I moved from New York to California, people made fun of my voice and my clothing.

In the third grade, people at the table next to me in Girl Scouts made jokes about me for not fitting in.

In elementary school, I was picked on for being tall at first. I was on the taller side of girls. People would call me a "boy" as a derogatory term.

When I moved to Massachusetts in the fifth grade, people called me "tomboy" as a derogatory term. Other people referred to me as "it" or "he-she," because I wore my brother's hand-me-downs. I began wearing a bright yellow GAP sweatshirt almost every day. Some people alleged it stood for "Gay and Proud" and reminded me that every time they walked by.

"You're too good at kickball to be a real girl," a boy "complimented" me at elementary school recess.

"You have a vagina so you are a girl," the same boy declared to me in high school.

I was screamed at in a women's bathroom that I was a "pervert" and should be "harassed to my death" as I was chased out.

I was cornered in a men's bathroom, being asked by some huge guy "how the fairy got in here."

A person once told me that my parents got a divorce because I made their lives miserable.

Another person wrote to me anonymously online to tell me that God gave my mom cancer to punish her for having me; they suggested killing myself as a way to have God forgive my family.

A person identifying as a lesbian called me a "freak" at an LGBTQ support group meeting.

I was called names for being "too skinny."

A person identifying as a transgender man told me I was not transgender because I didn't have debilitating body dysphoria.

A person identifying as a transgender woman told me that "anyone identifying as a transgender man is a misogynist."

A person identifying as gender fluid and non-binary verbally attacked me for "reinforcing the binary" by identifying as a man which is "within the binary and therefore oppressive."

A person identifying as a bisexual woman told my girlfriend that she must be bisexual because she was with a transgender man. When my girlfriend defended her own sexual orientation and my gender identity, the woman told her that I was "a messed-up mental freak who didn't know a penis from a vagina anyway," and still proceeded to hit on my girlfriend after this.

When I was sixteen, someone told me that I should go out on the corner of a street and "whore myself out because no one else would love me and the best-case scenario would end with me being murdered by them and putting me out of my misery sooner rather than later."

When I got into a college that a peer of mine got rejected from, I overheard them say, "but even the tranny got in!"

I have had many people ask me repeatedly about my genitalia, disregarding my refusal to disclose. When I finally got the strength to physically walk away from one such conversation, I was called an "overly sensitive asshole."

This list goes on and on. Most of these instances happened face to face, but it's important to know that now, some of the worst bullying seems to happen online.

Anonymity does a funny thing.

It makes us feel like we can say or do anything without consequences. Maybe we could say nice things instead.

In today's day and age, with transgender suicide rates in the double digits, with transwomen of color being murdered at an unbelievably high rate, what we say and what we do matters, whether we're online or face to face.

The National Center for Transgender Equality states, "transgender people face discrimination and violence throughout society, from their family growing up, in school, at work, by homeless shelters, by doctors, in emergency rooms, before judges, by landlords, and even police officers."

One of the biggest factors in the US Trans Survey, a survey that gauges factors like housing, health, employment, and acceptance among transgender people, is whether or not the transgender person has a supportive family.

When I count my blessings, I look back and thank my family for coming around. They did not kick me out. They did not threaten me. They did not fully accept me right away, but they let me exist and have a safe-ish space to come home to. They gave me shelter from a world that told me I wasn't going to belong and to get out.

I'm here, but if you need assistance, if you have been bullied, if your family is not there for you, and you need someone to talk to—please call the Trevor Project help line at (866) 488-7386.

That Time I Almost
Fist-Bumped Joe Biden

I T WASN'T A NORMAL TUESDAY. SITTING in the Somerville Hospital's lobby, I was filling out paperwork to get a skin infection treated. The whole process was a hassle, was going to cost me thousands of dollars, and it was all due to having unprotected sex with someone who I hadn't trusted. I was lucky there was a definite cure, though it was going to be painful and take many months.

As I was trying to figure out if my health insurance listed me as M or F (they had me as F) my phone buzzed. It was a private number. I silenced my phone.

They called again and it somehow bypassed my silencing. Who were these people?

I quietly answered, "Hello?" as the other person in the lobby turned to stare at me.

"Hi, is this Skylar Kur-gail?" a man asked.

"Ummm . . . yes. Who is this?"

"Oh great! This is the White House staff calling on behalf of President Obama. We wanted to make sure you received your invitation to come to the LGBTQ Pride Month reception tomorrow evening here in DC." He introduced himself as Peter.

"What?" My eyes were bugging out.

"Yes! Did you see it in your email? It should have come through this morning!"

He explained that if I and a plus one were able to get down there by tomorrow late afternoon, we were cordially invited to attend the first ever LGBTQ Pride Month reception. It was June of 2015 and Obama had declared June national LGBTQ Pride Month. I imagined the reception was to honor that commitment.

I dialed Amy's number.

"What? What is going on, dude?" We lived together at the time and Amy had been super supportive of my advocacy and events, helping me organize them. "Why hadn't I heard about this?"

"The invite came to my other email early this morning, but it didn't seem legitimate. Now, White House staff is on the other line, I'm about to get this STI treated, and I don't know what the heck is going on but give me your info and we will figure it out when I get home in a few!"

"Do we go? Do we not go? How do we afford to go? Are there flights? Should we go? What is this?" Amy and I were both reeling in our heads.

I told Peter our information and he replied he looked forward to seeing both of us tomorrow. While the doctor used an icy gun type thing to freeze these spots of infection, she asked me how I was.

"To be honest, I just got a call from the White House and I don't even know what to do." I felt excited but nervous about this last-minute plan.

That afternoon, Mom informed us that she had booked our tickets. When we woke up early the next morning, we were thankful Mom had gotten us seats that were one in front of the other, so I spent most of the flight turned around chatting with Amy. We still had no idea what to expect but were excited.

The flight was quick and we landed in DC with time to spare. As we got on the subway to head to the White House, it hit us.

"Dude, we are going to meet the president." I shuddered at the thought. I had started hormones when he was inaugurated and I couldn't even believe this.

We saw so much security in front of the White House, people gestured for us all to leave the area as someone important was driving in.

"Maybe it's Michelle coming back from the grocery store," Amy said, laughing. "And we're all here peering out at her!"

Heading toward the White House, we had no clue which gate to go to. There were many entrances, and thankfully, a snaking line of vibrantly clothed human beings appeared in front of us. Rainbow pins, amazing hairstyles, and androgyny left and right. We knew we had found our crowd.

Right when we entered the White House, the actual reception area, someone approached me with a clipboard and said, "Skylar, we need you to come with us."

I looked at Amy, confused. I didn't recognize this person. How did they know me? I was shooed into a room behind giant wooden doors. They closed softly behind me and I heard Amy getting instructed that she could hang out on the bench outside.

A photographer was in the room alongside another staff member. The staff member approached me.

"President Obama will be releasing a video, should the Supreme Court ruling go according to plan. Because of your work on YouTube, we wanted to see if you would offer your thoughts on what this historic decision means," she said.

"Of course!" I couldn't believe it.

After my clip was recorded, I let Amy know what it was all about.

"Oh my god. This makes sense then, why they invited you down! And even last minute, because the ruling is about to come out! Holy shit!"

Walking through the White House, we had time to schmooze and explore before Obama was set to speak to the crowd. Some of the rooms had special purposes, such as the one that displayed much of the old presidential china. Lincoln had some long plates. We posed in front of a picture of JFK and sent it to our parents, looking goofy even in our formal wear.

Upstairs, the crowd at the event began to gather. When Obama took the stage, we could see him pretty clearly if we stood on our tiptoes. Maybe twenty to thirty people away from him.

He spoke about the progress we had made. He spoke with optimism, strength, and unity. I had never heard such an eloquent man.

Once he was finished, the crowd went wild. Things began to calm down after that, but Amy and I noticed that Obama had had to head to a meeting with some foreign officials in the room we had been in. Standing outside was another marine, but this one set to guard the entrance.

We had had a couple of glasses of champagne. And by a couple, I mean there was free champagne and Amy and I were not used to free champagne or champagne at all. As we chatted with the marine, joking about if he would let us in, I was feeling tipsy. Oh well.

After waiting for ten or fifteen minutes outside this door, the marine told us he would do his best, but he couldn't guarantee a handshake or anything with the president. We settled for a selfie with the marine.

As he opened the door for Obama and his VP, Joe Biden, to come out, everyone around seemed to rush forward. They did a great job protecting them from the crowd, but it was a very pleasant crowd overall, so nothing too pushy.

Obama scooted by quickly, but he did stop for a few handshakes. My arms were too short to reach out. *Sigh*.

A few minutes later, a lot of the folks had disappeared. That's when Biden came through the door. Barely a few feet away from him, I reached out my closed fist for a fist bump. He saw me and extended his arm toward me, but was ushered into the elevator at the same time. I was about six inches away from having fist-bumped the VP. Dang.

Flying home, Amy and I reflected on the experience.

"It felt like we were a part of history, with all that Obama has done for our communities, and all that is still left to be done," I said.

"I still can't believe we were there." Amy was floored for days. I was, too.

Wednesday night, we were back home in our apartment, gushing to Winnie about the trip.

Thursday morning, I went back to work.

And on Friday, June 26, 2015, Obama lit up his house in rainbow colors. The Supreme Court ruled in favor of same-sex marriage, effective in the whole of the United States.

I had long sworn that, even though Massachusetts had allowed marriage between same-sex couples for a long time, I wouldn't feel comfortable getting married until I knew all my queer friends in this country would be afforded the same rights.

Hey, I guess I may get married someday. Thank you, President Obama, for being the first president to truly listen to the decades of pain and injustice our community has tried to communicate. We are still far from where we need to be, but that was a truly momentous day.

Tell Me a Story

song lyrics, 2015

Strangers stare and they want to be the first to
ask for my life in one word
But it's not that simple
Why do you care to know
am I a boy or a girl?

But I don't care about the answers
The questions were boring
Please tell me a story

"What did your mom say?"
"What is your real name?"
"How about those drugs that you take?"
"And does your voice change?"
"How come you don't feel ashamed?"
"What kind of love do you make?"

But you don't care about my answers
Your questions ignore me
Let me tell you a story

Well, alright
Ask me anything you want to
and I will tell you the truth

My mom is my best friend
and this is who I am
All of it adds up to keep me sane
Yes, I've dropped octaves
'cause I am a mountain range
and any kind of love is good enough to be made

But I don't care about the answers
The questions were boring
Please tell me a story

Camping

"HMMMM . . . THIS LOOKS GOOD." Alix approached the campfire after he and I had taken turns trying to get it started. Eventually, we got the fire going, a combined effort between the four of us.

Behind him, Reed was pulling sausages out of our cooler.

"Which wieners do we want?" Reed waved them in our faces.

"Ewwwwww but both!" yelled Micah from the tent.

Laughing, I wrapped some of them up in tin foil and stuck a stick through them while saying "ouch!"

As they cooked over the fire, we sat back in our camp chairs and chowed down on scalding hot sausages and barely cooked potatoes after a long day of hiking and exploring an old quarry.

"Hey, grab me an America." Alix winked as I was by the cooler.

There was a gigantic family camping near us—about forty to fifty folks spanning three camp sites—having some sort of reunion. Because alcohol is banned in the state parks, we resorted to calling our beers "America."

The fire crackled at our feet as we shot the breeze.

"So this girl I'm talking to . . ." Reed filled us in on some of his love life.

"Dang, I can't believe my scar strip is still hanging on!" Alix remarked; he had had top surgery a month prior.

"Do you ever feel like an old man? Just like, wanting to say to the kids—get off my yard!" I was half serious, but we joked all the time that we were aged souls.

There was no cell service, a blessing in disguise. Silence or stories were all we could bring to the camp sounds. Sitting back, infinite stars up in the sky and the cool air coming in from the mountains, I felt at home.

I was at home.

I was with three of my best friends, all of us identifying as transgender individuals and all in various points of our physical and social transitions. I fell asleep in a sleeping bag in the middle of the woods next to these people I loved, thanking my lucky stars for the path we had chosen. It was hard to believe that I wouldn't have met them had we not all identified as trans.

In the morning, we took off to get brunch before heading back to Boston, where we had all met over the past three years.

"What can I get ya, boys?" The waitress had a southern accent.

Looking up from our menus, we exchanged smiles and glances.

It never gets old to be seen as who you are.

"For a Moment,
I Didn't Feel the Pain"

S TANDING IN MY BEDROOM, I pick off the pieces of fluff that my cat has left behind on all of my clothes. Black pants? Check. Plain T-shirt? Check.

I pull my guitar case out from under my bed. The college wasn't too clear about whether or not I was speaking, performing, doing a Q&A session (which is my favorite part), or all of the above—I ended up practicing an hour's worth of songs in case. I know my own story but can never remember my chords or keys to songs I've written over the years. Those numbers and words get written on the back of my hand in case of emergency.

I hop into my car, exhausted. This past week, I started a new job working as an office assistant in the heart of Boston's downtown. The hours are consistent, the team is creative, and it will lend me a better day routine than the bank had. *I've been so busy*, I think to myself, *that it's okay to be this tired*. Lately, I haven't been making regular YouTube videos nor frequenting social media. There are many role models in the trans community—Janet Mock, Logan Ireland, Tiq Milan, Chandler Wilson, and Ash Hardell, to name a few—who put forth their best foot in the community, both in person and online.

Because they (and infinite others) exist, I don't feel I need to be on the Internet 24/7. When I began vlogging, it was primarily for myself. I did not anticipate an audience to come from it, nor did I see myself ever traveling to schools to share my story, nor did I imagine myself receiving an award for my work, my YouTube channel, that I had kept hidden from my friends and family for so long.

Looking back, if my channel hadn't turned into a conversation, one so vibrant and moving, I wouldn't have continued making videos. And I wonder how different my life would be had that been the case. Probably not so full of diversity, thought, and love.

I am blessed to be transgender.

I have given so much of my life to the Internet, to the transgender community. What of it have I given to myself? This time. This time alone in my car, chugging up the highway, knowing I won't get back home in time for more than five hours of sleep before beginning my job again in the morning. This time, flicking from radio station to radio station. This time, pondering what I will say, what message I want to leave behind. This time, thinking about how hungry I am and wishing I could pull over and buy a pack of Oreos (except that I'm trying to go sugar free next month and gearing up to that is difficult).

Two hours later, I pull into the driveway of a small, private college in New Hampshire. I meet up with some energetic students, a couple of lovely transgender student leaders, and the sound tech guy. The students caution me that it may be a small crowd, since the school is pretty small. I joke that I prefer fewer people—then I get less nervous. Well, the nervous part wasn't a joke at least. I always get anxious before my gigs, even four years into doing it. We grab dinner in the dining hall—the food makes me burp a lot during my performance, though. Oh well.

Sitting on the stage, fifteen minutes before I start, I feel tired and distracted. I forgot my guitar cable at home and my mind keeps fixating on my inability to remember everything I need.

I wipe the sleep from my eyes and meet the eyes of a familiar blond-haired boy. He's too young to be in college; I hadn't realized the event was open to the public. Next to him is his mom, who I immediately recognize from a performance I had done in Connecticut last year. I decide to face my own nervousness and pop over to chat with them until I perform. We catch up about our lives and they encourage me to volunteer at a trans camp, and I begin to seriously consider it, when I see the lights dim.

The president of the school's pride alliance introduces me. I list off my many disclaimers before playing a cover of "Use Somebody" by Kings of Leon—one of my favorite childhood songs. I mess up a few of the notes, but I smile and wink to the audience after I do.

Time flies by on stage. It's like a time warp. We spend as much time on the Q&A as possible, and because of how late it was getting, I wrap things up and invite anyone who wanted to approach me, to come up after for a few minutes before I head out.

A stranger approaches me, twiddling their beanie hat in their hand, shaking slightly.

"Is it okay if I tell you something? It's personal." They seemed nervous, but they were smiling.

"Of course! If you want we could talk privately after these folks disperse, but I may have to leave this space pretty soon, so it's totally up to you."

"Oh that's fine." They lower their voice to an almost inaudible volume.

I lean in close to hear them clearly. They explain how they had been struggling with their body and gender identity for a long time, not knowing what to do, or what to think—feeling like a swarm of information about identities, hormones, surgery had just been released from a dam and was heading right toward them at the speed of light. They didn't know how to juggle it.

"You don't need to carry it all right now," I say. "Close your eyes and think about what is most important for you to focus on right now; self-care, your identity, finding words, whatever that may be." I take a deep breath alongside them.

"While you were on stage, for a moment, I didn't feel the pain. I didn't feel the anguish and the despair and the drowning feeling that I experience all the time. Thank you," they said, and asked for a hug.

"Thank you for existing," I said, and I hugged them tight.

Thank you for existing.

Conversation with Mom

Why did you choose the name Katherine Elizabeth for me?

We tried to name both you and JT after family members. We had to go pretty far back to get a "normal" female name (Henrietta, Bertha, Lottie . . . you get the idea of what we had to work with). Anyway, Katherine is for your third-great-grandmother Katherine Curtin. Your Grandmother Betty Lou remembers her funeral, but was not allowed to go as she was deemed "too young," so likely in the early 1930s. So, your middle name Elizabeth is homage to your Grandmother Betty Lou.

How did you feel when I asked to get that bowl cut and be called Mike for a summer?

I don't recall any issues with it. I found it so funny when you introduced yourself at Jay Baker with Grandpa. We all went with the calling you "Mike" until you didn't want that anymore.

Growing up, I felt pretty free to learn from my own mistakes—like getting scraped knees from roller blading. Did you and Dad make a conscious choice to give JT and me that much freedom? Do you wish you had done anything differently?

I felt it was important for both you and JT to try things and succeed or fail and deal with that on your own. I definitely did not make a big deal about cuts and scrapes (your Grandmother Betty Lou didn't either

. . . unless it was bleeding profusely or an obvious broken bone . . . it didn't merit a doctor visit). If you signed up for a sports team, you had to complete the practices and season (even if you didn't like it), as you made a commitment. Otherwise, I let both you and JT pick your friends, your activities, gave you lots of freedom. I was not a helicopter or dragon mom. You know the only thing I would have done differently is to try to help JT earlier . . . I enabled him too much.

Have you ever questioned your gender identity?

No.

How did you know I was dating girls even when I didn't tell you?

You had dated Tyler and talked about it. When you started hanging out with Ashley, it was clear to me that you were more than just friends. All okay with me, but I appreciated it when you came clean to me about that.

Did you ever think about my gender identity and if I differed from those around me?

You were pretty "male" in your expression from a young age, but since you had an older brother and liked sports, it seemed okay to me. I grew up with two brothers and was never a "girly girl," so I wasn't feeling that you had to be expressing in a more female manner.

When I came out as transgender, how did you feel?

I wish I had written things down, because I don't think I can give an honest gut reaction so many years removed from it. I think I didn't know a lot about it, and wanted to find out more. I was adamant about not starting physical irreversible changes until I knew more and could confirm you were sure. We had lots of things going on in our family . . . divorce, my cancer diagnosis, JT dealing with his issues, and I wanted to know that it was what you needed to be you.

Is there anything you wish you could change about our coming out conversation?

I don't know . . . I remember talking at the kitchen table in Acton and discussing it, with the result being you would see a therapist to talk about things. I guess I felt you were still figuring things out, so we had time to "look into it." I would love to know how you felt it went. I understand now how hard that must have been for you, with so many parents being non-accepting and even violent in their reactions. I hope you knew I wouldn't respond that way, but you were taking a big risk anyway.

When you told me that you would always love me, but not support me financially, I understand that—now—was to make sure I wasn't about to rush into hormones, surgery, etc. At what point did you realize that I wasn't choosing to be transgender and that these steps were needs and not wants?

Yes, the lack of financial support (for that which wasn't covered by insurance . . . remember, my insurance covered lots of your therapist visits and eventually hormones) in your mind, was putting the responsibility for your decisions about how you wanted to proceed with your transition on you. I did not want to jump in and quickly move through hormones and surgeries without you being 100 percent sure what was right for you. When you started testosterone, and I saw how much that made a difference in how you felt about yourself, I realized that you knew what you wanted and needed and I was fine with moving along as quickly as you wanted. I am sorry that I didn't recognize that in time to have your top surgery before you went to college . . . that is the one thing I would change (but knowing what I learned along the way and know now . . . hindsight is wonderful).

What name would you choose for me now, if I hadn't chosen Skylar Tucker?

I think Skylar is you! You chose it and it defines how you moved through your gender questioning and transition (Skye, then Sky and Skylar for legal purposes). Tucker seemed a bit of a stretch and I don't sense you are "attached" to it. I would have liked to have gone through the family tree a bit. Since you are unique, perhaps you would have been okay taking Grandpa's Spurgeon or Struven for your middle name. Both are as strange as Tucker in my opinion, and I think Struven being the name of your great-grandpa's sailing ship would have been sort of neat . . . Sky and Sea.

When telling our family and your friends, were there any moments or responses that stood out to you?

People were pretty good (at least to my face). Something that was a recent reaction made me feel good. While I was visiting your Uncle Eric and Aunt Angie, Eric noted that he doesn't understand "all that transgender stuff," but that you were a depressed, unhappy girl and now you are confident, interesting young man. He didn't like that miserable girl much (although he always loved you), but really likes the young man you are. I think that reaction is what most folks had/have. You are a wonderful person.

The fact that you are transgender is sort of like having blue eyes to people once they know you. I think by being pretty matter of fact about it (in my Christmas newsletter update the year you came out, as well as in person), it allowed folks to take it in stride. People like you for you. We discussed this in relation to one of your chapters . . . I wanted family to see you and talk to you as part of learning about your transition as you are you . . . both your past you and future you.

I always felt like you were my number one advocate when it came to my needs, once you saw me on testosterone and realized my potential to be happy. You still give so much to parents out there who have trans kids, as well as talk with other trans kids, too. What advice would you give to parents who want to support their children like how you supported me?

Thanks! I do love you unconditionally. I suppose there are a couple of things I tell folks/kids a lot: (1) There is no wrong/right way to support transition. (2) Keep talking and communicating. One of the best things I had going for me is I saw you every day and you didn't hesitate to talk about it all. That really helped me. (3) Allow yourself time to grieve . . . you are "losing" a son or daughter and depending on how much you "pictured" your child's future based on gender, you need to "break" that picture, grieve over it, and start creating a new "picture." (4) I think a gender therapist is necessary, both for the kids and the parents.

Do you feel things have progressed since 2007 when it comes to trans issues and education?

Very much. There was very little out on the web when you came out to me. Books tended to be academic and hard to read through. Lots of talk of "mental illness" about transgender folks. I feel very lucky that we were able to see Dr. Spack for your endo . . . he was great! I think if every parent of a transgender individual had someone of his caliber (and Rachel . . . she was great too) to talk with, it would be such a help. Fortunately, there is much more information online to help, as well.

If I had been born four years ago, asking to be called "Mike" now, what do you think may have been different?

I'm not sure. If you were insistent on it for more than a summer and said things like "I'm a boy, not a girl," I would like to think I would have looked things up online, determined that you may have gender dysphoria and made appointments with appropriate professionals, we would be looking at you transitioning before starting school, using puberty blockers and taking the appropriate steps. I think the key is what I heard at a presentation at Colby . . . if your child is consistent, persistent, and insistent that they are not the gender prescribed at birth, it is highly likely they are transgender as three or four seems early, but can be the beginning of when children develop their gender identity.

What has been your favorite memory of me since I have begun transitioning?

I am so proud of you and the support/activism you provide to the transgender community . . . any of the moments that I have seen you in public qualify. From your speech at the Trevor Awards, to watching you in a crowd of folks at Philadelphia Trans Health Conference this past June, noticing the shy person on the outer edge of the group and making a point of reaching out to them and introducing yourself and asking them about themselves, fills me with pride in what a wonderful person you are, and how much you are dedicated to helping others.

When it comes to coming out, what can a parent do to be supportive?

One of the things I've learned from you is to advise parents to ask their child what they can do to support them. Every individual has a different journey and there is no single answer or way for a person to address their gender identity.

What were you doing when you were twenty-five? What advice would you give your twenty-five-year-old self?

Hmmm . . . I was just starting at Reader's Digest, *in a relationship with someone that was fun, enjoying myself . . . going out a lot to eat, movies, visit friends. Typical twenty-five-year-old! Advice: be true to yourself, be honest with yourself and others. My biggest issues have always been in relationships with others and I think being honest about everything is the only way to do it.*

What do you hope for in this world?

Tolerance. If everyone accepted others for who they are and didn't try to force them to change to be the same as they are, we would be much better. Unfortunately, it seems we are entering a period of great intolerance in the world. I believe in letting everyone live their lives, with the caveat that I don't expect folks to be intolerant of me and my family. Don't hurt me, I won't hurt you. My entire life, I have believed in treating others as you would like to be treated, to work hard, take responsibility for myself. I realize as I have aged that I came from and still exist in a "bubble" of privilege. I appreciate what I have, and hope as I go forward to try to help others.

Conversation with Dad

Can you tell me about a noteworthy memory from my childhood?

One thing that was really neat, when we would go to the beach, you would really get a kick out of looking through the sand and rocks and glass. You'd get super excited when you found something, like every time it was your first time finding it. And that's always a neat thing when you're a parent, raising children—it's the look in their eye when they've discovered or recognized something they didn't know yet, even the simplest thing, and so it becomes this exciting, new experience every time.

Alright, so I worded this next one strangely, but what I wanted to ask was—did you always want a son and a daughter? Like, was that combination ever important to you?

No. Literally never. I never once thought about the gender or sex of my children. It just didn't matter.

Awesome. Mom said something similar, so I'm really thankful for that. Next is—when I first came out as queer, you knew I was dating women, and then after you already knew that, I came out to you as a transgender boy. How did you feel when I told you all that?

You were young. My first thought was, "How can anyone know who they are at this age?" And after getting past that, I began to think more deeply. You know Debra, from the TV show Dexter? *She wears clothes that a man wears, not necessarily clothes a woman wears, so I figured maybe that's more what it was. Like she doesn't dress like a woman, but she's still very masculine—there's a word for it.*

Androgyny?

Yes! That's it. So I thought you just meant you were going to be androgynous. And you were so young, I didn't want any permanent choices being made about these things. I always wanted the best for you, but I didn't want you to make the wrong choice that wouldn't end up being the best for you. There are a lot of different angles to the LGBT community and different circumstances—I just wanted to make sure you knew what you were doing. I saw you every couple of months, unlike Mom who could see you daily, and so I think it took me a bit longer to be fully on board, but I got there.

Did me being transgender ever make you uncomfortable?

I think, if anything, it just opened my eyes to the real world. When I was a kid, a guy could be gay and a girl could be a lesbian. Sometimes, a guy dressed up as a girl and a girl dressed up as a guy and that's just who they were, I figured. Then, all of a sudden, I began to hear all the classifications and variations, which I think is really cool. You can't put people in a box. No two people are the same.

But no, it never bothered me one way or another. All I needed to know was that you were true and being true to yourself and that this was your honest feeling. It wasn't something fashionable. It wasn't "Oh I wanna be goth." No. It was who you really were and that's all that matters.

The only life I can lead is my own. I can't lead your life though. I can love you till the end of the world but I can't lead your life, bottom line.

This is very true, Dad! So what advice would you give to other dads or parents out there who may have a transgender child?

Be as open and free as you can—as far as allowing them to be who they are. Whatever you do—and I've seen this on TV a lot, and you hear about kids committing suicide—you can't do this. You can't kick your kid out of your house. You've got to be kidding me. It boggles my mind to even think that someone could be that hardened to treat their child that way because of what they think.

You don't own your kid—you're the parent. Let them be who they are.

What name would you choose for me now, Dad?

Well, the thing you did, and I don't even know why, but I thought it was cool when you picked your name—Preston Tucker invented so many automobiles and then the Buick Skylark is also a combination of your name. Skylar Tucker just works well. I like it. Keep it.

Thanks, dude. I'm pretty clever, what can I say. But truthfully, the sky-lark thing came about as an accident, although a happy one.

Oh yes, lots of good accidents become good choices, you see.

What were you doing when you were twenty-five?

Oh man, what was I doing when I was twenty-five? I was doing a lot of stuff. I got a lot of things out of my system, went a lot of places, always had money, had a good job, ran around. Met your mom when I was thir-ty-two. I saw this happen to all these other people I knew who got married at an early age—they felt like they were missing out. Like being married was holding them back—which is more psychological than true. I never had that, because between twenty-five and thirty-two, I ran around and did what I wanted to do. I never felt held back, so I never woke up every day going "Oh I wish I had done blah blah."

What advice would you give your twenty-five-year-old self?

I'd say to be true to yourself. Try to do the right thing, but enjoy your-self when you can. Have a good time. Don't do anything that would

*harm others, but enjoy yourself. You know, I guess the older you get—
the harder it is to answer those questions.*

*But there is one thing—I'll tell you this. I'm glad you and JT are
being successful in your own way, I really am proud of that.*

Thanks, Dad. I'm so happy to hear that. Well, I think the last thing I
want to ask is, what do you hope for in this world?

*Well, first, I'd like a cure for cancer. I think that would be nice and can
be done. I'd like to see—well, I'll tell you what I'd really like to see—
and I know it's a little far-fetched, but . . . I'd like to see something from
another planet land peacefully on Earth and wake people up to the fact
that there is way more out there than we could ever imagine. And once
that happens, I think it could sober up the countries on this planet to
realize—we should get over our petty differences. We are just a marble
in this thing. Let's put it all in perspective—stop the bickering, stop the
petty baloney, stop half the news you hear on a daily basis—something
to bring people together to realize we need to help each other. But I
don't know—who knows—someday that might happen—it just seems
impossible to think that we are the only living things in this universe.
There's gotta be so much more out there that we have no idea about. I'd
really like to see something come about, to bring that mindset about.
We'll see if we get lucky.*

I think we will in this lifetime, Dad. There seems to be signs!

*We're all in the same boat, here, on this planet. And we should be uni-
fied in whatever ways we can be, as opposed to always looking to get
the upper hand, to be the best, to always be fighting. We will see where
it all ends up, that's for sure.*

Conversation with JT

First things first—what is your favorite memory of your childhood?

Getting the kittens, Tiger and Olivia, as Christmas presents!

And what is your favorite memory of us together?

Playing the "Skate Park" game we made up with Mom and Dad—where we would use the tech deck finger skateboards and make the half pipes, bowls, and other parts of the park—then charge them if they wanted to play on it.

That was the best! So then, growing up, did you have any thoughts that maybe I was different than your friends' "little sisters?"

Not really when I was younger but as I started to get older, I definitely did.

I used to follow you around everywhere—was that annoying?

It was . . . but I'm sure it's the same for anyone with a younger sibling.

Almost forgot to ask, before we get super serious—what was your favorite N64 game we used to play?

Mario Kart for sure!

So high school was tough for both of us for different reasons. What was your favorite part of high school and your least favorite part?

My favorite part of high school was the people I met (friends) and the least favorite was the actual school part of it.

For a long time, you struggled with substance abuse and our relationship struggled as well because of it. Do you think that without the other family issues we had (Mom's cancer, parents' divorce, substance abuse) you would have been able to accept me as transgender sooner? I felt it all got mixed up together into one big mess.

I feel like I would have. My other issues have changed the way I look at things but ultimately I believe I would have arrived at the same place I am now without them.

I'm so glad to hear that. I know it took some time, I honestly never thought we'd even have an interview like this. Thank you for doing it, seriously.

Something I've never really asked you was—you never made fun of me for dating girls, but when it came to my gender identity, you denied it was possible and refused to call me Sky or by male pronouns for years. Do you remember why that was?

It was because I didn't want to accept that I was losing my little sister.

So, when I came out as transgender, how did you feel?

I was upset and angry because I couldn't accept it.

There were some times you would still call me your sister as a way of jabbing at me by outing me to others. It mortified me a bit pre-testosterone, but once I began passing 100 percent of the time as male, you still did it . . . even when those people clearly saw me as male. What was up with that?

That had more to do with my own insecurities about having a transgender sibling and I saw it as a way to get back at you for "doing this to me."

I see it so clearly now. What helped you to accept me?

After I realized that you were doing the transition because it was who you were and it made you happy, not to be rebellious or just to be different, I chose to stop fighting the idea and accept you for who you were, and that was as my little brother.

I appreciate that so very much. What advice do you wish you could give siblings of transgender people?

The best advice I can give is that anyone who is transitioning is not doing it out of spite for you or your family. They are not doing it just because they want to be viewed as different. People transition because it is who they are INSIDE and they feel legitimately uncomfortable in the gender they were born into. It is not easy, but I urge anyone who has a family member going through a transition to put your own personal feelings aside, take a step back, and see how it affects the person who is actually transitioning. If you do, I guarantee you will see it makes them happier to be on the path to becoming who they truly are.

What are you most proud of in your life today?

I would honestly say I am most proud of myself (selfish, I know) and how far I've come with the issues I've struggled with in the past.

I'm so proud of you, too. That's not selfish at all. You're amazing. So I guess I'll just ask, last but not least—what do you hope for in this world?

I hope that everyone can just learn to live peacefully. No matter what gender/race/religion or any mixture of those a person may belong to. Thanks for the opportunity. I hope it helps! I love you, Sky.

Resources & Inspiration

Resources are constantly changing and growing, so I've included these online! I'll be adding to them as they evolve. Similarly, I'd like to invite you to check out various people who have inspired and influenced me. Please check out these amazing humans, as well.

Join the conversation at beforeihadthewords.com/resources and beforeihadthewords.com/inspirations

I'm always looking to learn more, and welcome any thoughts or stories from you! Feel free to send me an email at skylar@beforeihadthewords.com if you want to share.